MESSAGE
to AZTLÁN

MESSAGE to AZTLÁN

Selected Writings

of

Rodolfo "Corky" Gonzales

Compiled, with an Introduction,
by Antonio Esquibel

With a Preface by Rodolfo "Corky" Gonzales,
a Foreword by Rodolfo F. Acuña and an
Editor's Note by Henry A. J. Ramos

Arte Público Press
Houston, Texas

This volume is made possible through grants from the Rockefeller Foundation and the Charles Stewart Mott Foundation.

Recovering the past, creating the future

Arte Público Press
University of Houston
4902 Gulf Fwy, Bldg 19, Rm 100
Houston, Texas 77204-2004

Cover design by James F. Brisson

Cover photo courtesy of The Denver Public Library.
Photo insert courtesy of the Gonzales family.

Gonzales, Rodolfo "Corky."
    Message to Aztlán / by Rodolfo "Corky" Gonzales; foreword by Antonio Esquibel.
    p. cm.
    Includes bibliographical references (p.).
    ISBN 978-1-55885-331-7
    1. Mexican Americans—Literary collections. 2. Mexican Americans—Civil rights. I. Title. II. Series.
    PS3557.O47 M4 2001
    818'.5409—dc21
                                   2001022314
                                     CIP

15 16 17 18 19 20   10 9 8 7 6 5 4 3 2

This book is dedicated first to my wife of fifty years, Geri Romero de Gonzales, who has supported and inspired much of my writing. It is also dedicated to our eight children: Nita, Charlotte, Gina, Gail, Rudy, Joaquín, Cindy, and Valerie; eighteen grandchildren; and great-grandchildren. The names of my grandchildren are: Arturo (PoPo's) Rodríguez, Estanislado Gonzales, Rodolfo Lucero, Indelecia Gonzales, Angelita (NeNa) Rodríguez, Mousita Lucero, Tula Rosa Rodríguez, Sergio Gonzales, Marcelino Alvarado, Serena Gonzales, Valentino Alvarado, Joaquín Gonzales II, Jacobo Gonzales, Teófilo Lucero, Maclovio Lucero, Vinchenzo Moscoso, Vitorrio Moscoso, Gabriela Lucero and Judea Beliza Lowe. My great-grandchildren are: Esia Gutiérrez, Estrella Guerrero, Luis Rodríguez and Octavio Lucero.

Rodolfo "Corky" Gonzales

Contents

Preface

I wrote the thirty-six pieces in this volume between 1966 and 1980, during the height of the Chicano Movement. We compiled them with the help of my *gran amigo* and *compañero* of more than thirty-five years, Dr. Antonio Esquibel. During the ten years he served on the Board of Trustees of La Escuela Tlatelolco, he researched, identified, collected, and typed the writings that appear in this book. These selections are not all of my writings of that time. We selected these because they represent my thoughts during the late 1960s and 1970s. At that time, I was not only writing and giving speeches on the Movement, but was chair of the Crusade for Justice, a full-fledged, multipurpose, Chicano-oriented, activist organization located in Denver, Colorado.

I published many of these writings as editorials, articles, or poems in *El Gallo: La Voz de la Justicia,* the newspaper that we at the Crusade for Justice published from 1967 to 1980. These are referenced in the text and in the end notes. The others, such as the two plays, *The Revolutionist* and *A Cross for Maclovio,* the speech I gave in 1976 in Colorado Springs for the Bicentennial, and some of my poems, were reproduced from my own personal files.

I believe it is important for future generations, and the older ones, too, to know and have access to my thoughts through my writings during the Chicano Movement. It was my intent to write my version of the Chicano Movement in a book that I began before I was injured in a 1988 auto accident. That book, entitled *The Chicano Revolution, A Poetic Account and Philosophy of the Chicano Movement,* is outlined, and I have written several chapters of it. I intend to finish it.

Until it is completed, *mi gente de Aztlán* can analyze the works in this volume. Even though this volume does not contain everything I wrote almost thirty years ago, it does capture my ideas, thoughts, and feelings during that era. I have not written anything new for this book. All the speeches, poems, and plays were written more than twenty years ago. We have included and retranslated into Spanish my only widely read poem, *Yo soy Joaquín/I Am Joaquín,* published more than thirty years ago.

It is my hope that these selections will inspire and motivate a new generation of Chicanos and Chicanas to write and get involved in improving our condition in this country and the world during the new millennium. You will have to judge for yourself whether or not we have made progress on the issues I raised in my writings and speeches three decades ago. *¡Qué viva la Raza y que viva Aztlán!*

Rodolfo "Corky" Gonzales
Denver, Aztlán, 2000

Foreword

Message to Aztlán: Selected Writings is the compilation of selected speeches, plays, poetry, and correspondence of one of the Chicano Movement's premier actors. Although authored by Rodolfo "Corky" Gonzales, the works go far beyond an individual. Most people forget that Corky, through the Crusade for Justice, represented a large and defined constituency whose frustrations and aspirations he, as an individual, expressed through an organization.

Understanding that the so-called science of history differs from the other social sciences in that it supposedly bases its narrative on documents, we understand the importance of Corky and the Crusade for Justice. In previous generations, the poor, not knowing how to read and write, or because of limited education and/or resources, did not leave documents. The ruling elites controlled the state, and state documents served the elites' interests. Few, if any, scholars cared what the poor were saying, so few records were left that told the side of the poor.

Even within Chicano history, written examples of the poor speaking for their class are rare. Middle-class Mexican Americans have left most written organizational records. Those organizations at times reflected the injustices of the times and at other times the interests and biases of its members. What sets the second half of the century apart from this tradition is that the voices of the poor are more distinguishable and louder, although traditional historians did not always respect them.

The legacy of the Crusade for Justice (and that of Corky Gonzales speaking through it) greatly influenced the times and its interpretation by present-day historians. It is a primary source for what happened in the 1960s. With time, it is a narrative that will grow in importance as the Chicano and Latino population in the United States zooms, from just under four million in 1960 to more than thirty million today. Because the Crusade for Justice was such a viable community organization, it gave Corky a base to express the interests of the Chicano Movement itself.

Corky had his greatest impact among the Chicano urban youth. He gave the *pocho* an importance that few other Chicano leaders have. This collection of readings includes his epic poem *I Am Joaquín*. This anthology takes us through the First National Chicano Youth Liberation Conference that gave a home to Alurista's "The Spiritual Plan of Aztlán," which popularized and gave a forum to the historic claim of Chicanos as indigenous to the Southwest. The symbol of Aztlán is influential to this day, although its extremes are open to debate. In retrospect, its importance is its historical context, and the reaction of many Chicano youth at that point in time, which amounted to self-identifying themselves. The notion of Aztlán went hand in hand with the self-identification of Mexican Americans as "Chicanos." It symbolized the break with the past, and the dedication of the movement to *la plebe,* the rabble.

If polemics and their documentation in writing are the engine of revolution, a study of the documents in this anthology proves this thesis. From the beginning to the end, they advocate for Chicanos. Many articles are from *El Gallo: La Voz de la Justicia,* the newspaper of the Crusade. His beliefs are uncompromising, and you know where he stands. All the writings in this book are by Corky Gonzales. They are poems, plays, speeches, and other writings that cannot be found in current university libraries. Their importance here is that the book makes them accessible to the children and the grandchildren of the group that Corky and the Crusade spoke for.

From reading the selections, however, one does not get the full impact of the importance of the Crusade for Justice or even Corky Gonzales. *Message to Aztlán: Selected Writings* only offers one side of the multi-dimensional man and organization. Just off hand, we need a volume on the role of the Chicana within the Crusade, and an in-depth analysis of the international involvement of the Crusade. Typed by critics as a nationalist organization, the Crusade was light years ahead of the movement itself in working with other Third World peoples. Besides the Poor People's March on Washington, D.C. of 1968, the Crusade championed the cause of the American Indian Movement, actively supporting it during the government siege of Wounded Knee. It championed the cause of black scholar and activist Angela Davis, and Mexican students and revolutionaries.

Scholars of the period must wait for Gonzales' autobiography that is in progress, titled *The Chicano Revolution: A Poetic Account and Philosophy of the Chicano Movement.* Ironically, although Corky and the Crusade are central to the Chicano Movement, there have been few scholarly works written about it. The only recent scholarly work on the Crusade is by former Crusade activist Ernesto B. Vigil. Vigil's *The Crusade for Justice: Chicano Militancy and the Government's War on Dissent* (University of Wisconsin Press, 1999) clearly demonstrates the importance of Corky and the Crusade and the extent that the U.S. government went to in disrupting its activities. The mountain of documents produced by that work validates what many of us were saying about the government at the time.

More than just a walk down a memory lane, *Message to Aztlán: Selected Writings* is about the polemics of struggle. The errors were errors of the time. However, this is hindsight. The importance is that it is about a time when people cared. It is about a time when they wanted a better world and joined others to struggle for this vision. They called themselves Chicano, which to them meant conquest and a history of racism that had denied them an identity and that typed Mexicans as inferior. It sends a message that we should listen to.

Rodolfo F. Acuña
California State University at Northridge

Editor's Note

Message to Aztlán: Selected Writings presents for the first time in one collection the ground-breaking writings of one of the most important Hispanic civil rights figures. Rodolfo "Corky" Gonzales was a leading protagonist of the 1960s and 1970s Chicano Movement, which challenged American society to recognize the building force and compelling voice of urban Chicanos west of the Mississippi River. Gonzales' work, remarkable for its range and depth of conviction, signaled the onset of major shifts in American cultural life: the ascendance of largely poor, working class, and immigrant Mexicans as the nation's emerging minority of record; and the unbending determination of Chicanos—contrary to past immigrant group experiences—to preserve their linguistic, cultural, and community traditions, even while aspiring to become a proud and integral part of American life.

Corky Gonzales' often nationalistic admonitions to Mexican American/Chicano people—and especially the youth—to learn and take pride in their pre-U.S. history, to develop their own community-controlled self-help institutions, and to reject conventional notions of American cultural assimilation were—and remain—controversial to many conventional U.S. observers. His forceful community advocacy, fiercely militant views, and effective organizing on the issues made him a prime target of the FBI and other U.S. law enforcement agencies. To be sure, Gonzales and his activist followers were viewed by many as a significant threat to established American traditions and values.

But Corky Gonzales was more than an angry, garden variety radical. He was essentially a sensitive, unusually insightful, self-taught man, whose life was consistently marked by constructive, community building efforts: to improve American democracy and inclusiveness; to elevate the status of Latinos and other disadvantaged citizens of the world; and to model through his own struggles and sacrifices the core principles he stood for. *Message to Aztlán: Selected Writings* reflects these truths about the man and underscores why leading Chicano Studies scholar Rodolfo F. Acuña, in his foreword to this volume, observes of Gonzales that "his words go far beyond the individual."

Corky Gonzales is an epic figure in the chronicles of contemporary Chicano struggles for justice. Notwithstanding that in retrospect much of his work and thinking seems politically outmoded, rhetorically excessive, and even naïve, Gonzales' comprehension of growing structural inequality in America—and especially its impacts on the outlook of inner-city minority youth—is perhaps as relevant and compelling today as when he first came forward, over thirty years ago. Arte Público Press is proud to include his collected works in this volume as part of our Hispanic Civil Rights Series. The series, which is supported by major funding from the Charles Stewart Mott Foundation and the Rockefeller Foundation, attempts to educate and inform Americans of all backgrounds—and especially younger Americans—about the many contributions of U.S. Latino leaders and groups to American history and cultural perspective since World War II.

At a time when the next half century will see the U.S. Hispanic community grow to comprise fully one quarter of the total American population, expanding public understanding of these contributions is particularly timely. *Message to Aztlán: Selected Writings* provides one of the most important—albeit controversial—stories we have to tell along these lines. While Corky Gonzales' views will inspire much debate and even discomfort among many readers, they are important views nonetheless for shedding light on a critical time and a significant figure in modern Latino civil rights history.

Henry A. J. Ramos
Executive Editor
Hispanic Civil Rights Series
Arte Público Press

Introduction

Nadie es profeta en su tierra. This *dicho,* that no one is a prophet in his own land, characterizes the paradox Rodolfo "Corky" Gonzales faced throughout his public career. Many believe that Corky had more influence on Chicanos outside of Denver and Colorado than on those in his own *tierra.* This was because many Chicanos outside of Colorado listened to his speeches as he made presentations all over the country; however, since most of his and the Crusade for Justice's local media coverage were negative and he was portrayed as a controversial radical, a violent and militant revolutionary, many Mexican Americans in Colorado avoided him.

The general Mexican American population of Colorado, therefore, knew little of his philosophy and thinking. Although he expressed his and the Crusade's ideas through *El Gallo: La Voz de la Justicia,* the Crusade for Justice's newspaper, and through hundreds of speeches, few in Colorado outside of the Crusade for Justice and the Chicano Movement really knew him. However, he was widely known and respected nationally for his one published work, *Yo soy Joaquín/I Am Joaquín,* studied in college Chicano Studies courses throughout the United States and other countries.

The goal of this book is to present Corky Gonzales' thoughts, ideas, and direction for the Chicano Movement as he expressed them in the '60s and '70s through his works and in his own words. It presents the writing of one of the most influential and controversial Chicano Movement leaders. It will also serve as a source of his writings for scholars who want to examine Corky's influence on the Chicano Movement, on Chicano literature, and on the Chicano in general.

College professors, who have had the luxury of attending college, those with graduate and doctoral degrees, have criticized Corky for being self-educated and only having a high school education. Some even question his writing of *Yo soy Joaquín*. The fascinating question, however, is how could a college dropout construct *Yo soy Joaquín* in which "theme and structure come together to produce a superior artistic experience?"[1] How could a college dropout compose the moving poetry found in this book of "Raíces . . . Raíces . . .," "El Movimiento Chicano," "América . . . América . . . América . . ." and also pen the sensitive verses found in "He Laughed While He Danced," "A Boy Juárez U.S.A.," and "Adiós Miguelito"?

Much of the answer is just plain, hard, exhausting work. As B. Vásquez observed, Corky spent time "writing, writing, eight hours, nine hours, ten hours, so the first draft of the play *Cross for Maclovio* took shape in a hotel room in Taos, New Mexico. For three days this went on interlaced in the evenings with booze and good talk."[2]

Another part of the answer is the other literature and individuals he was exposed to. He read Federico García Lorca, Pablo Neruda, Jorge Luis Borges, and Octavio Paz. He also read John Steinbeck, Ernest Hemingway, and Tolstoi. Corky interacted with the top civil rights leaders of the '60s and '70s. He interacted and worked with Martin Luther King, Jr., the Rev. Ralph Abernathy, and Black nationalists such as Angela Davis and Kwame Ture (Stokely Carmicheal). He worked with Indian leaders such as Thomas Bianca, Russell Means, Vernon Bellecourt, Dennis Banks, and John Trudell. He interacted with other Chicano and Chicana leaders, such as Reies López Tijerina, César Chávez, José Angel Gutiérrez, Bert Corona, Dolores Huerta, Olga Talamántez, and many others who visited the Crusade for Justice Building at 16th and Downing Street in east Denver. He also interacted with some of the liberal Anglos of the day, such as Father Groppi and William Kunztler.

Internationally, he followed activities of the Latin-American revolutionists Ernesto "Che" Guevara, Camilo Torres, and Fidel Castro. An enormous ten-foot poster of "Che" Guevara looked over the patrons of the lounge in the Crusade for Justice building.

One of Corky's personal heroes was *El General del Sur,* Emiliano Zapata. Emiliano Zapata was the Mexican revolutionary general from Anenecuilco in southern Mexico who fought for land reform for the peasants of Mexico during the 1910 Revolution. The Zapatistas' indigenous struggle for cultural survival and land in southern Mexico continues today.

Other influences were his own personal interactions with the common folk. His immediate family, especially his father and his wife, were important influences, as well as the hundreds of individuals with whom he came into contact as a boxer, politician, activist, and speaker. As he traveled around the country speaking, college students and community activists and their experiences influenced him as well.

These experiences come together to produce the writings presented in this book. It is very difficult to write about something that one has not experienced or observed. Corky's earlier *I Am Joaquín* expressed his painful self-evaluation search for his own identity.

This introduction presents Corky Gonzales, the person, the world-class boxer, the energetic politician, the devoted father and husband, the charismatic leader, all of whom produced Corky Gonzales, the influential Movement writer.

Several recent writers, and older critics as well, have questioned Corky's Spanish ability. Did he know Spanish well enough to compose in Spanish? Being a professor of Spanish and having known Corky for more than thirty-three years, I can attest to the fact he did know Spanish and speaks Spanish today. He may not have had the speaking fluency of those who have had the advantage of formally studying it in college. But make no mistake, he understood and could speak and write Spanish.

Many who came after Corky's time and who grew up in places like Denver, Colorado, and other big cities in states such as California, judge Corky's experience from their own perspective and negative experiences when the schools drummed Spanish out of them and Spanish was not encouraged at home. For example, until the mid-1960s, Colorado had a law on the books that made English the language of instruction in state public schools. However, for those of Corky's generation, Spanish was still important and stressed at home.

Many who speak Spanish mistake the hesitancy of one who does not speak Spanish as well as they do as a sign that he does not know Spanish. Usually, these same individuals insist on speaking in Spanish to show their superiority.

We consciously included some of his writings in Spanish in this work to prove his knowledge of Spanish. Still, there will be critics who will say he does not know Spanish. Does he know Spanish to the extent of scholars who studied it at the doctoral level? Certainly not. But he knows more Spanish than he has been given credit for in recent writings. He knows more Spanish than many of the critics younger than he, who judge him without knowing how to speak Spanish themselves.

Corky was a charismatic leader who provided leadership opportunities for young Chicanos. He encouraged the Chicano youth around him to get involved. He encouraged them to lead marches, to organize demonstrations, to plan conferences, to get involved politically and run for office. Equally important, he encouraged them to be creative: to paint, to sculpture, to dance, to act, and to write.

He believed that one of the reasons Chicanos had problems was because too many people did not get involved. He continuously challenged his young audiences to get involved, as he did in the ASU speech and in other writings in this book. He commands them to ask those who criticized the Movement, what they were doing for *la causa,* what they were doing for the Movement. He sees them as part of the problem because they are not doing anything for the betterment of Chicanos.

He placed Chicano Crusade members in their early twenties in charge of major Crusade for Justice activities and placed them in settings where they represented the Crusade for Justice. He inspired a whole generation of Chicano activists. He inspired and encouraged many of today's college professors and other educators. He is always challenging us to get involved, to do something for our people.

Corky wrote during one of the most turbulent times in our history for Chicanos. It was the time when we were questioning our own worth. We were questioning our own history and our own legitimacy in this country. These questions come through in his writings.

Because of his early involvement in the Democratic Party and his later founding of the Colorado La Raza Unida Party, he opened the doors for Chicanos to get involved in the political system. Federico Peña, Denver's mayor from 1983 to 1991, stated during the "1988 Tribute to Rodolfo Corky Gonzales" that Corky "cracked that door open for people like me to be successful in politics."

Corky As an Influential Writer

Through *Yo soy Joaquín* and his speeches, he encouraged and inspired a whole generation of Chicano activists to become writers in their own right. Many Chicano writers and poets were influenced by Gonzales' *Yo soy Joaquín*. This influence should be studied further. What has been Corky's influence on other writers? Now that we have presented a large body of Corky's works, others will be inspired to explore this question and others, such as the ones raised by Rodolfo Acuña in the foreword of this book. Acuña states, "We need a volume on the role of the Chicana within the Crusade, and an in-depth analysis of the international involvement of the Crusade."

We hope that this book and other recent ones, such as Ernesto B. Vigil's *The Crusade for Justice: Chicano Militancy and the Government's War on Dissent* and José Angel Gutiérrez's *The Making of a Chicano Militant: Lessons from Cristal,* will again inspire a new generation of Chicanos to get involved, to lead marches, to organize demonstrations, to plan conferences, to get involved politically and run for office, and most of all to be creative, to paint, to sculpt, to dance, to act, and to write.

Message to Aztlán

We divided this work based on the types of writing: speeches, plays, poetry, and correspondence. We decided to separate Corky's writing in this manner instead of chronologically so readers interested in a specific type of writing could go directly to that chapter or piece of work.

We present Corky's writings with minimal editing, although some may think the language used is vulgar and offensive. We decided to present his own words without cleaning them up for the easily offended.

The audiences for this book are Chicano scholars, college professors, college and high school students in Chicano Literature and Chicano Studies courses and the public interested in how his speeches and writings influenced the Chicano Movement of the 1960s and 1970s.

Personal Background, Boxing and Political Careers

Before introducing Corky's writings, a brief outline of his early life, including his boxing and political careers, is in order. Rodolfo "Corky" Gonzales was born at Denver General Hospital on June 18, 1928, to Indalecia and Federico Gonzales. He is the youngest of four brothers and three sisters: Federico, Tomás, Alfredo, Arturo, Nattie, Beatrice, and Esperanza. Corky's mother died when he was two years old. However, his father never remarried. Corky, his brothers and sisters grew up in Denver's tough northeast barrio during the disastrous depression of the 1930s. On life during the depression Corky later remarked, "though the depression was devastating to so many, as a child, we were so poor that it (the depression) was hardly noticed."[3]

Federico, Corky's father, was born in the state of Chihuahua, Mexico, and came to northern Colorado as a young man. He often spoke to Corky about the Mexican Revolution of 1910, in which he had fought. He talked to Corky about Mexican history and the pride of the Mexican people. This gave Corky a proud, strong, and positive self-identity.

During the summers of his early years, like many Chicanos of that time and later, Corky and his family worked in the sugar beet fields of northern Colorado and the potato fields of the San Luis Valley of southern Colorado. The family spent short periods in New Mexico, as well. The winter months found the Gonzales family in Denver's northeast barrio, where early in life Corky interacted with African Americans.

Corky attended many public schools, including schools in New Mexico, and Gilpin and Whittier Elementary Schools in Denver. He attended Lake Junior High School, Baker Junior High School, and West High School in Denver. He finally graduated from Denver's Manual High School in 1944 at the age of sixteen. He attended The University of Denver for one term and studied engineering, but was unable to continue after the first quarter because of the costs.

Corky next followed a boxing career. He was an outstanding Amateur National Champion. Weighing 126 pounds, Rodolfo, nicknamed "Corky" early in life by his oldest brother Tomás, became one of the best professional featherweight fighters in the world. Although he attained a number-three world ranking by *Ring Magazine*, he never received a justly deserved title shot. The official program of the Twenty-Fourth Annual Awards Banquet of The Colorado Sports Hall of Fame, held in Denver on February 15, 1988, states, "Ironically, Gonzales never fought for the featherweight title because he refused to play politics—yet he vaulted to the forefront of the Chicano Movement because he played them so well."[4] Corky was inducted into the Colorado Sports Hall of Fame at this banquet in 1988. He is the only Latino in Colorado's Sports Hall of Fame.

The official program of the Twenty-Fourth Annual Awards Banquet contains a summary of his boxing career. This program states that in 1949 *The Denver Post* referred to Gonzales as "Denver's number-one individual athletic drawing card."[5] According to the Colorado Sports Hall of Fame, Corky's amateur boxing record was fifty-three wins with four losses. He won the National Amateur Athletic Union (AAU) Bantamweight Championship in 1947. His professional boxing record was sixty-five wins, nine losses, and one draw. In all, he fought fifty-seven amateur and seventy-five professional bouts. His last professional fight was in 1955. In 1999, *The Denver Post* listed Corky as the fifth-greatest boxer to come out of Colorado in the last 100 years.[6]

For more on Corky's boxing career, see Ernesto B. Vigil's book *The Crusade for Justice: Chicano Militancy and the Government's War on Dissent.*[7] This is the best book available on Corky Gonzales and the Crusade for Justice to date. It is a comprehensive and meticulously documented account of Corky Gonzales and the Crusade for Justice, written by a Crusade insider. Also, see *Nat Fleischer's The Ring Record Book, 1950 Edition*[8] for the win/lost record of Corky's first thirty-nine professional fights.

While preparing for his last professional fight, Corky also ran for the Denver City Council. He won his last fight, but was not successful in his bid for the city council seat. Earlier, Corky had become a successful business person and had gotten involved in Democratic politics. In 1952, he established and ran one of the first sports bars in Denver: "Corky's Corner." He also was a life insurance agent and owned a bail bond company.

Corky involved himself in Democratic politics early. He helped Quigg Newton get elected as mayor of Denver in 1947, and after his own 1955 bid for the Denver City Council, he was selected as a Democratic district captain in Denver County. He supported other successful Democratic candidates, such as John Carroll in his bid for the U.S. Senate. In the 1960 presidential campaign, he headed the Colorado "Viva Kennedy" effort. In 1964 Corky ran for the Colorado House of Representatives. In 1965 Mayor Currigan appointed Corky director of Denver's War on Poverty. He resigned from the Democratic Party on June 13, 1967 (see his "A Message to the Democratic Party"). Later, in 1967, Corky ran unsuccessfully for mayor of Denver.

In 1963, he and others established an organization called "Los Voluntarios." This organization was the forerunner of the Crusade for Justice, which was founded in 1966.

Corky Gonzales is best known for four major contributions to the Chicano Movement. The first is the publishing of *Yo soy Joaquín* in 1967. The second is the Crusade for Justice's hosting of three National Chicano Youth Liberation Conferences in Denver in 1969, 1970, and 1971. The First National Chicano Youth Liberation Conference held at the Crusade for Justice from March 27 to 30 produced *El Plan Espiritual de Aztlán,*[9] which set forth broad general goals for the Chicano Movement and introduced the concept of Aztlán. The third is the establishing of the Crusade for Justice in 1966; this developed into a nationally known cultural center with a large building that included La Escuela and Colegio Tlatelolco. The fourth contribution to the Chicano Movement came through the speeches he presented as he was invited to speak throughout the country.

Corky's Writings

Only one of Corky Gonzales' poems, *Yo soy Joaquín/I Am Joaquín,*[10] has been published. Most Chicano Studies programs in the country and outside the United States use it as a major piece of literature emerging from the Chicano Movement. The 1967 edition published by the Crusade for Justice[11] sold more than 100,000 copies. The 1972 Bantam Books edition sold an additional 100,000 copies. In

1991, The Board of Trustees of La Escuela Tlatelolco[12] reprinted the original 1967 version. El Teatro Campesino[13] produced a film version of the poem in 1972, and in 1991, La Escuela Tlatelolco Board of Trustees reproduced this film version in video cassette format.[14]

This book is a compilation of selected writings of Corky Gonzales, written during the late 1960s, 1970s, and early 1980s. It includes seven major speeches, two plays, thirteen pieces of poetry, and eight pieces of other correspondence. The title of one of the speeches is the title of this compilation, "Message to Aztlán." This compilation also includes his famous bilingual epic poem, *I Am Joaquín: An Epic Poem*. We believe the selected pieces for this work were as important to Chicanos as *Yo soy Joaquín*.

This book fills the void in Corky's writings. It proves that Corky Gonzales was not a "one-piece author." He wrote much more. He wrote plays, speeches, letters, and other poetry. However, because of his serious automobile accident in 1987 and his 1988 double bypass heart surgery, he was unable to publish his other writings of the Chicano Movement. Except for *I Am Joaquín*, there are no other books of his writings.

In the introduction to the 1991 edition of *Yo soy Joaquín*, Corky talks of the project that led to this current work. He not only indicated that this project was in progress, but he hoped to finish *The Chicano Revolution: A Poetic Account and Philosophy of the Chicano Movement*, the book he began in the 1980s. This collection of Rodolfo "Corky" Gonzales' writings includes a new Spanish version and the original English version of *Yo soy Joaquín/I Am Joaquín*. More important, this collection includes many of his other writings that will establish him not only a poet, but a playwright. This compilation includes his two unpublished plays, *The Revolutionist* and *A Cross for Maclovio*.

Chapter I, *Yo soy Joaquín, un poema épico*, contains both a Spanish and English version of Corky's famous 1967 epic poem. David Conde, in his 1992 critique of *Yo soy Joaquín*, states there "is little doubt that *I Am Joaquín* was written as a social document that sought to instill Chicano pride as well as encourage community activism in support of self-determination."[15] In describing it as a literary work of art, Conde explains that the "literary merit of the work comes from the manner in which the poem is constructed and how theme and structure come together to produce a superior artistic experience" (11). He further explains that its epic qualities come "from the depiction of a dual journey into the post classic world of pre-Colombian meso-America as well as into the contradictions of the Chicano heritage. In doing so, the poem models the task of the modern hero, who must not only resolve the sociopolitical struggle for self-determination but, more importantly, come to terms with the contradictions of the cultural and spiritual reality that is Chicano identity" (111).

Yo soy Joaquín remains one of the most popular Chicano pieces written during the 1960s. The issues it raises are as applicable to young Chicanos and Chicanas today as when he wrote it more than thirty-three years ago.

Chapter II contains seven major speeches delivered by Rodolfo "Corky" Gonzales during the early part of the Chicano Movement. It includes speeches from 1968 through 1976. He delivered the first speech in this chapter, "El plan del barrio," on the steps of the Justice Department Building in Washington, D.C. The Crusade for Justice and Corky participated in the 1968 Poor People's Campaign. Before his assassination, Martin Luther King, Jr., recruited Rodolfo "Corky" Gonzales and Reies López Tijerina, the leader of the Alianza Federal de Mercedes, to coordinate the western portion of the Poor People's Campaign. It was during the Crusade for Justice's participation in the Poor People's March in Washington, D.C., that Corky delivered "El plan del barrio," in May of 1968.

"El plan del barrio" lists and elaborates on seven demands to improve the lot of Chicanos in the United States. The demands outline and elaborate the changes needed in the following areas affecting Chicanos: housing, education, job development, law enforcement, economic opportunities, agricultural reform, the redistribution of wealth, and land reform.

He delivered the second speech on the campus of Arizona State University on October 14, 1970. This version is from a tape recording provided by George Carrillo, the director of educational development at ASU in 1990. This speech is typical of the many speeches Corky delivered across the country and addresses most of his themes. He talks about *El Plan Espiritual de Aztlán,* the Crusade for Justice, *La Familia,* and the need for Chicanos to get involved in the Chicano Movement. He states that the Chicano has to organize himself around his culture, around nationalism, and use it as an organizing tool. He also speaks about the Chicano's need for cultural renewal, Chicano cultural renaissance, and the need for Chicanos to identify with their historical roots. He also declared that the Chicano Civil Rights Movement was dead.

The next speech, "Manteniendo una dirección positiva para el Movimiento Chicano," and its English version, "Maintaining a Positive Direction for the Chicano Movement," is from *El Gallo: La Voz de la Justicia,* April 1972. This speech was first given at a weekly Wednesday-night "Fisherman's Meeting" held at the Crusade for Justice. On February 27, 1972, Corky was freed from jail after having served thirty days of a forty-day jail sentence. Corky started his sentence at the Los Angeles County Jail, but was later transferred to the Wayside Honor Ranch. He was arrested for carrying a concealed weapon during his involvement in the Los Angeles Chicano Moratorium Against the Vietnam War, on August 29, 1970.

During his stay in jail, the guards marked Corky with a red wristband used to identify prisoners involved in the Movement or otherwise considered dangerous. Of the hundreds of letters mailed to Corky, he was given only a few.

His supporters held a "Free Corky Rally" at the Colorado State Capital Building during his absence from Denver. Upon his arrival back in Denver, a crowd of several hundred greeted Corky at the weekly Wednesday-night "Fisherman's Meeting," held at the Crusade for Justice Building. The theme of his speech at this meeting was the maintaining of a positive direction for the Chicano Movement. In this speech, he again calls on his followers to rededicate themselves to the Chicano Movement and to use nationalism to organize and unite people. This compilation contains the text of Corky's speech in both Spanish and English.

The fourth speech is the one Corky delivered at the La Raza Unida National Convention held in El Paso, Texas, on September 2, 1972. He gave this speech when he ran against José Angel Gutiérrez for the chair of the National La Raza Unida Party. He dedicated this speech to Ricardo Falcón, who was shot and killed by a gas station owner in Oro Grande, New Mexico, while on his way to attend the national convention. In this speech, Corky stresses the need to become one family, La Raza Unida. He states that La Raza Unida must take a position of not compromising with either of the two established parties and of not backing either of their presidential candidates, Richard Nixon or George McGovern. For more on the National La Raza Unida Conference, see José Angel Gutiérrez's book *The Making of a Chicano Militant: Lessons from Cristal.*[16]

Corky delivered "Message to Aztlán," the fifth speech in this chapter, on the steps of the Colorado State Capitol Building. He delivered it after a 16th of September Parade in 1975, celebrating Mexican Independence Day. This book takes its title from this speech. This speech sets out the roles for the various Chicano groups. It is the most commanding speech in this book. It outlines the roles for the Chicano critics, the *políticos,* the *campesinos,* the police, the educators, the artists and writers, the workers, the *guerrilleros,* the students, and the people in general, if the Movement is to be successful.

Corky delivered the next speech in Colorado Springs, Colorado, on July 4, 1976. He spoke as part of a Bicentennial Celebration honoring the two-hundred-year founding of the United States. This speech is from Corky's personal files. In it he stresses the role Chicanos had in the development of this country. He directs his comments to local heroes, such as Zebulon Pike, for whom Pike's Peak is named.

The final speech, "The Past-Present-Future of the Chicano Movement," is from the opening session of a 1978 workshop at the Crusade for Justice building. At the beginning of this speech, he reviews the past actions of the Crusade for Justice. He identifies its successes and shortcomings from his point of view. He criticizes the people who have benefitted from the Chicano Movement but who have not given back to the community. He ends by identifying future long-range goals Chicanos need to accomplish.

Corky crisscrossed Aztlán and the entire country, sometimes making twelve or more speeches a month. In one month in 1967, he spoke in Santa Fe at the anti-war rally sponsored by the Santa Fe

Peace Committee, in Albuquerque at the Alianza Federal de Mercedes Hall, at the University of Colorado at Boulder, at the Colorado State University Teachers' Conference in Fort Collins, at the University of Denver, at the Albuquerque Luncheon Club, and at the Crusade for Justice in Denver.

Corky's speaking engagements extended from California, across the nation, to Washington, D.C. The speeches in this collection and others helped lay the base for much of the thinking and ideas of the Chicano Movement of the 1960s and 1970s.

Corky Gonzales was a charismatic and magnetic speaker. One college professor likened the campus speeches by Corky to the arrival Emilano Zapata in a small town in Mexico, where he would summon his supporters to hear the latest in the Mexican Revolutionary effort and command them to join.[17] When asked where he learned to deliver a speech, Corky answered:

I don't recall who taught me how to give a speech. I don't remember where I learned how to give a speech. I do know that when you speak, you speak sincerely. You speak the truth. You speak how you feel. You speak not to what the other wants to hear. You speak not to impress somebody else, you speak your thoughts, the thoughts that are in you. You state the opinions you want to say, the ideas that you want to share with people. Don't shorten it and don't slide it down, and don't make excuses about it or pass it off. Say what you got to say and say it directly.

This is one of the skills that you learn in writing. Say it succinctly, say it clearly, say it with no added ornaments. This is one of the dangers of many modern writers: they decorate their words until you do not know what they are talking about. Only they know what they are talking about.

When I went out to speak, I spoke what I felt was true and I knew was true. I spoke directly to the people. I didn't go off to some other point of view or try to direct, to include anything else. I talked to the people. When I said something and was angry about the situation, the system, or a politician, I mentioned the situation. I mentioned the institution. I mentioned the politician's name. I said he was right or I said he was wrong. If he was an asshole, I called him an asshole. I looked him straight in the eye when I said it. And I never backed down from that.

Many times there were guys waiting for me out in the alley, to let me prove if what I said was what I really had meant to say. And I usually told them, "Well, I said it and I'm backing it up," and I did back it up. I had more *chingazos* in the alley than I did in the ring.[18]

Chapter III includes Corky's two unpublished plays. Chicano *teatros* throughout the country have performed the first, *The Revolutionist.* El Centro Su Teatro from Denver performed it at the 1988 Tribute to Rodolfo "Corky" Gonzales. A drama about a Mexican revolutionist who finds himself in a southwest barrio in 1950, it presents the problems of the aging revolutionist and his family in adapting to a large United States city. Corky wrote *The Revolutionist* in 1966, making it the oldest composition in this book.

The second play, *A Cross for Maclovio,* dates to 1967. Set in the home of Maclovio Gallegos in the barrio of a city in the Southwest, the drama depicts the Gallegos's family dealing with the father's activistism in the Chicano Movement. This volume marks the first publication of *The Revolutionist* and *A Cross for Maclovio.*

In an article in the August 31, 1967, issue of *El Gallo: La Voz de la Justicia,* B. Vásquez documented the creative process Corky went through in Taos, New Mexico, while writing *A Cross for Maclovio:*

He sat there, a clipboard on his knees, writing furiously, the *mocos* and water running from a savage head cold, dropping to moisten the paper. He wrote right through and over the damp surface. When he went to the head, the clipboard and paper went with him. Writing, writing, eight hours, nine hours, ten hours so the first draft of the play "Cross for Maclovio" took shape in a hotel room in Taos, New Mexico. For three days this went on, interlaced in the evenings with booze and good talk.

Gonzales was mining the ore of his soul, and that mine is rich. Okay, that was spring, early spring, and the beauty of the play had to lay fallow in its rough state until after the middle of August, because the man was hung up on troubles. His and other people's troubles, property losses for him, all kinds of problems for those others. This work of beauty had to wait for its final milling until another Taos trip could be squeezed in between those problems.

This time no head cold, just two days of straight concentration interspersed with walks on the mountain mesa land, drinks of booze in the evening, then bravo: the readings. This ore, this creative gold, now had the necessary shine, and I laughed and wept to hear the words of the play "Cross for Maclovio"—another fine, strong piece of creative evidence to the credit of the Chicanos of the Southwest, has gone to the copywriters.

Chapter IV contains thirteen of Corky's poems written after *Yo soy Joaquín/I Am Joaquín.* Corky published most of these poems first in *El Gallo: La Voz de La Justicia,* the newspaper that Crusade for Justice published from 1967 to 1980. Four of these poems are from Corky's personal files and have never before been published.

The first poem, "Tlatelolco," refers to La Escuela y Colegio Tlatelolco, established by the Crusade for Justice in 1970, and was published in part in La Escuela's 1973 brochure to commemorate the founding of La Escuela and explain its educational philosophy. The poem is historical in structuring, beginning with the ancient Tlatelolco civilization of Mexico and proceeding to contemporary Chicano culture.

"El Ballet Chicano de Aztlán," written in 1970, celebrates the Crusade's own Chicano dance troupe, which included dancers who had traveled to Mexico to study dance with the Ballet Folklórico Nacional de México. Instructors from this world-famous company also came to the Crusade in Denver to teach dancers from the Ballet Chicano de Aztlán. "Adiós, Miguel" was a farewell to the young son of a Crusade family: Gloria and Leonel Ruybal. Miguelito was nine years old when he passed away in 1969. This is a touching eulogy to a young member of the Crusade for Justice. "A Chicano's Trial" criticizes the court system in this country. The other, "The Revolution," foresees revolution coming to the United States. "Mis hijos guerrilleros," honoring the youth of the Chicano Movement, exhorts activists to resist as they fight for freedom.

"He Laughed While He Danced," the killing of Luis Jr. Martínez, commemorates a young member of the Crusade for Justice. Corky was very close to the young Luis Martínez, who was shot and killed March 17, 1973, by a Denver police officer in what has become known as the St. Patrick's Day Massacre. The poem remembers Luis as a dancer and active member of the Crusade for Justice. His death was a turning point in the history of the Crusade for Justice. Immediately after he was shot, the Denver Police stormed the apartments next to the Crusade building. During the shootout, the apartment building was blown up, and the Denver police arrested more than thirty Crusade members. After this incident, *El Gallo: La Voz de la Justicia* incorporated the subtitle *El Año de Luis Jr. Martínez* in all its editions to honor him. This poem captures the turbulence, confusion, and fear on the night the Denver police killed Luis Jr. Martínez. It is one of the longer poems in this book.

"A Boy, Júarez U.S.A.," a poem about a young boy without a dream, is reproduced here in its entirety for the first time. "Raíces . . . Raíces . . ." and "El Movimiento Chicano" honor the roots of the Chicano and the Chicano Movement. The latter, as well as "América . . . América . . . América" first appeared written in *El Gallo: La Voz de la Justicia* during the Poor People's Campaign and March on Washington, D.C., in 1968, "América . . . América . . . América" demands that the United States pay its debt with social justice or pay the price in blood!

"¡¡Cuídate, Méjico!!" warns Mexico to look out for the United States. It warns about the dangers of what was to come much later in the form of the North American Free Trade Agreement (NAFTA). In it, Corky implores Mexico to "watch out." This is advice from its Mexican sons, the Chicanos of the United States of America, who know how to live in the belly of the shark and are well aware of its brutal racism and hatred of Mexicans, Blacks, and people of color.

Gonzales referred to himself as "the poet of the revolution." In his introduction to the 1972 Bantam Books edition of *Yo soy Joaquín/ I Am Joaquín,* he states, "There is no inspiration without identifiable images, there is no conscience without the sharp knife of truthful exposure, and ultimately there are no revolutions without poets (1)." Stan Steiner, one of the first to write about the Chicano experience, in his 1969 book *La Raza: The Mexican Americans,* referred to Corky as "The Poet in the Boxing Ring."[19]

Many of his writings in this book were taken from *El Gallo: La Voz de la Justicia.* We have also included three editorials from the newspaper that Corky edited and published from 1967 to 1980.

In Chapter V, the first of the editorials comes from the very first number of *El Gallo.* He states, "*El Gallo* was born out of frustration and determination for the truth. The truth about our people is never printed in the major newspapers. The sponsors of *El Gallo* found it necessary to establish and financially support a newspaper that would be the voice of the people."[20]

The second piece is the letter he wrote to the chair of the Denver Democratic Party when he resigned from the party on June 13, 1967. Corky had been involved in the party since he was district captain in 1957 and, subsequently, he ran for several political offices on the Democratic ticket, including City Council in 1955 and the state legislature in 1964. He headed the "Viva Kennedy" Colorado campaign in 1960. In this letter he closes by stating, "I can only visualize that your goal is the complete emasculation of manhood, sterilization of human dignity, and, that you not only conscientiously, but purposely are creating a world of lackeys, politico boot lickers and prostitutes."[21]

He wrote the Western Union telegram to Tomás and Berta Rodríguez of Dallas, Texas, included next, in a show of support after the Dallas police and federal officers had demolished their apartment. The police had mistakenly shot them in a search for two people accused of killing three deputies.

Corky's letter to Reies López Tijerina, the leader of La Alianza Federal de Mercedes, on October 20, 1972, explained why he would not be attending the Congress on Land and Cultural Reform. In it he states, "In the past years I have dissociated myself from those people who confuse and mislead the gullible government representatives. I want no type of alignment with political prostitutes; I have no intention of creating a reaction for the profitable benefit of the professional program managers." He further states, "One of these great issues on which all struggles are based is land. Land is the greatest issue with which to organize our people."[22]

Corky sent this "Discurso al Congreso de la Tierra" to Tijerina with the letter mentioned above. We present it here in Spanish and English, as printed in *El Gallo: La Voz de la Justicia* in October 1972. In this position paper he lays out the importance of land and its relationship to Chicanos and the Movement. In addition, Corky identifies the responsibilities of Chicanos in the Movement and quotes Ricardo Flores Magón, the exiled Mexican Liberal Movement leader and publisher of *Regeneración* and *Revolución* newspapers: "When I die, my enemies will say, here lies a madman; my friends will say, here lies a dreamer and a fool; but no one can say that I was a coward or a traitor to my ideals and my principles."

Corky wrote the "Letter to the Editor," the next piece, in response to criticism of the Crusade by the editor of the *Denver Rocky Mountain News*. In this letter, he points out the importance of the Crusade's independence and self-determination. In another response to a newspaper, the *Denver Post,* Corky's letter "We Will Endure" responded to the paper's attempt to link the Crusade for Justice to the two car bombings on May 27 and May 29, 1974, in Boulder, Colorado, that killed six Chicano and Chicana students. He states, "We intend to survive no matter what the odds against us are. We will continue with our work and encourage our people to continue the struggle for liberation, despite coercion, threats, or death."

Corky Gonzales wrote the way he boxed and played his politics. He wrote the way one of his heroes, Emilano Zapata, lived his life. According to Enrique Krauze, "Zapata era un hombre de convicciones absolutas."[23] (Zapata was a man of absolute convictions.) In reading Corky's writings, you come to the same conclusion. Corky lived his life and wrote "con convicciones absolutas." He never backed down from his convictions or changed his direction. In his "Message to el Congreso on Land and Cultural Reform," Corky stated,

> Personally, the direction I chose some years back is still the same direction I choose today. The man who makes compromises based on politics, personal gain, and personal financial interests is as enslaved when his pocket is full of money as when he was poor. When they gave us powdered milk, we were slaves; when tomorrow they give us cream, there will be a financial or political hook in our bodies and we will still be slaves. Those people who see victory in the form of full stomachs and pockets full of money while they still squat and bow to the establishment, who still have inferiority complexes, are not any more liberated than animals in a cage.[24]

Later he makes the point, "I personally cannot change my views from yesterday for promises of tomorrow. I cannot and will not change philosophy for fear of disagreement, discomfort, prison, or death."[25]

Throughout his writing we see Gonzales' major themes: nationalism, building the nation of Aztlán, *la familia*, economic independence, self-determination, cultural and historical pride, *mestizaje*, Chicano unity, liberation, brotherhood or *hermandad*, self-defense, inclusion of all La Raza, and political independence. All of these were major issues of intense debate during the Chicano Movement.

As the Crusade for Justice became more powerful and better known, it also became the target of local, state, and federal police agencies. It even drew the interest of the U.S. Congress. On October 1, 1975, U.S. Representative Larry McDonald of Georgia read into the *Congressional Record* an extensive report on the Crusade for Justice under the title of "Colorado Terrorism." The report accused the Crusade of "being an enemy of the system" and of various attempted terrorist activities: it spoke of "evidence of national and international revolutionary support for the Crusade."[26] For a detailed account on the relations between the Crusade for Justice, the FBI, and local police agencies, see Ernesto B. Vigil's book, *The Crusade for Justice: Chicano Militancy and the Government's War on Dissent.*

Corky wrote while leading one of the most influential and controversial Chicano civil and human rights organizations, the Crusade for Justice. During this period, the Crusade for Justice established La Escuela y Colegio Tlatelolco, a primary, secondary, and undergraduate school. The Crusade building, located at 16th and Downing Street in Denver, had a bookstore, a curio shop, a large lunchroom, a boxing gym, a 500-seat auditorium, twenty-four classrooms, several offices, a lounge, art studios, and a print shop. The Crusade also had one of finest Mexican ballets outside of Mexico, The Ballet Chicano de Aztlán, and the theater company "El Teatro Pachuco."

The Crusade for Justice was a comprehensive human rights organization. It provided a full array of community services in employment, legal defense, education, civil rights, political action, immigration, and recreation. Chicanos and others who had a problem, especially with the police, schools, or jobs, came to the Crusade for help, comfort, and relief.

The 1967 edition of *Yo soy Joaquín/I Am Joaquín* describes Rodolfo "Corky" Gonzales as a poet, playwright, lecturer, political activist, community organizer, and a publisher. This book presents these facets of Rodolfo "Corky" Gonzales through his own writings and in Corky's own words.

Antonio Esquibel
Denver, Colorado, 2000

Notes

1. David Conde, "Rodolfo (Corky) Gonzales," *Dictionary of Literary Biography* (Detroit: Gale Research Co., 1992) 111.
2. B. Vázquez, "Cross for Maclovio," *El Gallo: La Voz de la Justicia* August 1967.
3. "Tribute to Rodolfo "Corky" Gonzales," Paramount Theatre Program, Denver, Colorado, 10 Apr. 1988.
4. "Twenty-Fourth Annual Awards Banquet, Colorado Sports Hall of Fame, 1967-1988," Denver, Colorado, 15 Feb. 1988.
5. Ibid.
6. "The Denver Post's List of Colorado's Greatest Athletics of the 1900s," *The Denver Post* Dec. 1999: D11.
7. (Madison: The University of Wisconsin Press, 1999.)
8. (New York: The Ring Shop Inc., 1950) 393.
9. Rudolfo A. Anaya and Francisco A. Lomelí eds., *Aztlán: Essays on the Chicano Homeland* (Albuquerque: University of New Mexico Press, 1993).
10. Rodolfo Gonzalez, *I Am Joaquín/Yo soy Joaquín: An Epic Poem* (New York: Bantam, 1972).
11. Rodolfo Gonzalez, *I Am Joaquín/Yo soy Joaquín: An Epic Poem* (Denver: The Crusade for Justice, 1967).
12. Rodolfo Gonzalez, *I Am Joaquín/Yo soy Joaquín: An Epic Poem* (Denver, La Escuela de Tlatelolco, 1991).
13. *I Am Joaquín: An Epic Poem*, dir. Luis Valdez, perf. and produced by El Teatro Campesino, 1972.
14. *I Am Joaquín: An Epic Poem*, dir. Luis Valdez, perf. and produced by El Teatro Campesino, 1972. Available from La Escuela Tlatelolco Centro de Estudios, 1949 N. Federal Blvd., Denver, Colorado, 80211.

15. David Conde, "Rodolfo (Corky) Gonzales," *Dictionary of Literary Biography* (Detroit: Gale Research Co., 1992) 111.
16. (Madison: The University of Wisconsin Press, 1998) 221–235.
17. Arnulfo Casias, remarks, "Tribute to Rodolfo "Corky" Gonzales," Denver, 10 Apr. 1988.
18. Rodolfo "Corky" Gonzales, personal interview, 10 Apr. 1999.
19. (New York: Harper & Row, 1969) 378.
20. "Editorial," *El Gallo: La Voz de la Justicia* 13 June 1967: 2.
21. "A Message to the Democratic Party," *El Gallo: La Voz de la Justicia* 13 June 1967.
22. "Discurso al congreso de la tierra," *El Gallo: La Voz de la Justicia* Oct. 1972: 11.
23. Enrique Krause, *Emiliano Zapata: El amor a la tierra* (México: Fondo de Cultura Económica, 1987) 64.
24. *El Gallo: La Voz de la Justicia* Oct. 1972: 3.
25. Ibid. p.3.
26. *Congressional Record*, 1 Oct. 1975.

CHAPTER I

Epic Poem

Yo soy Joaquín: Un poema épico, 2000

Yo soy Joaquín,
Perdido en un mundo de confusión,
Atrapado en el remolino de una
  Sociedad gringa,
Confundido por las reglas,
Despreciado por las actitudes,
Suprimido por manipulaciones,
Y destruido por la sociedad moderna.
Mis padres
  han perdido la batalla económica
y han ganado
  la lucha de supervivencia cultural.
¡Y ahora!
Yo tengo que escoger
Entre la paradoja del
Triunfo del espíritu,
a pesar del hambre física
    O
  existir en el puño
del neurosis social americano,
esterilización del alma
Y un estómago lleno.

*The following Spanish version was translated from the original 1967 English version of *I Am Joaquín,* published by the Crusade for Justice. Juanita Domínguez, an original board member of the Crusade for Justice, translated Corky's original English version into Spanish. Juanita Domínguez was also responsible for many of the Spanish translations in the Crusade for Justice's newspaper, *El Gallo: La Voz de la Justicia.*

We have translated the original English version with Corky's permission, adding accent marks, Spanish punctuation and articles, as appropriate. We used verb tenses that agree with the English version. In places where the original Spanish version used the preterite tense, we changed them to the present perfect tense to agree with the original English version. In some cases we substituted Spanish words that best convey the sense of the English text.

We made these modifications so the Spanish version would retain *el alma y el sentido* of Corky's original English version. Corky considers the following translation as a new Spanish edition of his original poem.

Sí,
He llegado desde muy lejos a ninguna parte,
de mala gana arrastrado por ese
monstruoso
   gigante técnico industrial llamado
   Progreso
y éxito angloamericano.
Me miro a mí mismo.
Veo a mis hermanos.
Lloro lágrimas de lamentación.
Siembro semillas de odio.
Me retiro a la seguridad dentro del
Círculo de la vida . . .
   MI PROPIA RAZA
Yo soy Cuauhtémoc,
Orgulloso y Noble
   Líder de hombres,
Rey de un imperio,
civilizado más allá de los sueños
   del Gachupín Cortez,
Quien también es la sangre,
el reflejo de mí mismo.
Yo soy el Príncipe de los Mayas
Yo soy Nezahualcóyotl,
Gran líder del los Chichimecas.
Yo soy la espada y la llama de Cortez
   el déspota
     Y
Yo soy El Águila y La Serpiente
   de la civilización azteca.
Yo era el dueño de toda la tierra que se podía
ver bajo la corona española,
Y trabajaba mi tierra
y daba mi sudor y sangre india
   al amo español
Quien gobernaba con tiranía a hombre y
bestia y todo lo que él podía pisotear

Pero . . .
LA TIERRA ERA MÍA . . .
Yo era ambos tirano y esclavo.
La iglesia Cristiana tomó su lugar
en el buen nombre de Dios,
para tomar y usar mi virgen fuerza y
Fé confiada,
Los sacerdotes
tantos buenos como malos
tomaron
Pero
dieron la verdad perdurable que
español,
indio,
mestizo
Todos eran hijos de Dios
Y
de estas palabras surgieron hombres
quienes rezaban y peleaban
por
su propio mérito como seres humanos,
por
aquel
MOMENTO DORADO
de
LIBERTAD
Y fui parte en sangre y espíritu
de aquel
valiente padre aldeano
Hidalgo
que en el año mil ochocientos diez
repicó la campana de la independencia
y dio el grito perdurable:
"El Grito de Dolores, Que mueran
los gachupines y que viva
la Virgen de Guadalupe . . ."
Yo condené al

que era yo.
Yo descomulgué a mi sangre
Lo desterré del púlpito para encabezar
una revolución sangrienta para él y para mí . . .
    Yo lo maté.
Su cabeza,
que es la mía y de todos aquellos quienes
han pasado por aquí,
La puse en la pared del fuerte
a esperar la Independencia.
¡Morelos!
  ¡Matamoros!
    ¡Guerrero!
Todos Compañeros en el acto, se pararon
EN FRENTE DE AQUELLA PARED DE
    INFAMIA
a sentir el arrancón caliente de plomo
  hecho por mis manos.
Morí con ellos . . .
Viví con ellos . . .
Pude ver a mi patria libre.
Libre
del dominio español, en
  mil ochocientos veinte y uno.
    ¿¿Méjico estaba Libre??
Ya no había corona
      pero
permanecían todos sus parásitos
  y gobernaban
  y enseñaban
con el fusil y la llama y el poder místico.
Yo trabajaba,
Yo sudaba,
Yo derramaba sangre,
Yo rezaba
  Y
esperaba silenciosamente que la vida

comenzara de nuevo.
Yo luché y morí
por
Don Benito Juárez
Guardián de la Constitución
Yo era él
en los caminos empolvados
en los campos áridos
cuando él protegía sus archivos
como protegía Moisés sus sacramentos.
Él tenía su Méjico
en la mano
en
el terreno más desolado
y remoto
el cual era su patria,
Y este Gran
Pequeño Zapoteca
no dio
ni lo que cubre una mano
de la tierra de su patria ni a
Reyes ni a Monarcas ni a Presidentes
de potencias extranjeras.
Yo soy Joaquín.
Cabalgué con Pancho Villa
rudo y cariñoso.
Un tornado a toda fuerza,
alimentado e inspirado
por la pasión y el fuego
de toda su gente de la tierra.
Yo soy Emiliano Zapata.
"Este terreno
Esta tierra
es
NUESTRA"
Las Aldeas
Las Montañas

Los Arroyos
 Son de los Zapatistas.
 Nuestra vida
  O la Tuya
es el único cambio por la blanda tierra morena,
y el maíz.
¡Todo lo que es nuestra recompensa,
 Un credo que formó una constitución
  para todos los que se atreven a vivir libres!
"Esta tierra es nuestra . . .
 Padre, te la devuelvo.
  Méjico debe ser libre . . ."
Cabalgué con los revolucionarios
  en contra de mí mismo
Yo soy el rural
 vulgar y bruto,
Yo soy el indio de la montaña,
 superior sobre todo.
Las pisadas tronadoras son mis caballos.
El chirrido de las ametralladoras
 es la muerte para todo lo que soy:
 Yaquí
  Tarahumara
  Chamula
  Zapoteca
  Mestizo
   Español
Yo he sido la Revolución Sangrienta,
El Vencedor,
El Vencido,
Yo he matado
 y me han matado.
   Yo soy los déspotas Díaz
    y Huerta
y el apóstol de la democracia
   Francisco Madero
Yo soy

las mujeres fieles
con sus rebozos negros
quienes mueren conmigo
o viven
según el lugar y el tiempo.
Yo soy el
 leal,
  humilde,
   Juan Diego,
    la Virgen de Guadalupe,
y Tonantzín, la Diosa Azteca.
Cabalgué las montañas de San Joaquín.
Cabalgué al este y al norte
 hasta las Montañas Rocosas
      Y
todos los hombres temían las pistolas
      de Joaquín Murrieta.
Maté a esos hombres que se atrevieron
 a robar mi mina,
  que violaron y mataron a
          mi Amor
          mi Esposa
Luego
Yo maté para sobrevivir.
Y fui Elfego Baca
 viviendo mis nueve vidas plenamente.
Yo fui los hermanos Espinoza
 del Valle de San Luis.
Todos
fueron añadidos al número de cabezas
que
 en el nombre de la civilización
se pusieron a la pared de la independencia.
Las cabezas de hombres valientes
que murieron por causa o por principio.
Buenos o malos.
      ¡Hidalgo! ¡Zapata!

¡Murrieta! ¡Espinozas!
son unos pocos.
Ellos
se arriesgaron a enfrentar
la fuerza de la tiranía
   de hombres
    que gobiernan
    con farsa e hipocresía
Aquí estoy mirando hacia el pasado
y ahora veo
   el presente
y aún
  Yo soy el campesino
  Soy el gordo coyote político
     Yo,
del misno nombre,
   Joaquín.
En un país que ha borrado
toda mi historia,
   sofocado todo mi orgullo.
En un país que ha puesto un peso
diferente de indignidad sobre
   mi
     agobiada
       espalda
         anciana.
   Inferioridad
es la nueva carga . . .
  El Indio ha perdurado y todavía
ha emergido el vencedor,
  El Mestizo todavía tiene que superar,
  Y al Gachupín solo lo ignoraremos.
Me miro
y veo la parte de mí
que renuncia a mi padre y a mi madre
y se disuelve en la mezcla de esta sociedad
para desaparecer en la vergüenza.

A veces
traiciono a mi hermano
y lo reclamo
como mío cuando la sociedad me otorga
autoridad nominal
     en el mismo nombre de la sociedad.
Yo soy Joaquín,
que se sangra de muchas maneras.
Los altares de Moctezuma
     Yo manché con sangre roja
Mi espalda de esclavitud indígena
fue desnudada y enrojecida
por los azotes de los patrones
que perderían su sangre tan pura
cuando La Revolución les exigió recompensa
Parados en frente de las paredes de
Retribución.
     Sangre . . .
     ha corrido de
          mí
en todo campo de batalla
          entre
Campesino, Hacendado
     Esclavo y Amo
          y
     Revolución.
Yo me tiré de la torre de Chapultepec
     al mar de la fama;
La bandera de mi patria
     mi sudario;
Con los Niños,
     cuyo orgullo y valor
no pudieron entregar
     con indignidad
          la bandera de su patria
A extranjeros . . . en su tierra.
Ahora

me desangro en una celda hedionda
del garrote,
o de la pistola,
o de la tiranía.
Me desangro mientras los guantes viciosos del
hambre me parten la cara, los ojos,
mientras peleo desde los Barrios hediondos
al encanto del cuadrilátero
y las luces de la fama
o el pesar mutilado.
Mi sangre corre pura sobre los cerros
helados de las Islas de Alaska,
sobre la playa esparcida de cuerpos
de Normandía, la tierra ajena de la Corea
  y ahora
   Vietnam.
Aquí estoy
  ante la corte de la Justicia
   Culpable
por toda la gloria de mi Raza
  a ser sentenciado a la desesperanza.
Aquí estoy
 Pobre en cuanto a dinero
 Arrogante de orgullo
  Valiente de Machismo
  Rico en valor
   y
  Rico en espíritu y en la fé.
Mis rodillas están costradas de lodo.
Mis manos llenas de callos por el azadón,
Yo he hecho al gringo rico
    pero todavía
 La Igualdad es solamente una palabra,
  El Tratado de Hidalgo se ha quebrantado
 y es solamente otra promesa traicionera.
Mi tierra está perdida
  y robada,

Mi cultura la han violado,
  Alargo
  la fila de la puerta de la asistencia social
y lleno las cárceles con crimen.
  Estos son pues
  las recompensas
    que esta sociedad tiene
Para los hijos de Jefes
    y Reyes
    y Revolucionarios sangrientos.
Quienes
dieron a gente extranjera
    todas sus habilidades e ingeniosidad
para prepararles el camino con su Inteligencia y Sangre a
aquellas hordas de Extranjeros hambientos
        por el Oro.
Quienes
cambiaron nuestro idioma
y plagiaron nuestros hechos
        en hechos de valor
        suyos.
Despreciaron nuestro modo de vivir
  y tomaron lo que podían usar.
        Nuestro Arte,
        Nuestra Literatura,
        Nuestra música ignoraron
y así dejaron las cosas de valor verdadero
y arrebataron su propia destrucción
        con su Gula y Avaricia.
Ignoraron aquella fuente purificadora
        de naturaleza y hermandad
La cual es Joaquín.
  El arte de nuestros grandes señores
        Diego Rivera
        Siqueiros
        Orozco es sólo
otro acto de revolución para

la salvación de la raza humana.
La Música del Mariachi, el
corazón y el alma
de la gente de la tierra,
la vida del niño
y la alegría del amor.
Los corridos relatan los cuentos
de la vida y de la muerte,
        de la tradición,
    Las Leyendas viejas y nuevas,
    de la alegría
        de la pasión y del pesar
    de la gente . . . que soy yo.
Yo estoy en los ojos de la mujer,
    amparada bajo
su robozo negro
    ojos hondos y
    dolorosos,
Que llevan la pena de hijos enterrados desde hace mucho tiempo
    o agonizando
        Muertos
sobre el campo de batalla o alambre de púas
    de la lucha social.
Su rosario lo reza y lo toca
sin cesar
    como la familia que
trabaja un surco de betabel
    y da vuelta
    y trabaja
    y trabaja
    No hay fin.
Sus ojos un espejo de todo cariño
    y todo el amor por mí,
Y yo soy ella
Y ella es yo.
    Juntos enfrentamos la vida con
    pena, coraje, alegría, fé y

sueños dorados.
Lloro lágimas de angustia
cuando veo a mis hijos desaparecer
tras el velo de mediocridad
para jamás mirar hacia atrás para acordarse de mí.
Yo soy Joaquín.
Tengo que pelear
y ganar esta lucha
por mis hijos, y ellos
nececitan saber de mí
Quien soy Yo.
Parte de la sangre que corre profundamente en mí
No pudo ser vencida por los Moros.
Los derroté después de quinientos años,
y yo perduré.
La sangre que es mía
ha obrado continuamente quinientos
años bajo el talón de los europeos
lujuriosos
¡Todavía sigo aquí!
He perdurado en las montañas escarpadas
de nuestro país
He sobrevivido los trabajos y la esclavitud
de los campos.
Yo he existido
en los barrios de la ciudad,
en los suburbios de la intolerancia,
en las minas del esnobismo social,
en las prisiones del desánimo,
en la porquería de la explotación
y
en el calor feroz del odio racial.

Y ahora suena la trompeta,
La música de la gente anima la
Revolución,
Como un gigante dormido lentamente

alza la cabeza
al sonido de
  Patulladas
  Voces clamorosas
  Tonadas del Mariachi
  Explosiones ardientes de tequila
  El aroma de chile verde y
  Los dulces ojos morenos de la esperanza de una
                                        vida mejor.
Y en todos los campos fértiles,
        los llanos áridos,
las aldeas de las montañas,
las ciudades contaminadas
    Comenzamos a movernos.
¡La Raza!
¡Mejicano!
  ¡Español!
    ¡Latino!
      ¡Hispano!
        ¡Chicano!
o lo que me llame yo mismo,
        Tengo la misma aparencia,
        Tengo los mismos sentimientos,
        Yo lloro
          y
        Canto igual
Yo soy las masas de mi gente y
me niego a ser absorbido.
      Yo soy Joaquín
Los retos son muchos
pero mi espíritu es fuerte
          Mi fé inquebrantable
          Mi sangre pura
Yo soy el Príncipe Azteca y el Cristo Cristiano
      ¡YO PERDURARÉ!
      ¡YO PERDURARÉ!

I Am Joaquín: an Epic Poem, 1967

I am Joaquín
Lost in a world of confusion,
Caught up in a whirl of a
       gringo society,
Confused by the rules,
Scorned by attitudes,
Suppressed by manipulations,
And destroyed by modern society.
My fathers
 have lost the economic battle
and won
 the struggle of cultural survival.
And now!
 I must choose
Between the paradox of
Victory of the spirit,
despite physical hunger
       Or
 to exist in the grasp
of American social neurosis,
sterilization of the soul
 and a full stomach.
Yes,
I have come a long way to nowhere,
Unwillingly dragged by that
 monstrous, technical
 industrial giant called
       Progress
and Anglo success . . .
 I look at myself.
 I watch my brothers.

*Reprinted from original 1967 book.

I shed tears of sorrow.
I sow seeds of hate.
I withdraw to the safety within the
circle of life . . .
        MY OWN PEOPLE
I am Cuauhtémoc,
Proud and Noble
    Leader of men,
King of an empire,
civilized beyond the dreams
of the Gachupín Cortez.
Who is also the blood,
   the image of myself.
I am the Maya Prince.
I am Nezahualcóyotl,
Great leader of the Chichimecas.
I am the sword and flame of Cortez
                    the despot.
                  And
I am the Eagle and Serpent of
          the Aztec civilization.
I owned the land as far as the eye
could see under the crown of Spain,
and I toiled on my earth
and gave my Indian sweat and blood
   for the Spanish master,
Who ruled with tyranny over man and
beast and all that he could trample
               But . . .
    THE GROUND WAS MINE . . .
I was both tyrant and slave.
As Christian church took its place
in God's good name,
to take and use my Virgin Strength and
               Trusting faith,

The priests
  both good and bad
              took
But
 gave a lasting truth that
    Spaniard,
      Indio,
        Mestizo
Were all God's children
And
 from these words grew men
    who prayed and fought
              for
 their own worth as human beings,
    for
      that
        GOLDEN MOMENT
        of
        FREEDOM.
I was part in blood and spirit
 of that
    courageous village priest
                  Hidalgo
in the year eighteen hundred and ten
who rang the bell of independence
and gave out that lasting cry:
 "El Grito de Dolores, Que mueran
 los Guachupines y que viva
 la Virgen de Guadalupe . . ."
I sentenced him
        who was me.
I excommunicated him my blood.
I drove him from the pulpit to lead
 a bloody revolution for him and me . . .
    I killed him.
His head,

which is mine and all of those
who have come this way,
I placed on that fortress wall
to wait for independence.
Morelos!
    Matamoros!
        Guerrero!
All Compañeros in the act,
STOOD AGAINST THAT WALL OF
                  INFAMY
to feel the hot gouge of lead
  which my hand made.
I died with them . . .
  I lived with them
    I lived to see our country free.
Free
  from Spanish rule in
  eighteen-hundred-twenty-one.
    Mexico was free ? ?
The crown was gone
    but
all his parasites remained
    and ruled
    and taught
with gun and flame and mystic power.
I worked,
I sweated,
I bled,
I prayed
  and
waited silently for life to again
              commence.
I fought and died
    for
    Don Benito Juárez
Guardian of the Constitution.

I was him
   on dusty roads
     on barren land
as he protected his archives
 as Moses did his sacraments.
He held his Mexico
    in his hand
      on
     the most desolate
     and remote ground
      which was his country,
And this Giant
    Little Zapotec
gave
 not one palm's breath
of his country to
 Kings or Monarchs or Presidents
of foreign powers.
I am Joaquín.
I rode with Pancho Villa,
 crude and warm.
A tornado at full strength,
nourished and inspired
 by the passion and the fire
 of all his earthy people.
I am Emiliano Zapata.
  "This Land
    This Earth
     is
     OURS"
The Villages
 The Mountains
 The Streams
  belong to the Zapatistas.
  Our Life
Or yours

is the only trade for soft brown earth
and maize.
All of which is our reward,
  A creed that formed a constitution
  for all who dare live free!
"this land is ours . . .
    Father, I give it back to you.
    Mexico must be free . . ."
I ride with Revolutionists
        against myself.
I am Rural
  Coarse and brutal,
I am the mountain Indian,
   superior over all.
The thundering hoofbeats are my horses.
The chattering of machine guns
 is death to all of me:
 Yaqui
  Tarahumara
   Chamula
    Zapotec
     Mestizo
      Español
I have been the Bloody Revolution,
The Victor,
The Vanquished,
I have killed
 and been killed.
    I am despots Díaz
    and Huerta
and the apostle of democracy
    Francisco Madero
I am
the black shawled
faithful women
who die with me

or live
depending on the time and place.
I am
faithful,
   humble,
     Juan Diego
     the Virgin de Guadalupe
Tonantzin, Aztec Goddess too.
I rode the mountains of San Joaquín.
I rode as far East and North
   as the Rocky Mountains
      and
all men feared the guns of
      Joaquín Murrieta.
I killed those men who dared
to steal my mine,
   who raped and Killed
                  my love
                  my Wife
Then
I Killed to stay alive.
I was Alfego Baca,
   living my nine lives fully.
I was the Espinosa brothers
   of the Valle de San Luis
All
were added to the number of heads
that
   in the name of civilization
were placed on the wall of independence.
Heads of brave men
who died for cause and principle.
Good or Bad.
      Hidalgo! Zapata!
      Murrieta! Espinosa!
are but a few.

They
dared to face
The force of tyranny
    of men
      who rule
        By farce and hypocrisy
I stand here looking back,
and now I see
      the present
and still
  I am the campesino
  I am the fat political coyote
        I,
of the same name,
        Joaquín.
In a country that has wiped out
all my history,
      stifled all my pride.
In a country that has placed a
different weight of indignity upon
      my
      age
      old
      burdened back.
    Inferiority
is the new load . . .
The Indian has endured and still
emerged the winner,
  The Mestizo must yet overcome,
  And the Gauchupín we'll just ignore.
I look at myself
and see part of me
who rejects my father and my mother
and dissolves into the melting pot
  to disappear in shame.
  I sometimes

sell my brother out
and reclaim him
for my own, when society gives me
token leadership
    in society's own name.
I am Joaquín,
who bleeds in many ways.
The altars of Moctezuma
        I stained a bloody red.
My back of Indian slavery
        was stripped crimson
from the whips of masters
who would lose their blood so pure
when Revolution made them pay
Standing against the walls of
Retribution.
    Blood . . .
    Has flowed from
        me
on every battlefield
        between
Campesino, Hacendado
    Slave and Master
        and
    Revolution.
I jumped from the tower of Chapultepec
    into the sea of fame;
My country's flag
    my burial shroud;
With Los Niños,
    whose pride and courage
could not surrender
    with indignity
        their country's flag
To strangers . . . in their land.
Now
I bleed in some smelly cell

from club,
or gun,
or tyranny,
I bleed as the vicious gloves of hunger
cut my face and eyes,
as I fight my way from stinking Barrios
to the glamour of the Ring
   and lights of fame
   or mutilated sorrow.
My blood runs pure on the ice caked
hills of the Alaskan Isles,
on the corpse strewn beach of Normandy,
the foreign land of Korea
               and now
                  Vietnam.

Here I stand
         before the court of Justice
              Guilty
for all the glory of my Raza
         to be sentenced to despair.
Here I stand
         Poor in money
   Arrogant with pride
         Bold with Machismo
         Rich in courage
               and
   Wealthy in spirit and faith.
My knees are caked with mud.
My hands calloused from the hoe.
I have made the Anglo rich
         yet
 Equality is but a word,
   the Treaty of Hidalgo has been broken
   and is but another treacherous promise.
My land is lost
         and stolen,

My culture has been raped,
          I lengthen
    the line at the welfare door
and fill the jails with crime.
     These then
are the rewards
          this society has
For sons of Chiefs
          and Kings
          and bloody Revolutionists.
Who
gave a foreign people
     all their skills and ingenuity
to pave the way with Brains and Blood
for
those hordes of Gold starved
Strangers
Who
changed our language
and plagiarized our deeds
               as feats of valor
               of their own.
They frowned upon our way of life
 and took what they could use.
          Our Art
          Our Literature
          Our Music, they ignored
so they left the real things of value
and grabbed at their own destruction
          by their Greed and Avarice
They overlooked that cleansing fountain of
          nature and brotherhood
Which is Joaquín.
   The art of our great señores
          Diego Rivera
          Siqueiros
          Orozco is but

another act of revolution for
the Salvation of mankind.
　Mariachi music, the
　heart and soul
　of the people of the earth,
　the life of child,
　and the happiness of love.
　The Corridos tell the tales
　of life and death,
　　　　of tradition,
　Legends old and new,
　of Joy
　　of passion and sorrow
　of the people . . . who I am.
I am in the eyes of woman,
　　　　sheltered beneath
her shawl of black,
　　　　deep and sorrowful
　　　　eyes,
That bear the pain of sons long buried
　　　　or dying,
　　　　Dead
on the battlefield or on the barbed wire
　　　　of social strife.
Her rosary she prays and fingers
endlessly
　　like the family
working down a row of beets
　　　to turn around
　　　and work
　　　and work
　　　There is no end.
Her eyes a mirror of all the warmth
　　　and all the love for me,
And I am her
And she is me.

We face life together in sorrow,
anger, joy, faith and wishful
thoughts.
I shed tears of anguish
as I see my children disappear
behind a shroud of mediocrity
never to look back to remember me.
I am Joaquín.
      I must fight
      And win this struggle
      for my sons, and they
      must know from me
      Who I am.
Part of the blood that runs deep in me
Could not be vanquished by the Moors.
I defeated them after five hundred years,
and I endured.
      The part of blood that is mine
      has labored endlessly five-hundred
      years under the heel of lustful
         Europeans
         I am still here!
I have endured in the rugged mountains
 of our country.
I have survived the toils and slavery
 of the fields.
         I have existed
in the barrios of the city,
in the suburbs of bigotry,
in the mines of social snobbery,
in the prisons of dejection,
in the muck of exploitation
and
in the fierce heat of racial hatred.
And now the trumpet sounds,
The music of the people stirs the
      Revolution,

Like a sleeping giant it slowly
rears its head
to the sound of
    Tramping feet
    Clamoring voices
    Mariachi strains
    Fiery tequila explosions
    The smell of chile verde and
    Soft brown eyes of expectation for a
                  better life.
And in all the fertile farm lands,
           the barren plains,
the mountain villages,
smoke smeared cities
    We start to MOVE.
La Raza!
Mejicano!
 Español!
  Latino!
   Hispano!
   Chicano!
or whatever I call myself,
    I look the same
    I feel the same
    I Cry
       and
    Sing the same
I am the masses of my people and
I refuse to be absorbed.
    I am Joaquín
The odds are great
but my spirit is strong
      My faith unbreakable
      My blood is pure
I am Aztec Prince and Christian Christ
    I SHALL ENDURE!
    I WILL ENDURE!

CHAPTER II

Seven Major Speeches

El Plan del Barrio

We are basically communal people . . . in the pattern of our Indian ancestors. Part of our cultural rights and cultural strengths is our communal values. We lived together for over a century and never had to fence our lands. When the gringo came, the first thing he did was to fence land. We opened our houses and hearts to him and trained him to irrigated farming, ranching, stock raising, and mining. He listened carefully and moved quickly, and when we turned around, he had driven us out and kept us out with violence, trickery, legal and court entanglements. The land for all people, the land of the brave, becomes the land for the few and the land of the bully . . .

Robbed of our land, our people were driven to the migrant labor fields and the cities. Poverty and city living under the colonial system of the Anglo has castrated our people's culture, consciousness of our heritage, and language. Because our cultural rights, which are guaranteed by treaty, and because the U.S. says in its constitution that all treaties are the law of the land . . .

Therefore we demand:

Housing: We demand the necessary resources to plan our living accommodations so that is possible to extend family homes to be situated in a communal style . . . around plazas or parks with plenty of space for the children. We want our living areas to fit the needs of the family and cultural protection, and not the needs of the city pork barrel, the building corporations, or the architects.

Education: We demand that our schools be built in the same communal fashion as our neighborhoods . . . that they be warm and inviting facilities and not jails. We demand a completely free education from kindergarten to college, with no fees, no lunch charge, no supplies charges, no tuition, no dues.

We demand that all teachers live within walking distance of the schools. We demand that from kindergarten through college, Spanish be the first language and English the second language and the text-

---

Delivered at the Poor People's Campaign, Washington, D.C., May 1968.

books to be rewritten to emphasize the heritage and the contributions of the Mexican American or Indio-Hispano in the building of the Southwest. We also demand the teaching of the contributions and history of other minorities which have also helped build this country. We also feel that each neighborhood school complex should have its own school board made up of members who live in the community the school serves.

Job Development: We demand training and placement programs which would develop the vast human resources available in the Southwest. For those of our people who want further choices in employment and professions we wish training programs which would be implemented and administered by our own people.

In job placement, we demand that, first of all, racist placement tests be dropped and, in their place, tests be used which relate to the qualifications necessary for that job. Further, we demand nondiscrimination by all private and public agencies.

We demand seed money to organize the necessary trade, labor, welfare, housing, etc. unions to represent those groups. We further demand that existing labor, trade and white collar unions' nondiscriminatory membership practices be enforced by a national labor relations act.

Law Enforcement: We demand an immediate investigation of the records of all prisoners to correct the legal errors, or detect the prejudice which operated in those court proceedings, causing their convictions or extra heavy sentencing. As these cases are found, we demand that the federal government reimburse those prisoners for loss of time and money.

We demand immediate suspension of officers suspected of police brutality until a full hearing is held in the neighborhood of the event.

We demand suspension of the citywide juvenile court system and the creation of a neighborhood community court to deal with allegations of crime. In addition, instead of the prowl-car, precinct system, we want to gradually install a neighborhood protection system, where residents are hired to assist and safeguard in matters of community safety or possible crime.

Economic Opportunities: We demand that the businesses serving our community be owned by that community. Seed money is required to start cooperative grocery stores, gas stations, furniture stores, etc. Instead of our people working in big factories across the city, we want training in our own communities. These industries would be co-ops with the profits staying in the community.

Agricultural Reforms: We demand that not only the land, which is our ancestral right, be given back to these pueblos, but also restitution for mineral, natural resources, grazing, and timber used.

We demand compensation for taxes, legal costs, etc., which pueblos and heirs spent trying to save their land. We demand the suspension of taxation by the acre, and institute instead the previous taxation system of our ancestors; that is, the products of the land are taxed, not the land itself.

Redistribution of the Wealth: That all citizens of this country share in the wealth of this nation by institution of economic reforms that would provide for all people, and that welfare in the form of subsidies in taxes and pay-off to corporate owners be reverted to the people who in reality are the foundation of the economy and the tax base for this society.

Land Reform: A complete reevaluation of the Homestead Act, to provide people ownership of the natural resources that abound in this country. A birthright should not only place responsibility on the individual but grant him ownership of the land he dies for.

Arizona State University Speech

This is probably the first time I've spoken in Arizona, at a university. It pleases me to hear that the young leadership, like López and Guerrero and the young people of MATA, are taking an active part. They are active not only in the university but down in the community. And that is what is important.

Our youth's minds, something that Gustavo was telling you, should not be suppressed in these universities. In the past most of our youth only went to high school. If they were lucky enough or had enough money or were sharp enough to get a scholarship, they attended college. Some did it, like a friend of mine from Denver, Louis Rubalid, who sits out in the audience. He fought his way as a professional fighter through college.

It's important to know that you have to not just evaporate or disappear after you get out of the college scene. College is not the launching pad out of the community. We want to see our youth come back to the community, but not on the basis of some of the lawyers that we have or some of the professional people.

I hate lawyers, especially because I know so many of them that are *cagados*. They have gone out and they crossed the bridge and they become like an astronaut and a satellite. They go out into gringo land and they never come back. However, if they do come back to the community, it is because the police are arresting our people. When the oppression hits our people, then they are needed in the community, and they live and feed off the needs of our people. If they come back to contribute, not to exploit, that's an important difference. You're not here only to obtain a professional level of educational attainment. You are not here only to learn something to take it out for your own economic freedom.

You see, the reason we have problems, is because too many people do not want to get involved. When the guy in the *cantina*, the pool hall,

Arizona State University Speech, October 14, 1970.
Transcribed from tapes recorded by George Carrillo, archived in the library of Arizona State University.

or the barber shop tells you, "Man, those Movement people are out of their minds. I take care of me, that's what is important, me." Ask him what he's doing for *la causa*. Ask him what he's doing for the Movement.

He's not going to be able to say anything. He is part of the problem because he's not doing anything. So, never fear that because you are involved, you're isolated from your people. Actually, you are going to be the leadership that draws your people together. It is important that our young people bring back their expertise, their professionalism, their degrees, their humanity, and their compassion, back home where it belongs, to the community.

As long as we cross that bridge and disappear, our people will be on the lowest ladder of educational attainment, as they are. They'll have the highest rate of unemployment, as they do have. They will have the biggest social and economic problems of any other group of people, because some people said that they don't count and that they don't have to get involved.

Now, many people say, I am involved on certain levels. We have to look at that and we have to ask what do you mean? People ask me, "What are your long-range goals? What are the solutions?" And I say, "Well, first we need to find out what the problem is." And we all say, we can all say the problem is unemployment. The problem is bad education. The problem is bad housing. The problem is bad hospital and medical care. The problem is narcotics. The problem is crime.

We say these are all the problems, and we all say that's right. How do those problems come to rest on our backs? How do those problems develop on a total mass of people, not on individuals? It is because the educational system teaches you that you can make it as long as you conform to society. This means that you must become a robot. You have to become another one of those human beings out there in that no man's land of a neurotic society. This is what you have to become to be what they want out of their schools.

There is one fact they do not want to admit. They do not want to admit that we have a different set of values. The white radical says it is a class struggle, and we say, that's fine! The Chicano comes along and tells me it's only a class struggle. I tell him no, it's just an ass struggle. You want to justify that you are with a radical white broad.

And often we are right. And we want to say that it is a class struggle, but with the class struggle, the Black agrees that it is also a racist struggle.

However, for us it goes even further. It is that we have a cultural difference. This is why the educational system does not want to teach you that the very government that you support in wars in Vietnam and Korea and other areas, the very government you're talking about, is the same government that committed genocide against the Indian, took over his land, and controls his money.

You know what the Pima Indian Reservation is like. If you haven't been there . . . that's one place I've been; I was there to see Ira Hayes's mother. We consider him one of the great heroes for raising the flag at Iwo Jima. They are still living in poverty that dates back a hundred years. You can still find that same type of poverty.

This is the same government that says you must fight for us. We say this is the same government that enslaved all the Blacks. The great white father is theirs, not ours; he belongs to that side of the Mississippi River. He was a cheater, and the new book on the bookkeeping system of George Washington, proves that he gained 30 pounds while his soldiers were freezing at Valley Forge. Also, while he was fighting for freedom, he had hundreds of black slaves on his own plantation.

We can evaluate that. Then evaluate that this part of Mexico, Aztlán, was taken in an aggressive war of expansionism even worse than the war in Vietnam.

They don't want you to know that, either. And they keep out Section 10 of The Treaty of Guadalupe Hidalgo. If you notice, when you go to the library, it's not part of the treaty, because it has to do with cultural autonomy. It has to do with the preservation of the ownership of land.

Now when we think on these bases, then we start to say we have ownership here. We are not born into this country just to fight for it. I say we were born into it to own it—that every living man is born to own part of the land, the economy, and everything else that goes with it.

So we look at the problem: the problem is the mass majority of society. It's true. It's true that only six percent of the population of this country controls more than sixty percent of the wealth of the world.

It's true that two percent of this nation makes all the decisions. And everybody thinks they are living in a democratic society.

So the problem is on our backs, and the way to get rid of it is not to deal with it. Now, we can deal with it by saying we are going to go into an armed revolution with four percent of the people against maybe fifty percent of the people.

Most of this society is brainwashed by their own TV, by their own literature, their own news media. Is there any part of that we control? In a democratic society, or in the Democratic and Republican parties, only the majority rules. The minority has no say-so, other than to become window dressing or a puppet.

So what do we have to do with ourselves? We have to start to organize ourselves around ourselves. We have to stop going to human relations conferences to educate the gringo on how to like us. We have to stop going to people and saying, "Please help us," because when you say "help us," it means I am inferior and only you can help me.

Many people base it right away, immediately, on the idea that we need money to fight this, to get what they've got. To get what we want, we have to come together and control our own economy. First, we have to create cultural awareness.

Five years ago we were saying that we needed to create a cultural renaissance, a cultural revival of whom we were. Many people, especially the radicals, said, "That is cultural revolution, and we don't want to buy into that."

However, when you have that layer and that step into liberation, when you can understand that you can love yourself for the contributions of your people, for the nobility of your heroes, for everything that we have done for this economy and this country, you can then look into the mirror and say, I am a man, I am a woman.

We are the schizophrenics of this society. We have guys walking around like John Wayne and singing like James Brown. They don't know who in the hell they are. You know it and I know it. I don't mind the part about James Brown, because music is universal. The fact is that they are not identifying with their historical roots!

Their historical roots are that they predate any gringo from that side of the Mississippi by nearly 500 years on one side of us and 20,000 years on the other side of us, because we are mestizos. We are

"La Raza Cósmica." We are the only integrated people on these two continents. We're not a minority. We're a majority, when you stretch us from here to Mexico to Peru.

When we start to think on those levels, when we start to teach in the barrio how we are colonized people, then we're able to understand how we live in this country and how this economy is based on the farm workers' struggle and the farm workers' production. Our people still use their hands in a society that is the most advanced technologically in the whole world.

When we can understand this concept, we can teach in the barrio. You are not going to teach it with radical statements, but you can teach it with grassroots, positive, simple-to-understand reasoning.

I stopped in Los Angeles. I was going to speak at UCLA, and Antonio Salazar, chair of MECHA, took me to his home. His folks still live in Hazard. They still live in the barrio. You know how these freeways cut and make little islands of barrios all across California. They don't care about it. They call it urban renewal. It's human removal.

When we were there, we walked down to the store to pick up some food. We walked to the store, and there were some guys standing around the corner in front of the store. They sell beer and wine there. And a couple of guys were hustling for a bottle. The little guy, Little John, who had gone to one of our conferences, came up and asked, "Hey, how you doing, man?"

I said, "I am fine."

"Hey, where are you going to speak at? Maybe we'll come down there tonight."

Then he told the other barrio guys, "Hey, come here, I want you to meet this cat."

We started shaking hands. He asked, "Hey, are you the guy that's fighting for some land?"

I told him, "No. I'm from Denver. We support the land issue and we support the farm workers. We support every problem that involves our people, and we have to start to organize our communities to control them ourselves."

"Ah," he said, "no sweat, look *ese*. There is not one gringo nor one black guy in this barrio. We control it."

I asked them, "Who runs the store?"

"Ah, some gringo."

"And who owns that clothing store across the street?"

"*Pues un pinche gringo.*"

"And who runs that housing project?"

"So what are we going to do, man?"

And then Little John says, "Yeah. They are all gringos in there! We're in occupied country."

Then the guy says, "You're from Denver, huh?" He looked into the distance to see if he could see it. He had never been out of that barrio. You see, he could relate only to that barrio. But he was not running the barrio.

I told him, "You guys are already organized. If someone came here from any other barrio and said, 'Hey, I'm taking over here,' you guys would kill him in a minute. You'd wipe him out because you're organized. Since you don't have anyone else to fight tonight, if you get pedo, instead, you are going to kill each other."

That comes from self-hatred, taught by the news media, by the institutions, by these institutions that we are in right now.

You see, self-hatred, that's why we kill each other, not self-love. If they organize, they'll take over Hazard. They will take over Hazard once they understand that they are already organized and they know what the direction ought to be.

That is what is taking place all across the Southwest. We are a family and we deny it. We say, and we preach, that the biggest organizing tool that we have is nationalism. Right away our intellectuals and some of our youth that almost think they have a degree, say, "Oh that's reverse racism." We tell them, "That is fine." If a father has children and doesn't take care of them, but goes across the city to take care of someone else's children, and lets his children go to the dogs, what do you call that in this society? Irresponsibility, irresponsibility to the very family that you have created.

That's why we're saying that's not reverse racism. That's "La Familia." First we must take care of our family. Nationalism is a tool. Now a lot of the young heavies that get started late get angry and use this as hate. Now we say nationalism is a tool for organization, not a weapon for hatred. Nationalism is a state of being a nation, not a state of creating an outside group that hates another group.

This is the difference. See, we created La Raza Unida, in Colorado. We have some thirty-five candidates there. The Democratic Party, which is hurting the most, took us to court and protested the candidates we have. They said no, and objected to our petitions. The Democratic chair of that state said, "To become part of La Raza Unida is reverse racism." What he was really saying was, "We already have a racist institution; why create your own?"

You see, we are telling them that we are creating our own political block, which has nothing to do with their legislature. Sure, we are running on the La Raza Unida ticket. We have thirty-five of the most beautiful, young, aggressive, progressive activist candidates. People who lead marches for farm workers. People who organize in the community. People who fight in the universities. These are the types of people we have. We don't have politicos. We have activists. We have people who are about the problems of their people.

That is what they are doing. They are using the political forum and getting the TV coverage, the press coverage, to relate and organize us all. So we now have a web of communication across the state. In addition, we have communication with south Texas, which has a La Raza Unida Party that has been successful in all their school board elections.

Now, you see. This becomes very important. We have to realize that we have a political philosophy. We don't care for *políticos* because many of our politicians in the past that we have supported have not done anything. I know because I was a stooge for the Democratic Party. I was the first Chicano Democratic district captain in the history of Denver. I knocked on doors and registered more people than anybody in Denver ever did. The only thing they offered me was the liquor license under the table to get a zone change for a rich company and get a cutback.

We wanted progress. We wanted social changes, and they would not give them to us. They wanted *vendidos*, and they wanted window dressing. We keep saying that you cannot go into a house full of disease with a bottle of Mercurochrome and expect to cure anybody. You are going to get sick.

We have seen that with some of our politicians, haven't we? Young people do not relate to political success symbols anymore, anyway, those young people who think. Political success symbols are the ones that have gone over and licked boots and rubbed elbows and sit at conferences and drink cocktails. They brag about how they went to the mayor's house, but make no changes.

The minute you have an issue, and you have one here at Union High School, right? You have an issue. I'd like to say to the leadership, and I'm not saying we're right, we make many mistakes in what we do, and what we have done in the past. We keep learning by making mistakes. This we do know: don't allow the *políticos* to come in and make the decisions for the community that has to deal with the establishment at Phoenix Union High School.

They have to sell out or they cannot keep their positions. They have to condone the actions of the administration or they have to sacrifice their positions.

We organize so that when one strong man stands up and says, "*Ya basta,* I will not condone the acts of a racist institution of any university or school," the other people stand up with him, not wait and just say, that's his bag. Because many of us know, those of us out of the barrio, we remember when the *placa* walked in, picked one Chicano, *palo,* hit him on the head, and the other guy from the barrio turned around and said, "That's not my bag."

No, we want to put into the heart and mind of every Mexicano that when one Mexicano is poor, we are all poor. If one is in jail, we are all in jail. If one of us has a bad education, we are all badly educated. If one of us has a problem, we all have a problem. We must understand that when they put one of our people up against the wall, that everybody needs to come up to see what's wrong.

The masses will make the difference. We are educating young people. Our young people here and across this country are saying, I am leading a "RESISTANCE," against institutional racism, racism or oppression, but when no one stands up with him, he commits suicide.

I was running from policemen up until the time I was eighteen years old, and still afraid of them, practically getting to middle age. Today we're teaching our youth at our school. We have decided to create a core leadership untainted by the confusion of these cookie-making-machines. Really! It is a cookie-making machine that goes boom, boom, boom, boom, and all the cookies come out looking alike. The only thing wrong is that some of them have names like Trujillo, Quintana, and some of them are black cookies. They don't fit the slots. We are creating our own school, Tlatelolco. Tlatelolco is our new school. We have primary, secondary, and college levels. Our students will be untainted. Our youth at the age of fourteen and fifteen will not turn around and run from the policemen, from any establishment man. And if he is alone, he commits suicide. That is why we have to educate the total masses of our people to understand what "La Familia" is about. This is why we have to organize ourselves in these universities. MASA means something; it means your own community in these universities, because this city is a city of tourists. The only original people here are the Indians and the Mexicano.

This city has grown how many times? It has doubled its size every few years. They are all tourists. And who controls the income? Who controls the finance and who controls the politics? You know who controls the politics. You know who runs the administration at any school. That is why, when you come to the college, you have to organize a community here. Those who aren't with MASA today should come to MASA tomorrow. Those who are complaining about what MASA's leadership is doing should get in there and get involved in their decisions and share their ideas to make those leaders do what they believe is right. Do not bum-rap it. That is what we say. In the community where you have people who are saying you guys are not doing the right thing, you ask, what are *you* doing? And you put the burden of proof on them.

We talk about this because we understand when someone says, "Oh, you are out of your mind." I made a speech in Colorado Springs, the seat of imperialism. There are more millionaires there per square foot probably than there are in any other area in the Southwest. I talked about Aztlán. While there, I was talking to a Jewish lawyer.

He told me, "I really agree with you." He said, "I realize what you are doing. You got a lot of guts, and the people who are with you, man, you guys are not afraid of anything and you will tackle any problem." He said, "I really admire you for fighting for civil rights."

I told him, "We're mostly fighting for human rights."

"However," he said, "I can't dig this Aztlán concept."

I asked him, "Well, what about Israel? Can you dig Israel?"
He responded, "You're damn well right, I can dig Israel."
I told him, "Well, but it belongs to the Arabs, the Palestinians."
He yelled, "The hell it does! History will prove it's ours!"
And I told him, "History will prove that Aztlán is ours!"

I then had a discussion on the same topic, on this same notion of the imaginary nation within a nation. I told another guy, he was an Irishman; he said, "I agree with what you're doing. The Irish did it. You guys can do it." And a little band of western Europeans all did it. They are all immigrants. They all came here to share and they got right in the society. That is why in this society the head of the Mafia can live to be eighty-six years old. That's right. They killed Che at thirty-eight. They killed Malcolm X at thirty-eight and Martin Luther King at forty. In this society crime and corruption can exist because the politicians are bought and sold. The double standards practiced out there are not what they teach you in here.

You see, when we talk about how they involve themselves in society, but fine, they bought into the society. However, we have a cultural difference. We have a value system that relates more to people than it does to money. That is why we are poor. Because we have also been taught to relate to "*en los cielos*," about heaven and all that: "*sea por Dios*," and we believe it.

More of our people plead guilty in front of a judge than any other ethnic group in this country. It is because they have been taught fatalism. When a *Dios* with a black judge's robe says, "Five years," all they say is, "*Sea por Dios*."

Look at it from the point of view of what we have to teach our people. This is why I do not talk to any more gringo audiences. There are Anglos here. Gringos are racists, and maybe there are some gringo racists in here. I don't know. They know it.

The Anglo supporter will try to discuss the war with us. I went out against the war five years ago. We create leadership out of our organization. Our men, our women, and our children, they're all involved in a leadership capacity. They all take part, and they all do what is necessary to support the organization, whether they are artists, writers, or fighters.

You know, it doesn't make any difference. We put them all into the same organization. You know yourself that if the dog catcher came to our house and was looking for our dog, we would hide him anywhere we could. We would take him to our neighbor. We would hide him in the basement. We would put him in the toilet. We would cover him up and act like he was the baby. We would say, "We don't have that dog here." However, when the President sends a letter for our son, we dress him up, give him an *abrazo*, and say, "Here, you can have him." Don't we? Kill or be killed, and that is what we do.

We are conditioned to the point that some of the guys would say, you are a bunch of sissies. Well, I would like some of them to face five years, instead of going to war, based on their principles and their conscience, based on the fact that they know that the war is not in Vietnam. It's not in Korea. It's not in Cambodia. It's right here in these barrios. It's right here in our community. Even in your middle-class home, you can't avoid it.

Middle-class people, our people . . . And let me explain that I don't condemn them. We have to learn this, too. I heard that parents here in Arizona, here in Phoenix, are supporting the union in Phoenix. I believe we should give them a big hand. I think that is the most beautiful act taking place in the Southwest.

Now we have to look at the fact that we have survived as people because our parents survived. That is why we are here. We have survived as people because our parents survived racism a hundred times as heavy as what we face. They survived labor ten times harder than any of us will ever work. They survived these problems and, in doing so, they had to withdraw. They withdrew and protected their families, and in some cases they put some of the young people in a cocoon. Their children later had to come to Chicano Studies in colleges to find out they were Chicanos. You don't have to go into the barrio or the *campos* to tell our people they are Chicanos, but you do have to tell middle-class youth they are Chicanos.

We understand that part of it. Now we have to teach ourselves that the whole world is at our back door, our back yard. We need to go out there and decide what we are going to do with our lives. Nobody is going to decide for us.

When we come to that conclusion, then we start looking at ourselves differently and we look at other people differently. It is going to be harder for you to live when you do these three things, when you stop, look, and listen. Many people have not listened, they have not looked, and they have not even stopped. They go to high school where their gringo friends say, "Hey, Chico, come on, let's go," and the guy's name is Carlos or Pepe or a common name that they think is Chicano or Mexicano. And the guy accepts it, or he makes a racial joke about it. "You pay so much for hamburger that the Germans or the Italians made, and for every ten they throw in a Mexican." And you say, "What's that for?" And they say, "For the grease." The Chicano goes along with it, and says it's all right, and he doesn't resist.

What we have to do is resist. Let no man get away with any word, we must stop looking at this and say, "You're not going to get away with that if you call me 'Chico.' You call me what I am; you call me my name, Rodolfo." To the guy that comes and says, "Hey, boy," he is going to find out that I am a man.

They try to patronize you or act condescending, like coming up and telling you, "Yeah, I like tortillas, too," and try to bullshit you that they are nice guys because they ate a taco yesterday.

You have to evaluate what they are within their soul, not this condescending bullshit. Now *gabachos* are finding out that we used to call ourselves Chicanos and we still call ourselves Chicanos and it's caught on. Ever since I can remember, from every barrio I was ever in, we called ourselves Chicanos, Chicanitos. There was nothing bad about it. Now, there are some coconuts running around, you know, they are brown on the outside but white on the inside. They are saying, "You aren't going to call me no Chicano! I'm Spanish American or Hispano, or Spanglo," or something. "You see that's a very bad word." Right away you know where he came from.

We have to do what we are talking about: make men and women whole again. We have to stop, look, and listen and analyze. We have to understand our own inferiority complex. I know it. You know it. We all went through it. For some of us older guys it took us longer. But as I told some of the young guys who picked up one of our old newspapers, *VIVA,* that we used to put out. They said, "Say, man, you're here with some sellouts." And they started laughing at me. I told them, "Well, us older people had to chop the trees down so you guys could see."

The truth is, you'll go much further than we went, but somebody had to do it, somebody had to start it. The time is coming when we will have to understand all of our weaknesses and our strengths to become a whole person again. We have racism among ourselves, against ourselves.

I was talking to Gloria, and she was telling me about her little sister, that she was a *morena, pobrecita, morenita* . . . You know, she was not going to be white like her sister. Or do you remember in the neighborhoods when they used to come over . . . this used to happen in my house, 'cause I have a brother that has brown hair and green eyes, we called each other night and day. When he was little, all the *vecinas* used to come over and say, *"Ah, mira qué bonito, parece gringo."*

We are relating to a white superiority myth and success symbol. We need to chop that off. We need to study George Washington and know that he was an exploiter. We have to study all those people who came here and those pioneers. There are no heroes in the Southwest, understand that. There are no gringo heroes in the Southwest.

At the University of Colorado, they have a grill, a cafeteria. You know what they named it? The Alfred Packard Grill. Do you know why? They couldn't think of anybody who was a hero, so they took somebody whose name they knew. Alfred Packard was a hunter, a trapper, and he went up to the mountains with all his gringo trapper friends, and they got caught in the deep snow of the Rocky Mountains. So, he turned around and ate all his friends. You see, and then they glorify a cannibal. They used to think General Custer was a good man, until they exposed him as a psychotic.

We still have Chicanos basing themselves on the white success image. Even the Aztecs are part of us, the Mayan, the Toltecs, the Olmecs, the Chichimecas, the Indians, are part of us. Do you know how many medicines the Indian has contributed to modern medicine? Medicines they put into a tablet to sell to you and say it is modern medical science.

They were performing brain surgery in Tenochitlán at the same time during the Middle Ages in England and Western Europe. They were still drilling holes in the heads of the people who were suffering from brain tumors to let the devil out. They were already doing brain surgery over here in the Americas. One of the problems is that they probably didn't drill enough holes, because it seems that the devil remained in there for a whole long time.

We keep looking at these different examples about ourselves and we keep looking at the different contributions and comparisons. We look at other people and ask, where are the heroes of the Southwest? Well, they are buried. They are buried with your *abuelitos* and your *abuelitas*. They are buried and burnt by the people who came across, like Pike and Fremont and those people who came and buried and burnt all of our history, and wiped it out.

We have to start to realize and understand our history to know where we are going in the future. We have to understand those inferiority complexes we have, and the self-hatred we have. We have to get away from that. In the barrio one Chicano looks at another Chicano and says, "Hey, *ese*, you're looking at my girl." The only reason he's even going with the girl is 'cause he looked at her. He's proud of her, and if everybody's looking at her, then he has himself a prize. But then he will do this guy in, in a minute. Sometimes we have more killings by ourselves than we do by the *placa*, and that's bad.

We have to identify the enemy. The enemy is not our community. The enemy is controlling our community, but he doesn't live there.

So this is what we are talking about. We have to start to develop a positive self-concept of ourselves, understand our own inferiority complexes and drop them. Then we can grow and start to educate our own people, our own brothers, our own *carnales*, on what the Movement is all about. Some people think it's just a bowel ovement. That's the only kind of movement they know. They go, "Ah! The Movimiento, what's that all about?" We have to start to explain to them. In fact, in some areas, white radicals have to tell Chicanos they are oppressed people.

"We are?"

It's amazing. It's amazing how right now, today, we are being used as statistics, very beneficial to the white student structure. Everything is turning to mechanics. As strikes become more successful and more contracts are signed, you're going to see 35,000 less migrant workers coming into the state. One of our candidates for the senate, Señor Sánchez, organized and took over a labor camp last year, and they don't want him back. Young people organized in Idaho and Utah and had a confrontation in Idaho and Utah sugar refineries. Young people organized farm workers in Michigan and had a confrontation with a Michigan sugar refinery. They don't want them back because they were organizing these people to tell these people we will no longer give you slave labor. We will no longer give you slave labor of both men and women together.

So now they are mechanizing. They would have mechanized sooner, except they had some people who worked with their hands. Now, there are so many sciences you can go into, so many professions. One of the new professions that has developed is the social science industry. There are many young people coming out of the colleges with bachelor's degrees in sociology and in the social sciences because they went that route to get draft deferments. You know it's only one percent of your total university enrollment that is Chicano, and in a place that is our homeland! So, we are only talking about one percent trying to get through the educational system. We talk about the peace movement and the young people getting deferments. Now, they come out, and they don't want to work with their hands.

Who works with their hands? Who are the garbage collectors of Atlanta? They are Blacks. Who are the garbage collectors of Denver, Albuquerque, and L.A.? They are Chicanos and Blacks. Who are the ones who shake out the sheets at the motels and hotels? They are Chicanas and Blacks. Who are the domestic workers? They are Chicanas and Blacks. Who are the people who work in the restaurants cleaning tables? They are Chicanos. Who works in the laundry? They are Chicanas.

Those are the people who still use their hands. So the social science industry creates an industry where these guys can come in and teach us not to be culturally deprived, to teach us not to be hardcore unemployed and to be part of the nice white-right society.

Fifteen million of their young people are leaving their neighborhoods and their families because they do not want to be part of a racist society. They do not want to be part of a people who hate instead of love. They do not want to be part of people who do not want to take part but who would rather oppress. They don't want to be part of people who are inhumane, who have the highest rate of neurosis, the highest rate of frigidity. I don't know of any Chicanos who have that problem . . . or Chicanas . . .

Then they come around and they tell us, they bring these other things, these abstract things to us . . . They say, "You have a problem: birth control. You better control all your kids 'cause that's your economic problem. They are your economic problem." And we turn around and agree and say, "Yes, they are our economic problem. I'm not going to have any children this year."

I'm surely glad my mother had seven children. I was the last one in line, you know. Yet, if you look at statistics, Western Europe and England and the other technically advanced countries in this world are the most overpopulated countries. Then they turn around and tell us, for example, just go to Brazil, and they say, don't have any more children there 'cause they may turn out like that revolutionary we had to kill last year.

You see, they are looking at the population differences; they are looking at the new philosophy. The Mexicano, the Chicano who will no longer stand back and wait in line, he will no longer stand at the back of the church with his hat in his hand, waiting for God to save him and the priest to bless him.

They say that the church is ours, too, that the church belongs to the community. When you get *padres* who understand that, then he is a "Real *Padre.*" When you get an authoritarian who says, it's my church and you are the people, then he's not one of you.

The schools in our community are our schools. The service agencies are our agencies. The recreation centers and the parks are ours. If they are in our community, then we should run them. That is what El Plan Espiritual de Aztlán is all about: community control and controlling our own destiny, controlling ourselves.

Yet the great white father will tell us, "You can't take care of yourselves." Here are our social science experts going to do a study. They are going to find out why *cucarachas* run up the wall sideways. They are going to find out all about your sex life. They are going to find out why Mexican jumping beans move. They are going to spend $500,000 on this study, and they're going to have their own people do it. They are masters of study. If one of these guys went outside and lightning struck him and turned him green, there would be three thousand gringos waiting out there from this university and other universities to write a proposal for a five-hundred-thousand-dollar study.

You know it, and I know it, and that's where the money goes. It doesn't go to the poor. How hard do you have to fight for your Minorities Studies' money? They put it together and throw it for Blacks and Chicanos and then say, you have a fight over the bone, don't they? That's what they do in every university. That's why, let me tell you, the Chicano Civil Rights Movement is dead. Demonstrations on the basis of confrontation are dead. We came along and we watched too long. Sit-ins, lie-downs, and walkouts and other demonstrations are dying.

This year you are successful because it's new. We had blowouts in Denver. What they did then was freeze the leadership out, the student leadership, they froze them out, waited for one little error, and got them out. But that didn't stop the Movement because these students kept organizing.

Now we know that the Chicano Movement is affecting every family. A conservative *compadre* of mine told me about it. He is really conservative because he has land in New Mexico and his father sends him his share of the sales from the cattle. He has a good job, his wife has a good job and his daughter is in business. But let me tell you that his grandchild, who is two and a half years old . . . and while he's sitting there trying to forget there is a Movement going on, his little grandchild goes by him and shouts "Chicano Power," and blows his mind.

There are so many things I would like to say. And I hope to return to Arizona. There are so many topics I would like to discuss with you. But you see, when you get involved in organizing, you can become a ferocious violent speaker. We can hit you emotionally for that one moment, then you go home and turn on the TV and watch John Wayne kill Indians and Mexicans and forget about the Movement.

Then you forget everything. So we have to do a preparation, we have to survive. Right now in this country there is repression. It is coming down; you don't even know about it. You see it on James Bond and you see it on "Mod Squad." Let me tell you there is repression coming down; that is why I said the Civil Rights Movement is over.

They have it down to a science, how to stop us. How to kill you, how to stop you, how to injure you, how to put you behind those bars.

We have to learn how to have survival kits. To survive you must construct a family organization. The family is the organization that is going to keep you together. The family concept of "La Familia," is going to keep us going because it has helped us survive this long.

Let me just give you a fast example 'cause I have to run, to catch a plane. On my father's side, my *jefe* came from Chihuahua. I have relatives all across Chihuahua. My *tío*, his brother, lives in San Bernardino. So I have *primos* and *primas* all across California. On my mother's side, she came from San Luis, and her people came from Tierra Amarilla, and Española. And now they are in Berkeley, Oakland, Stockton, Hayward, and they are relating to the Movement. They are relating to ourselves as a family.

On my wife's side, her family stretches into the original settlers of San Luis, all the way into Mexico from her mother's side. And they are about three-quarters Indian. On her father's side, he stretches into Santa Fe. You should know it predates Jamestown.

So you see how we stretch across this whole Aztlán. We stretch into Michigan. There are more Mexicanos in Illinois than there are in Colorado. There are almost as many in Michigan. Every place there has been farm labor, our people are there. We are all the sons and daughters of people who came from the farms, the *campos* and the *ranchitos.*

And we are all the same family. When we can stand up as one, there is nothing that can destroy us. To survive we have to start controlling our own destiny, creating our own economic power. To do that, you first have to learn to love each other. You have to love yourself before you can love someone else. When you do that, then you can share; but you can't share anything if you are part of this competitive society. In fact, you end up cutting each other's throats.

When you have that cultural awareness, then you can create your own economic base. Then you can get yourselves together. You don't hear any Japanese running around hollering "Yellow Power." They have green power. They don't get a haircut anywhere else except a Japanese barber shop. They don't go to any church except their own.

We are strangers in our own church. We do not control who comes into our church. The time will come when we will, and we must. These are ideas are based on El Plan Espiritual de Aztlán, to control our own destiny.

I'll give you just a fast rundown on what we are doing with the Crusade. First, we have held two youth conferences; one brought in 1,500 young people, with Chicanos even from Alaska. The next year we had another one that had more than 3,000 participants. This last March, we even had Puerto Rican brothers that came in all the way from New York and Chicago. We had people who came in from different Indian youth groups.

We sponsored an Indian Youth Conference that was not too successful, but neither was our First Youth Conference three years ago. We created an atmosphere of uniting ourselves and understanding what *carnalismo* was and then developed organizational expertise. We taught how to organize, how to explain what needs to be done.

I believe one of the beautiful things that has happened here is that you are ready. You've done something that many of us were involved in supporting: school blowouts. You have immediately established in the schools a desire to teach our youth.

At "La Cruzada," we develop leadership. We have liberation schools in the summertime. And none of our children has any problems in our schools because of grades. They have problems about opinions. They let the teachers know that George Washington is not their father. See, they let the teachers know that we were here first. Teachers say that Jamestown was the first colony. They rattle off San Augustine, Santa Barbara, Santa Fe, and then maybe they came in somewhere.

But you know the students know it from five years old and up. Now we have completely broken away and created our own school, Tlatelolco. It is a primary, secondary, and undergraduate school. They are accredited, not that that's even necessary, as far as I am concerned, but they are in order to justify the parents taking their children out of the public schools.

We created our own schools. We have our own youth teaching in them. We are telling them, "You can be anything you want to."

We need leadership. We just don't need guys that can really rap. We need our writers and we need our poets. There are no revolutions without poets. We need our politicians, our negotiators, our diplomats—ours, not theirs. We need our chemists and our biochemists. We need the veterans coming back from overseas that have learned all that professionalism. We need them down in the barrio, too. One biochemist is worth a hundred demolition experts.

We need every type of leadership to bring ourselves together and to survive. That is what is important. We have to survive because right now there is going to be an upheaval, and it's happening in this country. Let me say that whatever is happening, it is keeping the man off the back of the Mexicano right now, but we need to start to bring ourselves together in a very positive movement.

Out of the West High School blowout in Denver, we didn't gain everything we wanted. However, it motivated the young people to nationalize and they took over Lincoln Park. It's now Aztlán Park. The director, the pool attendant, the swimming instructor, everybody is Chicano. Everyone is Chicano because it is a ninety-nine percent Chicano neighborhood.

The students on the north side saw what happened on the west side, that all their murals are painted by Chicano artists. They started arts and crafts centers run by young people who were twenty-one and twenty-two years of age.

The west side now has the best-kept pool. They said they didn't have money to build a baby pool or refinements, so I took some buses with two hundred kids and went swimming at the University Hills pool in the gringo nice middle-class area. They sent one hundred-fifty policemen to gas us. But they found the money to build a new pool and then replaced the directors with Chicanos. They said we did it. No, no, we took it. They just saved face by saying they gave it to us.

So the kids in the north side, over at Columbus Park, saw Aztlán Park, and they had a swim in and never left, so they gassed them all out. They now have Zapata Park. And it is all run by Chicanos, and they are now painting murals there with their identity and their culture. And the kids in Pueblo, a hundred and eleven miles away, saw what was happening in Denver's north side, and they marched on September 16 and nationalized and liberated a park and called it Zapata Park also.

These are the things that are taking place. Our youth do come to us. We don't have a generation gap because we are willing to bring in middle-aged people who put themselves on the line. And that is important.

But you can't leave your women out of it. Your women have to march with you. There were Zapatas and Pancho Villas but there were also Adelitas and Valentinas. And we find that whenever we have a problem, our women can assume the leadership and take care and keep the thing rolling and going on.

And we run a center, the Crusade for Justice, that is not funded by any outside source. It is funded by our own resources. We are poor, yet it's ours. No policemen can come into our center, and they know it. They cannot come into our yard, and they know that. They do not dare come in. When our youth have a dance, it's their dance. They secure it.

I just want to say that we can accomplish liberation. We can bring ourselves together as a *familia.*

As I told many young radicals five or six years ago, and I tell Blacks today, with whom we are friendly and have mutual respect, that until they are organized and they are doing their thing, and until we are organized, there will be no international coalition. There will be no international coalition until we have made Aztlán a reality and the Chicano has become a concentrated organized force. ¡QUE VIVA LA RAZA!

Manteniendo una dirección positiva para el Movimiento Chicano

Hay períodos en nuestras vidas en que cada uno de nosotros debemos de reevaluarnos, como individuos, familias, organizaciones, grupos y, más importante, nuestras relaciones con el movimiento. Tenemos que determinar cómo estamos envueltos, qué es nuestro compromiso, qué es nuestra dedicación, cuáles son nuestras habilidades, qué son nuestras limitaciones, cuáles son nuestras metas y objetivos, finalmente cuáles son nuestros ideales y la filosofía que nos guían.

Se ven muchos beneficios y realizaciones que son el producto del movimiento. Conocemos a la gente que utiliza el movimiento para su propio provecho. Hemos participado en la lucha de los pobres. Somos los precursores en la batalla para una educación positiva y pertinente para los chicanos. Hemos ayudado a crear una conciencia política y, más importante, hemos ayudado para que la gente se entere de sus tradiciones culturales, sus contibuciones históricas, su identidad y su amor propio.

Algunos resultados

Vemos los resultados y podemos señalar con orgullo al número de estudiantes, cada vez más grande, en los colegios y las universidades, el gran número de empleados civiles de la industria privada. Sí, vemos a actores, atletas y políticos identificándose con los Chicanos. Vemos un número pequeño de gente común sin educación, sin títulos profesionales aprovechándose de los programas y agencias apoyadas por el gobierno. Vemos progamas de Estudios Chicanos brotando en las universidades que rinden ingresos para los expertos de los Estudios Chicanos.

Éstos son, pues, los resultados de la lucha de la gente. ¿Pero qué hay de las metas? ¿Están basadas en la ganancia financiera personal e individual o podemos decir honestamente que a las masas de la gente

El Gallo: La Voz de la Justicia, 4/3 (April 1972): p. 3.

todavía no se les ha dado un lugar en la mesa, ellos no han participado, utilizado, ni siquiera entienden de qué trata el movimiento? ¿Podemos decir que compartimos con nuestros hermanos en las prisiones nuestras palabras, un poco de tiempo, y si no, por lo menos unos cuantos bienes materiales? ¿Podemos decir que estamos listos para dar protección a nuestros hijos, no solamente a los de la casa, sino a los que están en la calle, en las viviendas públicas y en los barrios? ¿Podemos decir que tenemos la paciencia para enseñar al ignorante, no solamente al pobre sino también al ignorante de la clase media o aspirante a la clase media? ¿Podemos decir que tomaremos el tiempo para explicarle al tapado? ¿Podemos verdaderamente decir que podemos dar sin quejas, o darle a alguien una puñalada por la espalda? ¿Podemos todos nosotros admitir que las estadísticas de nuestra gente son la verdad y que ni todos los GS-18s, ni los políticos, ni los programas del gobierno, ni los *vendidos,* pueden mejorar los problemas que afrenta nuestra gente?

Más trabajo y menos retórica

Como gente que participa en el movimiento tenemos la obligación de desarrollar en nuestra gente, carácter en lugar de actitudes, confianza en lugar de cabezas egotistas, humildad en vez de fanfarrones presumidos. Tenemos que reconcer que nuestros padres y antepasados nos enseñaron a sobrevivir, cómo actuar en lugar de hablar. Tenemos que entender que en algunos casos hemos usado la retórica de los militantes quienes nunca han tomado parte en una acción. Tenemos que trabajar más y tener menos planes parlamentarios. Tenemos que ser el negociante, maestro y líder visible, y además el defensor y protector invisible.

Si cuando hablamos estamos hablando de nuestro destino, del control por la comunidad, de la igualdad humana, nuestro respeto, el orgullo, el nacionalismo y el humanismo, entonces no solamente tenemos que vivir esos ideales de los liberadores, sino también usar los instrumentos de los organizadores. Los instrumentos consisten de la unidad de la familia; después la tribu, la nación y finalmente la de toda la humanidad. Hay familias individuales, hay diferentes tribus (organizaciones), finalmente hay una nación y la combinación de las naciones en una filosofía común de respeto y carnalismo. Esto no sucede por accidente o por naturaleza; esto viene en reconocer la igualdad y en planear la lucha contra los que controlan la economía, la *política* y la sociedad capitalista, y especialmente las minorías y los pobres. Tenemos que usar los instrumentos en un modo positivo para construir y no negativamente para destruir. "El nacionalismo es un instrumento para organizar; no es un arma para el odio." El nacionalismo trasciende todos los límites religiosos, financieros, sociales, políticos y de clase. El nacionalismo es nuestro denominador común para enseñar lo del movimiento. Aunque reconocemos el nacionalismo, no podemos ignorar a los vendidos, los de la derecha, los tío tacos, los explotadores y los malinches de nuestra nación. Ellos tendrán que sufrir las mismas distinciones que cualquier otro enemigo u opresor.

Somos testigos del nacionalismo de los grupos estudiantiles, las organizaciones obreras, los maestros, las monjas, los sacerdotes, los actores, los barrios, los pueblos, los pintos, los hombres de negocio, los contratistas, las organizaciones para los derechos civiles y las asociaciones políticas. En la mayoría de los casos han tenido éxito para el beneficio de unos cuantos grupos y afirman que el sistema es bueno para uno si uno recibe parte de la acción. Si no podemos unirnos y dedicar nuestros esfuerzos para la sobrevivencia colectiva de toda nuestra gente, entonces tenemos que aliarnos con la gente que tiene la misma filosofía y llegar a la conclusión de que la mayoría de la gente realmente desea la oportunidad para ser ávara, violenta, racista, inhumana, explotadora, represora y asesina. Si ése es el caso, entonces los que escogemos nuestro papel en el movimiento tendremos que actuar de acuerdo con las reacciones de los patrones del sistema y la sociedad. En el futuro, a pesar del nacionalismo, seremos aliados o enemigos, el perseguido o el perseguidor. Hacemos nuestra decisión; no hay lugar para los indecisos. Necesitamos la participación completa de la gente común, la juventud, los estudiantes, los pintos (los de adentro y los de afuera), los obreros, los profesionales, los maestros, los hombres de negocios, los patrones, los empleados, los sacerdotes, las monjas, los políticos y los batos.

El apoyo para el movimiento debe llegar en diferentes formas, medidas y métodos. Es verdad que necesitamos el apoyo moral, pero también necesitamos apoyo económico, recursos mentales y físicos; servicios de protección legal y política; asistencia financiera y económica, empleo y dirección creadora; puertas abiertas en nuestras casas y defensa física de nuestros derechos.

El movimiento ha sido delineado por muchos planes de nuestros tiempos, el más efectivo y positivo es El Plan Espiritual de Aztlán. Recomendamos que lo lean todo y lo entiendan completamente. Entonces podremos fortalecer nuestra participación basada en el conocimiento de nosotros mismos y del sistema dentro del cual existimos; eso es, el racismo, el clasismo y el genocidio cultural. Tenemos que aprovecharnos de nuestro poder y fortalecer nuestros puntos débiles. Esto no solamente debe incluirnos como grupos, sino también como individuos.

Minoría contra minoría

Somos presos de este sistema de competencia que pone a un hermano contra otro, familia contra familia, gente contra gente, braceros contra domésticos; un grupo étnico contra otro, color contra color; clase contra clase en lugar de las minorías o clases bajas contra la clase dominante. La competencia cría la división, la desconfianza, las sospechas y el aislamiento. Tenemos mucho que perder si nos permitimos caer en la misma trampa una y otra vez.

¿Qué hay en esto para mí, para ti, para nosotros? Toda la vida nos identificamos con héroes, superhombres, aventureros, los que andan en busca de oro, constructores de imperios y líderes imaginarios. Soñamos del elogio, el honor y el amor de otras gentes. Pasamos por la vida con la esperanza de dejar una muestra de logro histórico para nuestros hijos, para la posteridad, y terminamos viejos, cansados, arrugados, sin visión o sin memorias, y dejamos una herencia de debilidad, lambedores de botas, indignidad y desorden. Podemos hacer la historia y podemos cambiar la historia. Nuestra historia consistirá de aquéllos que intentaron, que resistieron, que dijeron, que se atrevieron a luchar, que se atrevieron a vivir libres. También expondremos a aquéllos que tienen miedo, vergüenza, arrogancia, y al egoísta, al ávaro, al vendido, al malinche, al prostituto social, al tío tacos, al explotador, al cobarde y al idiota.

Si debe haber un movimiento, entonces tiene que haber líderes. Esos líderes deben ser juzgados por su habilidad para dar y no de aprovecharse. Un líder debe comunicar confianza, no egoísmo; un líder es aquél que se sacrifica, no nadie que sea oportunista. El liderato es el acto de usar el poder para liberar a la gente, no para controlarla.

En general, todos tenemos que purificarnos de nuestros complejos de inferiordad, el complejo de peón y nuestro complejo de inmigrante. No somos inferiores, no somos peones de ningún hombre y no somos ni nunca hemos sido inmigrantes. Como hombres y mujeres completos, no sólo podemos construir una organización y empezar un movimiento, sino crear una nación también.

Para dar estos pasos tenemos que pensar positivamente. Tenemos que poner a un lado los pensamientos negativos que tenemos uno contra el otro, especialmente, la duda de nuestra capacidad para triunfar.

Mirando hacia el futuro, establecemos nuestras prioridades basadas en las primeras necesidades. Continuaremos la lucha por los derechos humanos. En el área de la educación, haremos de la Escuela de Tlatelolco un modelo para las muchas escuelas chicanas que empezarán a crecer para servir a nuestra gente. En la comunidad lucharemos por el control completo de la economía, las instituciones y la política. En las áreas rurales hemos de seguir la lucha por nuestras tierras. El partido de La Raza Unida será la voz ofical de nuestro movimiento, no olvidando que en el corazón de cada chicano existen las palpitaciones del nacionalismo. Recordaremos a toda nuestra gente la vida atormentada de los pintos. Intentamos estar todos juntos como una sola persona, no una que odia a los otros, sino una con el fuego y el coraje para proteger nuestras creencias y nuestros derechos.

Un Verso Indio
(Anónimo)

El individuo puede ser sacrificado
por consideración de la familia;
La familia puede ser sacrificada
por consideración de la aldea;
La aldea puede ser sacrificada
por consideración de la provincia;
La provincia puede ser sacrificada
por consideración de la patria;
Por consideración de la conciencia,
sin embargo, sacrificamos todo.

Maintaining a Positive Direction for the Chicano Movement

There are periods in each of our lives when we must reassess ourselves as individuals, families, organization, groups, and, most important, our relationship to the Movement. We have to determine what our involvement is, what our commitment is, what our dedication is, what our abilities are, what our limitations are, what our goals and objectives are. Finally, what are the ideals and philosophy that guide us?

We see many of the accomplishments and benefits that have been the offspring of the Movement. We recognize the people who have profited from the Movement. We have taken part in the struggle for the poor. We have been the forerunners in the battle for positive and relevant education for Chicanos. We have helped to create political consciousness and, most importantly, we have helped to make our people aware of their cultural attributes, their historical contributions, their identity, and their own self-worth.

Some Worthwhile Results

We watch the results and point with pride to the larger number of students at colleges and universities, to the larger number of civic employees, the greater number of teachers and professionals, the larger number of people in business and industry. Yes, we watch movie actors and athletes and politicos identify with the Chicano. We see a small number of grassroots people, with no education or professional titles, profit from government-supported programs and agencies. We see Chicano Studies programs sprouting at the universities that provide income for Chicano Studies experts.

These, then, are the results of the people's struggle, but what about the goals? Are they to be based on personal and individual financial gain, or can we honestly say that masses of the people have not yet been given a place at the dinner table? Can we say that they have not shared, profited or even understood what the Movement is all about? Can we say that we share with our *hermanos* in the prisons our words, a little time, if not at least a few material goods? Can we say that we are willing to protect our children, not only those at home, but those on the street, in the projects, and in the barrios? Can we say we have the patience to teach the ignorant, not just the poor, but also the ignorant middle class or aspiring middle class? Can we say that we will take the time to explain to the naive? Can we truthfully say we can give without grumbling and backstabbing? Can we all admit that the statistics about our people are true and that all the GS-18s, *políticos,* government programs, payoffs, and sellouts cannot correct or alleviate the problems that the majority of our people face?

More Work and Less Rhetoric

As people who take part in the Movement, we have to recommit ourselves to build in our people character instead of attitudes, confidence instead of big-headed egotism, humility in place of outspoken cockiness. We have to recognize that our fathers and forefathers taught us how to survive, how to act instead of talk. We have to realize that we have in some cases been using the rhetoric of militants who have never taken an action. We have to do more work and less parliamentary planning. We have to be the visible negotiators, teachers, and leaders, also the invisible protectors and defenders.

If when we speak, we are talking about self-destiny, community control, human equality, self-respect, pride, nationalism, liberation, and humanism, then we have to not only live up to the ideals of liberators but we have to use the tools of the organizers. The tools consist of the family as a unit, then the tribe, the nation, and finally, total humanity. There are individual families, there are different tribes (organizations), there is finally a nation, and the combining of nations in a common philosophy of respect and brotherhood. This doesn't come about by accident or even by nature; it comes about by recognizing equality and planning the struggle against those who hold the economic, political, and social reins of the total society and especially of the minorities and the poor. We have to use the tools in a positive fashion to build, not negatively to destroy. "Nationalism is a tool for organization, not a weapon for hatred." Nationalism transcends all boundaries: religious, financial, social, political, and class. Nationalism becomes our common denominator to teach about our Movement. While recognizing nationalism, we cannot be blinded to the *vendidos,* the right-wingers, the Tío Tacos, the exploiters, and the Malinches of our nation. They will have to suffer the same distinctions as any other enemy or oppressor.

We have witnessed the nationalization of student groups, union organizations, teachers, nuns, priests, actors, barrios, pueblos, pintos, businessmen, contractors, civil rights and political associations. In most cases, they have been successful to the benefit of a few cliques and the reinforcement that the system is good for you as long as you are getting a piece of the action. If we cannot unite and dedicate ourselves to a collective survival for all of our people, then we will have to align ourselves with people who have the same philosophical goals and come to the conclusion that what most people want is a chance to be greedy, violent, racist, inhuman exploiters, suppressors, and murderers. If that is the case, then we who choose our role in the Movement will have to act according to the reaction of the bosses of the system and the society. We will in the future, despite nationalism, be either allies or enemies, the hunted or the hunter. We make our choice; there is no room for fence riders. We must have the full participation of the grassroots, the youth, the students, the inmates (in and out), the worker, the professional, the teacher, the businessman, the employer, the employee, the priests, the nuns, the *políticos,* and the *batos.*

The support for the Movement must come in different forms, sizes, and methods. It is true we need moral support, but we also need economic support, resources, mental and physical; political and legal protection and service; economic and financial assistance; employment and creative outlets; sanctuary for our homes; and physical defense of our rights.

The Movement has been outlined by many of the plans of our time. The most pragmatic and positive is El Plan Espiritual de Aztlán. We recommend reading it thoroughly and understanding it fully. Then we can strengthen our commitment based on knowledge of ourselves and the system within which we exist, i.e., racism, classism, and cultural genocide. We have to profit from our strengths and strengthen our weak points. This includes not only us as groups, but as individuals.

Minority Against Minority

We are caught up in a system of competitiveness that pits one against the other, brother against brother, family against family, people against people, *braceros* against domestics, ethnic groups against ethnic groups, color against color, class against class, instead of minority or lower class against the ruling class. Competitiveness creates division, distrust, suspicions, and isolation. We have too much to lose to allow ourselves to fall into the same trap over and over again.

What is in it for me, for you, for us? All of our lives, we identify with war heroes, supermen, adventurers, gold seekers, empire builders, and imaginary leaders. We dream of praise and honors and love from other people. We go through life hoping to leave some sign of accomplishment to our children, to posterity, and we end up old, tired, wrinkled, with no vision or no memories, and we leave an inheritance of weakness, boot-licking, indignity, and confusion. We can make history. It will consist of those who tried, who resisted, who led, who dared to struggle, dared to live free, and it will also expose those who are afraid, ashamed, arrogant, selfish, greedy, sellouts, Malinches, social prostitutes, Tío Tacos, exploiters, cowards, and idiots.

If there is to be a Movement, then there must be leaders. Those leaders must be judged by their ability to give, not take. Leadership must convey confidence, not egotism—one who sacrifices, not one who is an opportunist. Leadership is the act of using power to free people, not to control them.

All in all, we have to cleanse ourselves of our inferiority complex, our peon complex, and our immigrant complex. We are not inferior, we are no man's peons, and we are not and never have been immigrants. As complete men and women, we cannot only build an organization, start a Movement, but create a nation.

To take these steps, we have to think positively. We have to put aside negative thoughts about each other, and especially about our capacity to succeed.

Looking toward to the future, we set our priorities based on first needs first. We will continue to support and struggle for human rights. In the area of education, we will make La Escuela Tlatelolco a model for the many Chicano schools that will begin to grow to serve our people. In the community, we will fight for complete control of the economy, the institutions, and politics. In the rural areas, we will continue the fight for our lands. The La Raza Unida Party will be the official voice of our Movement, not forgetting that in the heart of every Chicano there exists the throbbing of nationalism. We will place in all of our people the tormented life of the pintos. We intend to be together as one person, not one who hates others, but one with the fire and rage to protect our heritage and our rights.

An Indian Verse
(Anónimo)

The individual can be sacrificed
    for the consideration of the family;
The family can be sacrificed
    for the consideration of the village;
The village can be sacrificed
    for the consideration of the province;
The province can be sacrificed
    for the consideration of the nation;
For consideration of our conscience,
    however, we sacrifice everything.

Speech Delivered at the La Raza Unida National Convention

Hermanos y hermanas, first I'd like to thank the La Raza Unida General Assembly for giving me the honor to speak here. I want to take care of a little bit of business before we start.

First, I want to give congratulations to José Angel Gutiérrez, our dynamic chair of La Raza Unida. Second, I'd like to extend congratulations to Raúl Ruiz. He is one of the leaders and forerunners of La Raza Unida in California.

I'd like to make a symbolic contribution. It is not too much in money, but it is a lot in soul, a lot of *corazón.* I'd like to give the first check from Colorado, from my wife, to Ramsey Muñiz for his race. Next, I'd like to pledge whatever financial resources that we can come up with to help to support, especially, the Tejas delegation. The Tejas La Raza Unida Party hosted this conference, and we want to help. We want to find out what and how much money we're in the red, so we can take and give our just contribution.

And then I want to dedicate what I say, what I feel my philosophy is, the philosophy of many of us who believe the same . . . I dedicate this speech, talk, whatever you want to call it, to one of the great young heroes and leaders of the Chicano Movement. I dedicate it to his family, to Priscilla Falcón, who is in the audience today. For myself and for all of our brothers and sisters, because we shared with him the same struggle toward a better life for our people, although for many of us it's a painful date. Ricardo Falcón was the type of leader that developed after a long series of struggles, the kind of leader that many of us who are older are waiting to see emerge. And he was dedicated to the very last. And he resisted to the last; in doing so, he preserves the dignity of all of La Raza, not just that of Ricardo Falcón.

I'd like to start by relating La Raza Unida to the vehicle of the Chicano Movement. The Chicano Movement some years ago was

Liberty Hall, El Paso, Texas, September 2, 1972.

considered an impossible dream. La Raza Unida was considered an impossible dream. This is a historic day for everyone who is here. Maybe everyone's name who is here will not go down in the history books, but you've taken part in creating history.

The one point we want to establish is that the Chicano Movement, its concept and philosophy of self-determination, of our sovereignty, cannot be prostituted by politics, although politics can be incorporated into the Chicano Movement.

And La Raza Unida is that vehicle that can bring forth all the leadership, all the thoughts, all the feelings, and attack all the issues to change the lives for a number of our people, change the lives of the masses of your people who may not be here today but whom you represent. We need to incorporate the ideas into La Raza Unida of those who never go to conferences, those who are in the prisons, those who are in the streets, those young men who are in the barrios, in the *campos,* in the *ranchitos.*

We came here as an independent party, and our wishes are that we leave as a united independent party. We'll be discussing many issues. And I know there will be many resolutions and points of strategy passed today. The decisions of the young and old are in the hands of the people. The principles of this party will be decided upon by those resolutions. And we'll decide the strategy as to where La Raza Unida will go in 1972 to 1973 and forward.

In most of the states, I can speak for Colorado in particular, we have taken a position of no compromise to any other party or any other candidate of any other party. We cannot negotiate from a position of weakness for anything that we want for our people. We have to organize ourselves into a position of strength.

La Raza Unida is now born nationally. La Raza Unida, then, must become independent and concerned with the very sensitive needs of our own people.

Based on the past performances of the two-party system, to negotiate with Nixon is to negotiate with Spiro Agnew. It is to negotiate with Laird, with the generals in the Pentagon, with the industrialists in the powerful corporate structure. It is to negotiate with the golf partner, the godson of the godfather, who is protecting the interests of the Cosa Nostra and the Mafia.

And then we have to look at the other party. We have to look at McGovern, who comes into a candidacy, into a nomination, arm in arm with Richard "The Pig" Daley from Chicago, who has given more power, yes, more power to a racist white southern bigot.

Whether he wins or loses, George Wallace will have more power than fifteen million Mexicanos. Let me tell you that he will have control through the committees of the southern bureaucrats and dixiecrats. And that's McGovern's partner.

Promises can be made, but promises are hard to keep when you don't control a Senate or Congress. We've had promises made before; in either case, the Chicano has come out on the short end. In either case, the only results that have developed for the Chicano community have come from our reaction. They have come from marches, and the struggles, and the pickets. They have come from the demonstrations. They have come from the blood of our marches. They have come from the cries and the screams of our children who dared to face the Man. Meanwhile, the intellectuals sit in the back room waiting to come in to be the carpetbaggers, to pick up the program monies, after we fight the battles. And this can't happen anymore.

Then we view our candidates. We view our candidates not so much as politicos who try to out-shrewd each other, who try to play chess games; we view them as activists. We view them as leaders of people committed to their people. And this is the difference between La Raza Unida candidates and the two-party system candidates, who are beholden to all the vested interests in this country that relate to money and capitalism.

So we say, "That is a monster with two heads that eats from the same trough."

Nixon appointed your famous former Democratic Governor Connally, a Democrat, to a position of power within his cabinet. As his running mate, McGovern comes in with Shriver—he, who for three years served a Republican president and was appointed by Nixon, and today carries the banners of the Democratic Party. One year ago he resigned. Now, he becomes the chosen son, the candidate for vice president to George McGovern.

We cannot afford the contradictions. The Mexicano, the Chicano, has been confused so often, has been abused, has been used so often and continues to be used because the gringo *políticos* use our own nationalism to fool us and to get our vote. One gringo puts on a serape and a sombrero, eats a taco, *y los chicanos dicen, "Ah, mira, está comiendo tacos."* Then they vote for him.

Everywhere across the country there are "Amigo Committees" for every gringo candidate in the two-party system. The *políticos* can have those types of *amigos*. Those *amigos* are working for their own personal jobs, their own personal financial interests. They are working to liberate themselves financially. But they can never liberate themselves morally or spiritually in this society, when they become the stooges, the puppets of the men who control this country and the world.

We can never be free. We can have $25,000 in our pocket, but if you're a *cagado*, a *vendido*, a *tío taco*, a *malinche*, you're not free. You are not free because you're licking the white man's boots. We cannot base freedom or liberation on a dollar bill.

In the zoo there are seals that balance balls on their noses. They get a fish for it and they're fat. There are lions who stop looking at the guard ferociously because he's waiting for his piece of horse meat. He lays in the middle of the cage swatting flies off his ass, and he's not free. Monkeys do tricks and get peanuts and so do elephants, but they are not free.

So you cannot base any logical argument about it takes money to free us. It takes people in action. It takes people who are ready to stand up for their rights. It takes people who believe in what they say when they speak of Emiliano Zapata and Ricardo Flores Magón. They should believe in those principles that those men lived for, not just use their words and deeds as rhetoric and then squat down the minute we deal with the man. We, too, kill our own brothers.

Because you see, in this society, there are two types of classicism. There's financial classicism and then there's the other type, the moral classicism. What we have to understand is that we have people who are sick. We have people who are *tapados y ciegos*. They have cataracts in their eyes, wax in their ears, *y no quieren ver.* And then we have teachers. Those people of La Raza Unida become the educators to start to direct our people in one direction. They start to develop a philosophy and a direction that we can live with, in honesty and in dignity, not one of compromise or prostitution.

We have allowed ourselves, in many cases, to be passive. Government programs today are set up to pacify the masses while they keep them under a poverty-level income. We cannot allow our people to become passive or submissive. We must become strong. We must become confident. And if we're strong, we have to share strength. If we're weak, then we have to develop the weak. If we have *batos* in the barrios who are *tecatos,* they're infected. We have to help the infested, but we have to get rid of the infested. And this is what it comes to, in the Movement.

I read a book, *The Futile Life of Pito Pérez,* a great philosopher, who drank a lot of *vino* and spoke a lot of truth. He looked up at Jesus Christ, and he said 'about the *políticos,* don't bless them because they know what they're doing.' That's what we have to do about the *vendidos.*

And the people in the social structure of this country stuff their own pockets through the social sciences industry. They know what they're doing. Don't ever believe they don't know what they're doing. Don't ever believe that the *políticos* of this nation don't know what they're doing as they try passing legislation—immigration acts, immigration laws—passport laws, which will make you identifiable from our *hermanos* across the *frontera.* They know what they're doing.

And they know that any time that activity starts within the Chicano communities, immediately comes one of the most horrible enemies that we have and that's drugs. One note, especially to those young Chicanos: hard drugs and drug culture is an invention of the gringo because he has no culture. Chicanos who follow that route are copycats. We don't need any more copycats. We need *puros chicanos* who understand and identify with themselves and their needs.

I know that today we will discuss priorities. I'm very sure that those priorities coming from every state have to do with aid, with education, the forming of a powerful block of people who relate to their own needs. If we don't help ourselves, they won't, and they never will.

They never have helped on those levels that would help our people, the masses, to rise and the masses to elevate themselves. It can't be done in the social structure of this country. You understand that Chicanos will not be needed very shortly. As farm workers organize and resist, machinery will take over. Eighty-five percent of our people are in the barrios, in the urban areas. Next year it will be ninety percent because corporation owners, ranch owners, don't want to deal with human beings or men. They would rather deal with machines or with slaves, and that's the difference.

As our people start to struggle toward the trade unions and the skilled work, you'll find out that we're not needed any more and neither are the Black people. Go to the South and the garbage collectors are Black people. Go to El Paso and Albuquerque and the garbage collectors are Chicanos. They don't need us or don't want us in the top levels. And little by little when they invent a machine that handles all the garbage, that handles all the refuse, that handles all the dirty work, they'll only need experiments, biological studies of a people or a cultural group that once existed but didn't have the courage to struggle.

And we're going to prove differently, standing, teaching each other, starting to look at the system, the educational system. We're looking at the establishments and the institutions, and we're understanding those things. You see, there are people who are coming out of the barrio. We are understanding why we have the poorest level of education, why we have the highest percent of unemployment, why we have the largest number in percentages of those killed overseas.

You see, we're out of the *campos,* out of the mountains, saying, "I don't understand that, that's radical shit," until it affects him or he becomes an instant militant after he's hit across the head by a policeman's club. That's the fastest way to learn. One man said, the police helped to organize us. They beat us either into submission or into activity, and we're going to get started into activity.

That's the difference. There are those who know exactly what they are doing when they use the statistics of the poor and the Mexicano and the Chicano for every kind of poverty program to bilingual education. We're going to prove differently, that they can take their studies and take psychiatric, psychological, sociological bullshit and stick it. What we think is taking place here and has taken place, what we hope will take place far into the future, is a unified movement of one people, one nation.

Those people who served as coordinators did a tremendous job, because even though there is friction, there isn't one family in this country that doesn't have an argument. When we come in front of the public, and the masses of society, we come out together. We come out in praise of each other, as long as our philosophies and our dedication are to the betterment of our people.

So, we hope that La Raza Unida, that leadership that's developing in every barrio in every *campo* and all across, from Tejas to Michigan and Illinois, to California and Arizona, we hope and we're sure that although today it looks like an impossible dream, that there will not be one issue whether it be a day care center, whether it has to do with food for a hungry child or the control of a school board, the control of one park in one barrio, one center, one agency, one nation, that La Raza Unida spokesmen will be the negotiators, because they're the only ones that will have the courage and the support of a national body that has the fortitude and the courage to stand up and say this is what we want. And not only have the brains; we've got the muscle. That is what we need.

I'd like to say that in the area of leadership, that the leadership is here. The leadership is developing and there is leadership already established, and many of our dreams were, again, that one day Mexicanos will come together and have their fights, have their arguments, will come out as one and say that we have representative leadership from across this nation, that can sit in a *congreso* that relates to every element and level of the Chicano Movement.

And that means that it will be related to politics, economics, the social struggle, unions, the struggle for the land, and the tremendous battle for community control in every barrio that we exist in. It can be done. *Políticos* from the two-party system cannot provide that. We have already started community control in many areas with young leadership facing the man and gaining the support of their *jefitas* and *jefitos*.

And it is beautiful to see happen. One more of our dreams that can become a reality is to organize a *congreso*. This national representation will face and handle all our issues and use its collective expertise to communicate across Aztlán.

We need to let each other know of our tears, our sorrows, and our victories. We need to create symbols, such as Crystal City and Tierra Amarilla. We need symbols of resistance, such as all the high school and college blowouts, symbols that have led other people to further steps.

This *congreso* will handle the issues that are vital for us. It will take positions such as deciding to rid ourselves of the draft of our young men, the cream of our crop. It will decide to take us out of wars that we didn't make. We need to become allies with Indian nations who are sovereign. These Indian nations deserve sovereignty and deserve freedom and deliberation, the same as we do.

The *congreso* will make alliances with emerging people, to free colonies like Puerto Rico, to set up cultural, educational relationships with Mexico, Cuba, and all of South America, Our mestizo brothers will take up the battle in support of boycotts that are already in existence and take up more boycotts until someday, since we are tripling in the total society of this nation, we will be a tremendous political, social, and economic power—the Chicano is developing that fast.

We know what sex and family and love are all about. Yes, in the future that this *congreso,* having been established and renewed and refurnished with new blood, constantly as our young people arise, making sure that it never becomes a click situation, where people get old and conservative and tired and secure, that we always have new ideas, new progress, the teacher, the professor, the lawyers, the *políticos,* our students, our dropouts, wherever we are, we'll be one people; that wherever we are, we will speak for one people; we'll be La Raza Unida; we'll be una *familia.* I think that's the important thing, and I think that's the feeling we should all leave with. When we get through with all the work, that we have new ideas, new progress, and are always involved in the struggle.

Life in itself is a struggle, and the only satisfaction that we can get out of our lifetime is to be involved in creating a better world . . . the teacher, the professor, the lawyers, the *políticos,* our students, our dropouts, wherever we are, we'll be one people; that wherever we are, we will speak for one people; we'll be one people; we'll be La Raza Unida. We'll be *una familia*. I think that's the important thing, and I think that's the feeling of having created something worthwhile.

Before I end, I would like to read a *verso indio* that has a lot of meaning, and I can't forget it ever since I read it.

> *El individuo puede ser sacrificado*
> *por consideración de la familia;*
> *La familia puede ser sacrificada*
> *por consideración del pueblo.*
> *El pueblo puede ser sacrificado*
> *por consideración de la provincia.*
> *La provincia puede ser sacrificada*
> *por consideración de la patria.*
> *Por consideración de la conciencia*
> *sin embargo, sacrificamos todo.*

Message to Aztlán

I want to thank you for being here today to prove to the world that the Chicano Movement is alive and growing. While other people are taking abuse and misuse without taking a stand, without voicing their opinions or facing the raw truth, the Chicano still marches, sings, and carries on the struggle for justice and liberation.

Today, I have a message for all the people of Aztlán: to the children, the students, the *pintos,* the workers, the professionals, the critics, the *políticos,* the educators, the police, the *campesinos*—the masses of our people—and to the bloodsuckers, the parasites, the vampires, who are the capitalists of the world.

The Critics

First, I want to address myself to the critics, whether they be right-wing, left, radical, moderate, or conservative. What we express in the form of demonstration has made changes. We know that the conservative element wants the handcuffs of the law and justice taken in their hands so they can play "Cowboy and Indian," "slave and master," "greaser and Texas Ranger," "vigilante and victim," with all those who disagree with their violence, their repression, their jails, their prisons, their courts, their colonies, their wars, and their murders. The moderate who says, "I agree with your goals but I disagree with your methods," is like an anchor holding us back rather than an ally pushing us forward. The coffee shop and the cocktail leftists spout all the fine phrases and quotes of truly great leaders and continually remind us of our faults and errors, but take the easy way out when confronted with real revolution. And then there are those who could truly be our allies, but they spend more time using poison tongues against their own than they do against the power structure, the real ENEMY.

Speech delivered on the steps of the Colorado State Capitol Building, September 16, 1975, Denver, Colorado. See *El Gallo: La Voz de la Justicia: El Año de Luis Jr. Martínez,* 7/7 (Oct.–Nov. 1975): p. 8.

Remember that only those who do not take action or do not get involved are the ones who never make a mistake.

The *Políticos*

I want to say to the *políticos,* remember that we pointed at the establishment together and we said, "They are corrupt, they are two-faced hypocrites, they are liars, they are bought and sold political prostitutes." Then as the pressures of the truth became fully known to all people, those in the power structure opened their arms to embrace you and infect you with their political disease. Then you pronounced the same corrupt structure healthy, generous, democratic, and pure, because you were now part of it. We urge you to speak out. Don't be afraid to lose false friends; one action is worth a thousand meaningless, compromised bills. Because one work, one courageous stand based on principle will set the example for all of our people. If you are weak and you compromise, your children will compromise twice as much and be twice as weak. If you are strong and uncompromising, your children will be even stronger and never compromise to false rulers and false ideals. Don't perpetuate the same system that has enslaved the minds and bodies of those who are confused enough to believe it (the system).

The *Campesinos*

We are children of the same parents and the same tree. Our hearts and support have always been yours. As the farm worker wins victories in the fields and works toward politicizing to true liberation, do not fall to the fate of other unions who are more concerned with their pocket books than they are with humanity: unions who practice exclusion of minorities, the inclusion of criminals, and who create an appetite for power at any cost. We hope to see the farm workers win their great battle over the tremendous obstacles of the growers and the teamsters and, in the process, recognize that the reality of liberation is not being part of the system which tried to destroy them and that they use their organizing talents to change every facet of this society. Their victory is our victory and a victory for all humanity.

The Police

Let all police in this city, this state, this country, and around the world where the same mentality persists, understand that the real responsibility is to serve the people and not to profit the corporations and their political puppets. Their role is not to defend the privileges of the power structure, but to respect the rights of the people. For the future of our own groups and our name, I say remember that you have a position, a job, and a place in this society because of our stance to injustice and not because of your own great qualifications. We wear our identity as a Chicano as a badge of pride, not one of shame.

Serve, protect, and it can be reciprocated. Destroy it and treat our people with injustice, and you might only receive the same in return. Recognize that we have families and want respect, and that we too realize the same about you. Take your side with us, not against us. The Viet Cong forgave their brothers, the South Vietnamese. It is possible that we may become brothers again, as it was when you, too, were a spic, before our demands, our marches, our demonstrations, got you a job.

The Educator

Your responsibility is one of the most important in the Movement. To you lies the great task of teaching the truth about our history, our culture, our values, and our contributions to mankind. You, the Chicano educator, must encourage and develop confidence in our children and teach our people the history of our colonization and oppression, and you must in all honesty instruct and direct them to a sound political action that inspires them to commit themselves to the progress of our people and of all humanity. The schools are tools of the power structure that blind and sentence our youth to a life of confusion and hypocrisy, one that preaches assimilation and practices institutional racism. You, the educators, have to rise above this to be the urban missionary, to be the believer in the advancement of our youth to a new and progressive society, and to be totally dedicated to mold minds to learn to know their future role as builders, teachers, and leaders. The progress of a people is judged by their educational attainment. Yours is the responsibility of truly educating our youth to the ideals of character, principle, and complete liberation. A teacher who loves to teach, loves people, and a person who loves, teaches the truth and stands by the students.

Artists and Writers

To our artists and our writers, we say, paint no murals of disgust and commercial garbage; write of inspiration to all mankind. Influence for progress and truth and not for money and perversion. Your paintings, your words, will influence for better or for worse. We urge you to choose for better, speak of growth, of success, tell of tragedy and relate a social message. It's better to say nothing than to misdirect and confuse our youth, who rely on you to interpret life and its true meaning. We urge you to write and paint what we in turn will use as tools to teach our people.

The Workers

In every factory, office, packing house, laundry, business, relate to your group with pride. Share your talents and your work with your fellow workers, stand behind them and with them in the defense of their rights and yours. Organize yourselves as brothers instead of dividing yourselves as competing individuals. Recognize that our social problems are not created by the poor and disadvantaged but by the rich and powerful who take advantage of disorganization and division and use it for their empire building at the expense of the weak, confused, and misled. We are all part of the same struggle for survival. Don't let a few luxuries separate you from the reality that we are all economic slaves if we never share totally in the profits of their labor.

The Guerrillas

Yes, there are guerrillas not only in South America, Mexico, Africa, Asia; there are also guerrillas in North America who truly believe in their efforts and that armed repression and violence can only be met with armed resistance. Never commit a criminal act against those who struggle for justice; never use violence for violence's sake. Make sure that all acts have political intent, one understood by the people you struggle for. Don't criticize those who are not on your political level or battlefield. Seek respect and give love, and the same might be returned.

We are all heirs to the land. We, the mestizo, the Indian, and of Spanish birth, owners of the Southwest by precedent and by legal title. The struggle for our land cannot be based on a pot of gold at the end of the rainbow and a quest for riches. It has to be based on a people's struggle to regain land for all and not for the privileged few. Our goal should be not to make new dons, *hacendados,* and *hidalgos,* but a new order based on group and community ownership, shared by all of the people of Aztlán. The land belongs to those who work it and those who share their proper heritage of the earth.

The Students

All of our dreams and hopes are placed on the shoulders of our youth. They must think as we have, that we must plan our ages not in terms of minutes, hours, weeks or years but by generations. Each generation takes one more step up the ladder to liberation. We made some changes to open up those doors. Now it is your turn to keep them open. You study what has happened in history. Study what is taking place in the world today. Evaluate, figure out what is noble, what is truth, what has meaning? And then take your position as the vanguard, as the leaders, to use your professional skills and knowledge to change this society for the better. Never let the world change you. Change the world. It's yours.

The People

Everyone says, "I'm doing it for the people." We say to the people, "Compare the results and tell us who has done it 'for the people,' and you will find those who truly committed themselves to the people and those who did it 'to' the people." Remember, the changes that have come about, have never come by way of the *políticos.* They have come about by the resistance of Movement people to all the injustices heaped on us from the days of conquest to the present days of exploitation. I tell you this because we are watching the world change, and how it changes will affect all of us. In the past ten years we have witnessed the assassination of national leaders, and in the past we said the government was involved. Today we know that the C.I.A. is involved, with the approval of the past four presidents. We have seen men reach the moon. We have watched half a country defeat the most powerful industrial war machine in the history of mankind. We witnessed the exposure of a total administration as a gang of thieves and criminals, including the president. And now you have a puppet who was never elected, serving the corporate structure as president and the godfather of the corporate world, the butcher of Attica; Nelson Rockefeller serving as vice-president while he openly runs the country. In the next ten years we will no doubt witness the rise and fall of the total capitalistic, bureaucratic, corporate-owned empire. Chicanos cannot sit at the same table with those parties that exploit, corrupt, and rape the rest of the world.

Chicanos must take their place in the new world as liberators of the people, not the exploiters of the people. NO ONE HAS THE RIGHT TO OPPRESS THE PEOPLE, AND ALL OPPRESSED PEOPLE HAVE THE RIGHT TO REVOLUTION.

Colorado Springs Bicentennial Speech of July 4, 1976

You have to understand that in order to make progress, in order to gain justice from any society, you have to take a stand. So when we talk about organizing people, when we talk about organizing Chicanos, organizing La Raza, that we have to know about the history of our people, we have to know what our contributions were to this area and to this continent. We aren't just Chicanos, a minority in the United States of America; we are Chicanos and Latinos who are a majority of Aztlán, of Mexico, Central America, and South America. We are a part of a majority.

We have to look at it that way. We have to remember that those brothers and sisters that cross that border are the same people that came before there was anyone out here, except the Indians. We predate 1776 by more than one hundred and eighty years. That Pike's Peak, named after Zebulon Pike, and they say you're a "Piker" if you're a dummy and you get jived. Juan de Ulibarrí was here one hundred years, a whole century, before Pike ever reached here, and the *indio* was here possibly 50,000 years before he got here. So we understand that we have to look back at our history and realize what we read about. Just like the Bicentennial today, they're talking about a revolution, but let me tell you that the people who talk about that revolution don't know what they're celebrating.

They are celebrating that "All Men Are Created Equal," but when they signed that Declaration of Independence, remember that they were not considering Black people, who were their slaves, they were not considering Indians, whom they considered savages and whom they were murdering; they were not considering Mexicanos, who would be the people they would conquer in 1848, a hundred years later.

So you see, they were only considering themselves. So we have to look at that history and ask what have all the struggles been about? What about the *indios* and the Chicanos in Taos and in that area?

Previously unpublished speech.

When they were told that they were going to be ruled under a new flag by Governor Bent, they didn't mess around with a celebration. They shot him with arrows, scalped, and killed him. That's right. It took three expeditions to go in there and finally overcome those people who were in those mountains, who understood that the land and the culture and the history was theirs; it belonged to nobody else.

We are the children of those people; we're the children of Zapata, who gave his life for the idea that the land belonged to the people. We're the children of "Pancho" Villa, who was willing to stand up for a cause and gather hundreds of thousands of Mexicanos and Yaquis to fight the oppressor and to liberate Mexico. However, Mexico was not liberated because the despots remained there and ran Mexico. And today Mexico is not liberated, nor are we liberated. We are not liberated when the prison population in Canyon City consists of forty percent our people, sixty-five percent in Buena Vista, and sixty to sixty-five percent in every juvenile hall in every one of these cities across the Southwest. We're not liberated, not any one of us.

And the people in Mexico are not liberated as long as the corporate structure in this country controls that country. As long as it controls their businesses and controls their economy. When inflation comes up here five percent, in Mexico it goes up twenty-five percent; if inflation is up thirty percent in this country, in Mexico it's two hundred percent. And the people there suffer from the same things that the people here suffer, only ten to twenty times more. So you realize when the average American in this country suffers inflation, the poor people and the minorities, the Mexicano and the Chicanos, *los indios y los negros,* suffer twice as much.

When unemployment is 7.2 percent in this country, you have to realize that with us, it's anywhere from fifteen to thirty percent unemployment or underemployment. We can't get the jobs that we deserve to have. We say that the Movement has changed some things. Until we dared to speak, until we dared to stand up, until we dared to march, until we dared to confront everybody from the pigs to the mayors to the *políticos,* nothing changed. Not in the mass media, not in the jobs, not in affirmative action, not in programs, not in food stamps or anything else, until we said *"Ya basta."* And they say, "We'll give them just enough to keep them quiet," and they give us a program. They created some *políticos* and gave them some jobs. And now those *políticos* are saying, "I'm sorry, you're not qualified." But the only thing that qualified him were the people in the streets.

We have kids and young people in the universities who have to understand that they're there because of the blood of Freddy Granados and the blood of Ricardo Falcón and the blood and jailing of the young people, who dared to take a stand, to say that if we're going to be part of this nation, then we want an equal percentage in those schools. And you judge the progress of a people by how many we have in prison and how many we have in the university. And if we have too many in the prisons, then that is not progress; it's regression. When we don't have enough in the university, then that's regression, and somebody is cutting us short.

So when we look back at history, remember the land struggle, remember those union strikes in the fields, remember the strikes in the mines, remember the confrontations, remember that your children had to suffer because we were not able to take a stand. Now we are saying that there is a new Chicano. We didn't start the revolution; the revolution started with the first resistance of Cuauhtémoc, who dared to fight the Spaniard Cortez. And now when we have false leadership, false idols, we say analyze them.

Recognize whether they belong to the people or they belong to the establishment. Either you are the people or you are the pig; and realize that we have to get rid of them, too, or we have to change them into brothers and sisters to understand that they deserve what they have if they share with their people for getting it for them. We have to teach our young people that they have to go out there, not based on how much money they are going to make for themselves, but how much they can learn to bring home to their own community. I think that's taking place, but it's taking place slowly.

When you see the young people up here, don't criticize them, cheer them on, help in whatever they do. Because on different levels, the different levels of political attainment, some people talk about political power within the system, some people talk about fighting that political power, some people talk about reform, and some people talk about destroying the system that creates the problem. You don't build hospitals after they create the disease; we don't have to have the disease. So we have to evaluate, what is Bicentennial? Do you realize that if you would go and you would read about the statements made by the people who signed the Declaration of Independence, and would go to the average American citizen who watches Archie Bunker, who is getting fat in front of the TV drinking Coors, that if you would repeat some of the words of the Declaration to those people, they'll think that it's radical, they'll say it's communist, they'll say it's socialist, and they'll say it's un-American. So ask them, "What is American?" If a revolution means change, if a revolution means freedom, then we all deserve it. And if they have gotten fat and forgot what it meant, then we have to educate them to understand what it meant.

The Declaration of Independence states that we the people have the right to revolution, the right to overthrow a government that has committed abuses and seeks complete control over the people. This is in order to clean out the corrupted, rotten officials that develop out of any type of capitalistic systems. Now, if they had done that, they would have never gotten to the point of having Watergate, they would have never gotten to the point of having criminals like Nixon and Agnew and fifty-five in the administration found to be guilty as crooks in this society, in this free democracy. How do those people develop? Where do they come from? What happens when you wipe them off the cake? They're just the icing. Because you can change the icing but the cake remains, and the cake is full of maggots, it's full of disease, it's full of liars, it's full of hypocrites, it's full of murderers, and up at the top they change the icing of the cake, but the same structure remains.

I want to tell you why that structure remains. Any country based on capitalism is based on greed. They teach young people that if they go to the twelfth grade, they can earn so much money; if they get a B.A. in college, they can earn a little more, if they make a master's degree, they earn a little more, and if they have a Ph.D., they earn more. So it's all based on how much money, and not on what you can do for humanity. How much money they can make. So greed is infected into our veins, and everybody wants to hustle, everybody wants to jive. If you can't get a degree, put a piece in your hand. If you can't get a degree, be a pimp. If you can't get a degree, be a hustler. If you can't get a degree, be a jiver. And if can't do that, sell yourself to the corporations, and they take care of you for life, as long as they control your life. People say, "You can make those statements, but you have to have some facts to back them up."

Let me show you something. In Angola, the sons of African slaves from Cuba are going back to liberate Africa, the land of their birth, the land of their origin. Let us look at that. In Vietnam, there were ships waiting for the sons of the capitalists, ships waiting for the people who work at Bank of America, at Texaco, at Exxon, ships waiting to take home the sons of the capitalists; people were killing each other to get away from Vietnam. In Cambodia, there were ships waiting for Americans, for sons of capitalists, to come home. In Laos and Thailand, the same thing. In China, the same thing. In Mozambique, in Angola, in Rhodesia, in Arabia, in different areas where they (capitalists) have been forced out, they are getting on ships and coming home, because the sons of the indigenous peoples and the sons of the liberators are starting to stand up and are ready to do what they have to do, and that is to liberate their own people. So we understand that.

Just look at your everyday newspaper to learn what is happening. The sons of Mexicanos and the sons of Latinos are standing up against the oppression all across Latin America, Mexico, and Aztlán. We're looking at each other. What happens when we don't care about each other? We are one *familia,* we are one family, we are related across this country and across these two continents. From Chicago to California, every one of you has a *primo,* you have a *tía,* you have a *compadre* and *comadre,* you have a *suegro* and a *suegra,* you have an *abuelito* and *abuelita,* from San Francisco to San Luis to Mexico. All across, we are interrelated, and that's what makes us so powerful and so hard to destroy.

Here we are. We are in the belly of the monster and we are tickling him. Right over here you have Cheyenne Mountain, you have a city built under that mountain that is a part of NORAD; it keeps track of everything that happens around the world. A $176-million plant is being built here to record anything that goes into orbit across the world, even the size of a half-dollar. You have the United States Air Force Academy right over there; you have Fort Carson over here; you have a Central Intelligence office in this city. You have the National Rifle Association (NRA) that moved from Washington, and they've picked the most right-wing community, Colorado Springs. And Mexicanos don't care; we're here to speak out, and we don't care if they are sitting around here. If you don't know the guy next to you, check his I.D.; he's probably with the CIA, the FBI, or one of their undercover snitches that they buy, and they are here.

So I'm just telling you that it takes a lot of guts. Remember that everybody wants to be part of history. So two hundred years of bicentennial to them is saying, "This is our history." But we're giving them a new step in history, and we're saying, "We're here." In this city you've got more retired army generals than anywhere in the country, who are the most right-wing element of this country. Remember, they live off of war and murder. And they live in this city, and this is where most of the millionaires come to retire and build their houses. That is why your community is controlled politically by them: because they control the money.

So we look at that and say, "How does capitalism affect us?" Capitalism affects us because for every millionaire you find, you'll find too many people breaking their backs to make his million dollars. He's not making it off his own back; he's making it off the sweat and blood of working people. And he's making it off of our people. And we fatten this land. Our people have worked in the fields, they've been the economic slaves, and then the man comes and creates taxation. They tax the land instead of the produce, and if they would tax what the land produces, most of our people would have the land back in southern Colorado and northern New Mexico. If they would not have come in with crooks, with corrupted jive artists, we would still own that land, we would still have our homeland, we would still have our own method of governing ourselves, we would still be sharing our work and sharing our produce. We would still be sharing our songs and our culture, we would still be sharing the *cantos y cuentos del alma, de la raza nuestra;* we would still be doing those things. We would still be living in a humane fashion, believing in people and believing in the words "dignity" and "honor."

These are some of the things that are contradictory in this society, and that's because capitalism is based on hustle, jive, scuffle, ruining people. How many of the Congressmen will go to Congress and come out millionaires? How many Senators will go in and become millionaires? And not just Anglos, but some Hispanos will become rich off of what their people gave them, their vote, but the people will have nothing in return.

So we have to understand how that history affects us, individually, every day of our lives, and how we can start to change it. And we must always think positively. Just think. Just think. We are the fastest-growing minority in this country. Our families are bigger than any other families. We have doubled our population in the last twenty-five years. Most of our people are under the age of twenty-five: sixty percent of us. We are a young group: we are twelve to fifteen million people and we are growing. We have grown because our parents were strong enough to face racism, worse and harder than we've ever faced. They have faced work ten times harder than we have had to work. They've faced repression and oppression and brutality, just for us to survive, and we've survived. It's up to the youth now to carry it on, to develop it and to understand that we have a new political direction to take.

We have to destroy capitalism, and we have to help five-sixths of the world to destroy capitalism in order to equal all people's lives. We have to support our Indian brothers, who are the indigenous people of this country. We have to support the Asians, who are indigenous, and the Africans, who are indigenous, and the South Americans, who are indigenous. People should have the right to liberation and the right to control their own destiny, and the only way to do that is to have a formulated plan to say that some of us will learn. As a baby starts to crawl, then starts to walk, then starts to run. Some people are running faster. Some people understand politically and then take political action a lot heavier than other people. Instead of rejecting those who haven't learned, then we say, "I'm going to help my brother and I'll do it for them." And the masses of the people have to understand that when certain actions are taken across this country, when demonstrations are taken and formed, when this kind of thing happens, then people gather together and it's for our people. It's not for money, no. One cannot pay us.

People are loyal to corporations for the check. People are loyal to the Mafia for the payment. They kill for money. But our people, I have to say, liberate themselves for love of each other, and that is the most important thing that we can have. Nobody can destroy that; nobody can destroy the spirit of our people. And they can kill individuals, they can shoot us down in the streets, and they have. They can throw us in their jails, but they cannot destroy an idea or a philosophy, and they can never destroy love, because we're going to win. We're going to beat them, whether it takes this generation, the next generation, or the next generation. We're going to win. Viva La Raza! Viva La Raza Libre! Viva! Viva Aztlán Libre!

The Past-Present-Future of the
Chicano Movement, 1978

We have invited you to participate in a working conference, to share experiences and study our mistakes and our successes. We remember how we stimulated the masses of our people into action; in many cases the results were positive, and in many cases they have soured and have had negative results.

The most positive results were in the creation of political, cultural, and historical awareness, self-identity and self-worth.

In accomplishing this, we were able to bring about a collective concept of a unit: one family, one people. By identifying ourselves as an ethnic minority, we were able to escape the titles placed on our backs—"The Invisible Minority" and other names—which placed us as an unidentifiable group. By identifying ourselves, we were able to judge or compare our accomplishments and in most cases our lack of accomplishments in the areas of employment, education, politics, economics, and social standing. We then were able to place ourselves on a scale that proved our claims of racism and classism as compared to that of the majority society.

We then carried through the enactments of civil rights bills and "Affirmative Action." We made our demands based on the inequities within the socio-political-economic life of this country. The result was a move by the establishment to open the doors to the universities, the employment rolls, and a slight crack in the door to economic participation.

We marched, we protested, we resisted, we demanded, we conducted an overt war on a minor scale and a covert protracted guerrilla operation in some situations. Those who acted were punished by the police, the courts, and the penal institutions. They paid the heavy price in blood, time, fear, demoralization, and, in some cases, death. The nation and the people they fought for often rejected or carefully avoided and forgot them.

Speech delivered at the Crusade for Justice, 1978.

We only talk of the past, because of the effects it has had on the present and what we must prepare for in the future. The single most important act was our nationalism and the identification struggle produced through the cultural, political, and social forces which brought the masses of our people together. This presented a forum for the organizers, the philosophers, the artists, the educators, and, most important, the revolutionaries, to instruct, teach, and inspire our students, our grassroots people, our workers, our parents, and our children.

We were not alone in recognizing this phenomenon; other groups and political organizations, especially the establishment, also took note and made their attempts to use our gatherings as their forums for our destruction or their own political self-interests; i.e., the physical destruction of the Chicano Moratorium against the War in Vietnam, held in Los Angeles in 1970, provocations, political theorists, repression in many forms (violent or psychological), left-wing political groups who had never been able to penetrate, much less organize the Chicano masses.

We now fully recognize that because we were an emerging movement and because we were neither racist nor classist, we accepted everyone with open arms. The result was confusion, division, distrust, antagonism, and competitive disunity.

Over the past ten years we have witnessed Chicano organizations of every shape and form identify with the Movement, but in most cases they are still tied to the umbilical cord of the establishment: two-party politics, capitalism, economic dependency, and right-wing social classism.

Those who have made economic gains have done so at the expense of the Movement, but have never nourished or supported those who have maintained the spirit of resistance and progress. In many cases they have developed a guilt complex out of an inferiority complex and, therefore, reestablish and reinforce the classism that we seek to destroy.

There have been many worthwhile causes supported by and in many cases led by students, although other students have proven to be adventurists seeking to take part in internationalist identification before they take care of their homework and responsibility to their community. It is easier to identify with something abstract and do nothing, than it is to face the fire of reality in your own home or back yard.

Many students are relating to the theories of intellectual masturbators rather than to the realities of confrontation and change. Also, many of them are starting to be afflicted with the disease of egotism in their relationship with their peers and community, not realizing that their acceptance into universities and colleges resulted because of forced opportunity and not because of class qualification.

It is our duty and that of the educators to remind those of our own that the steps to their classrooms and the checks from their financial aid are stained with the blood of their predecessors. We know and have learned through trial and error, through murdered martyrs and exiles, through repression and oppression, that we must organize forces that can survive all obstacles. We must continue to organize, teach, inspire, mobilize, resist, and win!

So then we must utilize our identity, our cultural and social life to attract the masses of our people. We must provide for the everyday needs of our people (social services); we must keep in contact with every facet of our people (prisoners' rights); we must create economic reservoirs to sustain our forces; we must be prepared to protect our people through legal recourse (legal defense or physical defense); we must be able to inform our people (media and press and schools); we must face the issues that are important and of immediate necessity to the betterment of our total community.

We face a new crisis, such as the forces of the right-wing mentality throughout this nation. Witness the emergence of the Ku Klux Klan, the Fascist Hitlerites, the John Birch Society, religious institutions, and that subtle but racist mentality that persists throughout this society. All these forces are on the rises and the new targets are the Mexicano/Chicano/Latino people of the North and South America continents.

The historical facts of the war of 1846–1848, colonization, repression, racism, economic slavery, are the reason we must look at our Movement not on the basis of present short-term gains, but the future of long-range goals.

Short-term gains are the weekly paychecks from government programs or financial aid grants. Short-term gains are the minority representation in the majority legislature and the window dressing representation in agencies and on boards that control the handouts that pacify the masses.

Long-range goals deal with: the philosophy of self-determination and total liberation, the building of confidence and independent action, the right to make decisions that affect our children and their future, the right to select our allies, the choice to pick our friends and determine our own political direction, to control our economic resources and human values. We must support and advance our collective nationalism, which in turn will produce a profitable collective economy. We must use our human resources to full advantage and benefit of our nation. We recognize that we must offer solidarity to all liberation struggles and progressive nations, but never flinch or turn away from the immediate task that faces us in the barrios, the campos, the ranchitos, the rural areas, and the urban and suburban complexes.

We must begin to think, plan, and organize, not on terms of days, months, or years, but on terms of generations. Each generation must provide a positive step forward, and we must teach them that unless we have taken one small part in helping to take that step, we have failed as men and women in our obligation to our people and humanity.

We have the choice of simply having existed like a bedbug in the *colchón,* or to having contributed to the part of the most exciting, rewarding adventure in life . . . the Chicano Movement!

CHAPTER III

Two Plays

The Revolutionist

Characters in the Play

PAPÁ . . . . Father, The Old Man

MARÍA . . . . Mother

ESPERANZA . . . . Daughter

JOHN . . . . Second Son

CARLOS . . . . Third Son

JOAQUÍN . . . . Fourth Son

BEN . . . . Son-in-Law

DEL . . . . Teenage Grandson

TINA . . . . Teenage Granddaughter

MARIACHI . . . . Three Men, One Woman

PARTERA . . . . Midwife

HARTEK . . . . Collector

POLICEMEN . . . . Outsiders

FBI . . . . Outsiders

GOLDMAN . . . . Outsiders

WELFARE WOMAN . . . . Outsiders

Time: In the fall of 1950

Place: A metropolitan city in the Southwest. The living room of a housing project. A plainly furnished room: a table and chairs, a radio, a plaster statue of the Virgin of Guadalupe. A large picture on the back wall . . . of a *charro* astride a horse, cartridge belts crisscrossed over his chest and a rifle in his arms.

The Revolutionist

Prologue

PAPÁ: (*Dressed in a charro suit with cartridge belts strapped across his chest and holding his rifle, he walks to the front of the stage. He speaks to the audience.*)

I have been in many battles in my time. I rode with Pancho Villa when I was but a boy. The times were hard. Life was hard in those days of tears and blood. Hardship was a common partner. I suffered hunger, pain, misery, and sorrow. I can remember when we rode day and night, our rumps a mass of bleeding blisters, the flesh of our pants, the ants glued to our saddles 'til man and beast became one galloping, painful boil riding to death or glory. I sweated and toiled in the fields—the hoe became part of my calloused hand as we glided through rows of beets. Yes, it was hard, but I was man, master of my home, poor but honest. I had honor and my soul. I almost lost it all some time back. I sank to the very bottom of the muck of this society, and I lied to my son Joaquín. I was beaten to my knees and, worst of all, I almost robbed Joaquín of the only inheritance that I could leave him: pride, honor, dignity, and faith. We made it through that winter that almost killed me. I look back now and know it wasn't Ben's fault. I couldn't blame John, not even the Anglos. It was the city . . . we were all the victims of the city. We are safe now. Joaquín has forgiven me and now he knows who I am . . . (*He exits.*)

ACT I—SCENE ONE

The family is waiting for their father and mother and the youngest son to come. They are reminiscing, talking about the old times and the Old Man. They are sitting around the table.

ESPERANZA: (*Glancing pleadingly at* BEN *as she speaks.*) Papá will like it here. He can take walks in the park, and Mamá can baby sit for us when we go to the movies.

JOHN: If they don't roll him.

ESPERANZA: Papá can take care of himself. He may be old, but he's a tough old rooster.

BEN: (*Sullenly.*) What about the kid? (*The teenagers* TINA *and* DEL *rush in fighting.* TINA *turns on the radio and starts dancing the jerk.*)

DEL: That music is really lame . . . turn it to Station 990.

TINA: (*Pushing* DEL *away from the radio.*) It's my turn!

ESPERANZA: Tina, turn that off. Your grandpa will be coming soon, and I don't want him to think we run a rock-and-roll joint. Tina, go check the baby and see where Benito is.

TINA: Oh, Mom. I always have to watch the kids. (*She sulks and walks out.*)

DEL: Ain't Grandpa hip, Ma?

JOHN: Hip! He still thinks he sees Zapata's horse. He still has a *charro* suit that he wears on the 16th of September.

DEL: What's the 16th of September, man?

ESPERANZA: Don't call your uncle "man."

DEL: You are a man, ain't you?

JOHN: If I hit you with a left hook, you'll know. (*He feints a punch and* DEL *runs out.*)

ESPERANZA: Remember when we were working beets in Keensburg? Papá won the arm-wrestling contest at the cantina, and he came home with that money and groceries. We hadn't tasted candy for three months.

JOHN: (*Sourly.*) Yeah, then he got drunk again and we didn't eat for three months.

ESPERANZA: You exaggerate. We never went hungry, that's for sure.

JOHN: Yeah, we never stopped working either.

CARLOS: No one ever worked as hard and clean as Lino. I used to walk by his side when I was eight years old as he thinned beets. He never missed a stroke. He never left a double. (*They look at LINO's picture sadly.*) Well, anyway, he died a hero for this country.

JOHN: The Old Man should be getting here.

BEN: (*Looking at ESPERANZA.*) He has to understand this is my house.

ESPERANZA: He'll be no trouble, *querido.* (*The others laugh.*)

CARLOS: He'll only start a revolution.

JOHN: Or he'll talk one for hours.

BEN: How old is Joaquín?

ESPERANZA: He's only twelve. Papá's last boy.

CARLOS: We shouldn't have left him with the Old Man. The Old Man has him all alone and fills his head with crazy notions that we need a revolution. This city might ruin the kid.

ESPERANZA: He's a good boy. He's a good worker. He's like Lino, only quieter.

BEN: Sullen is the word. He better keep his nose clean—I won't have any trouble here.

JOHN: Can I borrow your car?

BEN: Yes, if you catch up with the payments . . . No sir, nobody's going to drive that car but me.

Sounds of revolutionary music. The door opens, the Old Man enters carrying his petaquilla (trunk), followed by JOAQUÍN and then MARÍA. The family rushes to meet them. The Old Man warmly embraces them all. The sons sit their mother down and ESPERANZA clings to her father. JOAQUÍN receives a kiss on the cheek from

ESPERANZA, *a pat on the back from* CARLOS, *and moves to the edge of the room and sits on the trunk his father has set down.*

BEN: *Bienvenido, Señor* Jaramillo.

PAPÁ: A fine home you have here, Benito, a fine home.

ESPERANZA: It's your home, too, Papá. (*Looking at* BEN.)

PAPÁ: Thank you, daughter. I will find work soon. I'll have a place in no time for María and Joaquín. We won't be here long. (*Then looking at all of them, he beams.*) It's good to be with all of the family again. *Por Dios,* I feel good. *Eh,* María? (MARÍA *smiles; she walks toward* ESPERANZA *and embraces her.*)

MARÍA: Yes, yes, it's good to be with our children again.

ESPERANZA: (Leaving.) We'll fix some coffee. Come, Mamá.

MARÍA: *Muy bien.* (*They walk out together, after* MARÍA *gets her coat.*)

PAPÁ: Well, Juanito, where do you work?

JOHN: Ah, I'm on unemployment. The last job ended and I was laid off.

PAPÁ: Unemployment? Is that a good job?

JOHN: They pay me while I find another job.

PAPÁ: They pay you? Like the pension! Heh! You receive a pension at the age of thirty? (*He laughs and slaps his thigh.*) *¡Ay caray!* I have worked since I was six and I am sixty-two, and I will still work. (*He laughs again.*)

JOHN: They owe it to me.

BEN: It's not that easy here in the city, Mr. Jaramillo.

CARLOS: (*Looks up from his book.*) You have to have an education, Papá. They won't hire you without one.

JOHN: What's wrong with unemployment or welfare? They got it, let them use it.

PAPÁ: Slavery, that's what it is, bondage, servility—that's what Benito Juárez said.

JOHN: This is America. You are living in the past, Papá.

PAPÁ: The past is the glory and dignity of man. The revolution meant something; it gave the poor something to hold on to, and if you died it was with honor. (MAMÁ *and* ESPERANZA *return with food and coffee.*) They were men, not weaklings, men not *mantenidos.* And your wife, and children, where are they?

JOHN: (*Uncomfortable.*) Ahh, I couldn't get a job. We aren't together. They wouldn't help her and the kids unless I got out of the house.

ESPERANZA: Papá, sit and have some coffee, times are different now.

PAPÁ: No, *gracias.* (*He pulls out a roll of bills and slaps it on the table.*) I work hard and earn money. Look at Joaquín, a fine worker.

MARÍA: He is a good boy.

CARLOS: Well, at least now he can start getting an education without missing a month and a half in the spring and a month in the fall.

PAPÁ: If he learns to work, he needs no one.

CARLOS: Times are changing, Papá. Joaquín needs all the schooling he can get.

BEN: (*His eyes on the roll of money.*) Yes, now he can get his schooling. The school is very close by. (*He smiles at* ESPERANZA *as she beams at him.*)

PAPÁ: I must find a house soon. We do not come like beggars to live off the relatives.

BEN: My house is yours, *señor.*

ESPERANZA: *Sí, Papá,* you will stay with us. Our home will always be yours. (*She smiles happily at* BEN.)

JOHN: How was the topping? Did you do as well as last year?

PAPÁ: Better this time—there was no cantina for sixty miles. (*He laughs, they force a laugh. The teenagers come in fighting.*)

TINA: No, you don't, you square.

DEL: Tonight it's station 990 . . . hip, man, hip.

ESPERANZA: Speak to your grandparents. I don't know why these children can't learn more manners.

BEN: (*Stands.*) Speak to your grandparents. They are going to live with us. (*The teenagers walk to the old people.* MARÍA *embraces them. The Old Man looks them up and down and nods.*)

DEL: Hello. (TINA *kisses her grandfather, they both sit down.*)

JOHN: I see you still have the old *petaquilla.* (*He looks at the trunk. The Old Man's eyes light up. He stands. He looks around at the uplifted faces.*)

PAPÁ: (*He walks to the trunk.* JOAQUÍN *jumps off and stands still and straight, watching the expressions of the rest eagerly.*) Yes, I have something here for all of you. (*He pulls out a rosary for* ESPERANZA.)

ESPERANZA: Papá, oh Papá, it's like old days after the thinning, when we got paid and you bought me a new dress and a new pair of shoes, and we would go to the dance.

PAPÁ: Juanito, a wallet. (*He hands* JOHN *a wallet.*)

JOHN: Thanks, I won't need it except for cards.

PAPÁ: (*Hands* BEN *a bottle.*) For the head of the house.

BEN: *Gracias.* (BEN *sets it on the table.*)

PAPÁ: (*Hands* CARLOS *a book.*) For the revolutionist.

CARLOS: (*Reads.*) Viva Villa. (*He sets the book down and continues reading his book.* PAPÁ *hands* TINA *a necklace.*)

TINA: Thank you, Grandpa. (*She puts it in her pocket and tries to get* ESPERANZA's *attention.* PAPÁ *hands* DEL *a hunting knife.* DEL *whistles and admires the blade.*)

ESPERANZA: (*Takes it from* DEL.) I'll save it for you. (PAPÁ *leans down into the trunk and comes up with the rifle. He shows it to everyone. Offers it. No one accepts.*)

PAPÁ: My most valuable possession. (*He throws the rifle to* JOAQUÍN, *who stands it at his side. Reaches into the trunk and comes up with a large silver cross.*) I took this in Torreón. The *curas* ran like chickens when we took the town.

BEN: Let's have a drink.

TINA: (*To* ESPERANZA.) Can I go to the dance?

PAPÁ: How old is she? Dances on a Monday night?

ESPERANZA: Tina is fifteen, Papá. They hold dances at the social center.

PAPÁ: At this time she is going to a dance alone?

ESPERANZA: Go to bed, Tina, and check on the kids. (TINA *leaves, gives the Old Man a haughty look.*)

BEN: You too, Del, hit the sack. (*The teenagers grumble as they leave. The adults sit at the table, pour drinks.*)

PAPÁ: (*Raises his glass.*) *Un brindis muchachos.* You are doing well, Benito, a fine home, good furniture, you are doing very well, *hijo.*

BEN: (*Shrugs his shoulders.*) I'm not doing so good. (*He looks at* ESPERANZA.) I'm not working.

PAPÁ: How do you live, are you stealing? . . . or do you get a pension, too? (*Looking at* JOHN.)

ESPERANZA: I've been working, Papá. It's hard for a man to find a job.

PAPÁ: Ha, a man must work. It's not healthy for a woman to work. It's sacrilegious. A woman's place is in the home.

MARÍA: (*She pats* PAPÁ.) Let's talk of other things, we have so much to talk about.

JOHN: You'll find out!

ESPERANZA: I'll fix Joaquín a place, Mamá. Come, little brother. (*She leaves.* MARÍA *gets up and leaves with her.* JOHN *pours everybody a drink.*)

PAPÁ: ¡Salud! (*They drink, there is a knock on the door.* BEN *answers.*)

JOHN: This is really good stuff. Man, where did you get it?

PAPÁ: Yes, it clears your throat, cooks your stomach, and fires up your passion.

STRANGER: Are you Ben Sánchez? I am John Hartek, John's Finance Co. You know you're three payments behind on your car?

BEN: I'm not working. I called the office.

HARTEK: We want money, not talk. I've come for the car or the dough. $105.00 at $35.00 per month, plus late charges and pick-up fee. That's $148.00.

BEN: I have no money. (*He looks at the Old Man.*) I have nowhere to get it.

PAPÁ: *¿Qué quiere el gringo?* We have money! (*He pulls out his roll.*) How much do you need, Benito?

BEN: $148.00.

PAPÁ: (*Hesitates, then peels the money off.*) Here, pay him and tell him to take care of his business at decent hours.

BEN: (*Pays.*) I'll try to have the next payment on time, sir.

HARTEK: I don't want to be wasting my time and I don't like being around this neighborhood at this hour of the night. (*He leaves brusquely.*)

PAPÁ: *¡Qué animales . . . !* Do they scramble for dollars all night long?

BEN: Thank you, thank you, *Señor* Jaramillo.

PAPÁ: It is nothing. Am I not in your home? We will suffer together. When you have the money, you can pay me.

JOHN: That was a narrow escape . . . (*Sits.*) Say, Ben, can I borrow your car tomorrow?

BEN: Yeah, I guess so.

CARLOS: Papá, you should take care of your money.

PAPÁ: We must help one another. *¿Qué no?*

CARLOS: Your money won't last long if you start paying everybody's debts. (*He looks seriously at BEN. BEN avoids his stare.*)

PAPÁ: It is nothing. It won't be the first time, and you, *hijo* (*To CARLOS.*), what are your plans?

CARLOS: I'm trying to finish my education. I want to be a school teacher. You can't make it nowadays unless you study.

PAPÁ: *¡Muy Bien!* Just so when you start wearing a fine suit, a white shirt, and a tie, you don't forget that you are a *mejicano.*

CARLOS: It is not easy to forget.

PAPÁ: We will see. Education is like money: it sometimes changes a man, and he only thinks of himself, his education, or his money.

CARLOS: It's too soon to worry about that. I don't have either one yet.

JOHN: Hell! It don't make any difference one way or the other.

BEN: It's just not like working in the farms—the city is something else.

PAPÁ: The city does not make the man! The man makes the city!

BEN: Aww . . . Let's have another drink. (*They drink. Revolutionary music.*)

PAPÁ: I remember when we were ready to take Zacatecas. I was ordered to stay behind. I had been shot in the leg at Torreón. The bullet is still here in my leg. I had started bleeding badly again, when we finally took El Grillo; but I knew that every man and gun was needed. We had to take Zacatecas and break Huerta's main force. Well, I was chosen to lead one of the first attacks on the outpost of El Grillo, which protected the city of Zacatecas. We had to knock out the cannons that were blocking our main force; myself and the young ones of the brigade loaded ourselves with grenades and got our horses ready.

Lights fade out slowly as PAPÁ *talks. Faint sound of a bugle . . . cannon shots . . . rifle fire. Spot on the Old Man, lights fade on* CARLOS, JOHN, *and* BEN.

PAPÁ: (*He is once more the young revolutionist.*) Listen, *muchachos. Tú, Tomás, cuidado con la carabina! Luis amárrate los huevos; Jesús ¿por qué llevas tu guitarra? Monten sus caballos. ¡Adelante a la gloria y la victoria! . . . ¡VIVA VILLA! . . . ¡VIVA MÉXICO! . . . ¡Libertad o Muerte!*

ACT I—SCENE TWO

The same room. The Old Man and MARÍA. *Music of El Revolucionario as the curtain opens.*

PAPÁ: We have been here two months now, and there is no work—
not for a man: washing dishes, sweeping floors . . . Women's
work! *¡Qué vergüenza!*

MARÍA: Maybe tomorrow, *Viejito.*

PAPÁ: *Mañana.* Everyday is *mañana.* These hands were made for
work. I have been working or fighting since I was six years old.
Now they say you are too old. I can outwork any of those ghosts
who stand on 20th and Larimer Street, but when the trucks stop,
they look at my hair and call the young ones.

MARÍA: We'll get along.

PAPÁ: Where is Joaquín? I want to know where that boy is.

MARÍA: He is in school—he'll be home soon. He's a good boy.

PAPÁ: Our money is wearing thin. Does no one buy groceries here
except me?

MARÍA: Carlos helps what little he can. He must keep up with his
studies.

PAPÁ: And Juan, where does his money go?

MARÍA: (*She bows her head.*) We have had bad times before.

PAPÁ: In the fields, yes, but there was always somewhere to work,
even if they paid us with eggs, milk, or vegetables, even when
they rob us and we work like animals. This city is a prison. Our
children speak English, I speak Spanish, I cannot understand
what they say. They call themselves Jar-mee-lo. My name is
Jaramillo. *¡Por Dios!* There is no respect, this city is a prison.

MARÍA: The children respect you.

PAPÁ: Ah! Respect, they don't know what respect is anymore. This
city is a curse. (JOHN *runs in and looks out the window. A loud
knock at the door.*)

MARIÁ: *¿Qué, hijo?*

JOHN: I don't know.

PAPÁ: *Y tú, ¿qué traes? ¿Por qué vienes como un perro con la cola entre las piernas?*

JOHN: Aw . . . speak English. (MARÍA *opens the door. A policeman walks in.*)

POLICEMAN: All right, you. You're John Jaramillo. I have a traffic summons for you.

PAPÁ: Answer him, you are Juan Jaramillo.

JOHN: Yes, officer.

POLICEMAN: What ta hell you running from? You hiding something?

JOHN: No, sir.

MARÍA: What has he done? My son is a good boy.

POLICEMAN: Sure, they are all good boys. Come on, Pancho . . . get a move on.

MARÍA: Wait, wait. What did he do?

POLICEMAN: Pay his $45.00 speeding ticket down at the courthouse and you can take him. (*He drags* JOHN *out.*) Come on. (MARÍA *stands with her head bowed,* PAPÁ *looks at her, slowly goes to the trunk, he opens it and pulls out the last of his money.*)

PAPÁ: *Ay, mujer, otra vez el burro al trigo.* Here, take it. Get Carlos to take you. Go release your chicken thief. Remember he must pay me back.

MARÍA: (MARÍA *takes the money and leaves hurriedly. As she exits she turns and speaks.*) I'll ask Esperanza or Carlos to take me.

PAPÁ: (PAPÁ *sits down. The two teenagers,* DEL *and* TINA, *run in followed by* JOAQUÍN. JOAQUÍN *sits on the trunk. They look at the Old Man and snicker.* TINA *turns the radio on and starts dancing.* DEL *starts pounding on a book using it for a drum.*) *¡Silencio!* (JOAQUÍN *jumps off the trunk, tensely waiting; the children keep it up.*) Quiet, you fools! Is this what you learn at school? One callous on your hands would make you faint. (ESPERANZA *and* BEN *walk in.*)

ESPERANZA: You kids keep quiet and get out of here.

DEL: Man! We can't do nothing around here anymore.

TINA: This house is really for the birds.

BEN: They ain't doing anything wrong.

ESPERANZA: That's not what you said two months ago.

BEN: Well, this is their home.

ESPERANZA: (*To children.*) Go on, go on. (*They leave.*)

BEN: They got as much right as anyone else around here.

ESPERANZA: As long as I'm around, they're going to have to learn to respect the folks.

BEN: I guess my damn word don't mean nothing around here.

ESPERANZA: Papá, we want to talk with you.

PAPÁ: Yes, speak.

ESPERANZA: Well . . . well . . . Papá. I don't want you to feel offended, but we have a large family and . . . and . . . You tell him, Ben.

BEN: We were thinking that you should go apply for welfare. You're too old to work.

PAPÁ: I'm stronger than you. I can out-work any of you.

BEN: Here in the city it's different. I know you don't have any money left. It's for your own good, you need help.

PAPÁ: Help! I will say when I need help.

ESPERANZA: Please, Papá. There are expenses. We need food and clothing. The children need books and dues at school. So does Joaquín.

PAPÁ: Well, sell your car, I have an investment in it.

BEN: Now, wait a cotton-picking minute. You and the family have been here for two months. What do you think we eat, revolutions? Man! How far do you go for your people? I'll help all I can, but sell my car, never!

PAPÁ: Then we are even, is that what you mean?

BEN: Oh, yeah, you bet we're even.

ESPERANZA: That's not what he means, Papá. You can get help from the welfare. You can get enough food and money to last you till spring.

PAPÁ: Never. I will find a job. No gringo fool with a white shirt and tie is going to put a spoon in my mouth, or, even worse, one of those pale blabbering women. (*He looks at* BEN.) We are even, eh? Very well. I will pay you until I can find a house. You will have your money. (*He walks to the trunk.*) Haste. (JOAQUÍN *watches him.* PAPÁ *opens it up and picks up his rifle. Then he puts it back down and picks up the cross. He stalks,* JOAQUÍN *trailing behind him.*)

ESPERANZA: Now you've fixed it! (BEN *gives her a dirty look.* MARÍA *comes in with* CARLOS.)

ESPERANZA: Did you get him out?

CARLOS: He'll be out, I gave the money to his buddy Dave. He went for him. (*He looks at* BEN.) Lucky they didn't take the owner of the car, too. (*He picks up his book and starts reading.*)

BEN: What is he talking about?

ESPERANZA: The police came after John. He had got a ticket for speeding.

BEN: (*He asks suspiciously.*) What money?

MARÍA: José paid for his ticket!

BEN: How much?

CARLOS: Forty-five smackeroos for dear old John.

BEN: (*Looking at* ESPERANZA.) I told you they had money, and your brother John hasn't bought a slice of bread since they got here. They're your parents, not mine, and your brothers, too.

CARLOS: (*Looks up from his book.*) I gave you five bucks last night. (*He looks back at his book.*)

BEN: Big deal!

ESPERANZA: (*Looks hard at him.*) Now just a minute! I know they are my family. I work, Carlos works, and Papá has paid for your car. Now shut up.

MARÍA: (*To* ESPERANZA.) Where is your father?

ESPERANZA: I'm sorry, Mamá, he left, he was angry.

BEN: (*Dejected.*) Oh what-ta-hell, it's late . . . Let's go to bed. (*They all walk out,* MARÍA *sits heavily on the sofa, picks up a pillow and starts to croon a Mexican lullaby. The room darkens, and the strains of heavy guitar music start. The shadowed form of an old woman in black enters.* MARÍA *is moaning in pain now.*)

PARTERA: They say Francisco Villa and his rabble have taken Torreón. (*She spits.*) Your man is out there fighting while you have another miscarriage, because you have nothing to eat. Bah! The government troops ride through this village, take the food from the mouths of babies and mothers, rape the women, and then with a full belly, they kill your men.

MARÍA: (*Between groans and clenched teeth.*) We will win. Our men will return with food and help. We must win.

PARTERA: (*Busy with a basin, pouring water and tearing a sheet into strips.*) Do you know that half of Villa's men are starving? Hah! Fool! They will come and eat you out, just like the *Federales*.

MARÍA: Have you no faith, old hag?

PARTERA: (*Takes out a coin, bites it.*) In this I have faith! In man, never. In revolutions (*She spits.*) never! As long as women have babies, I will eat. (*She laughs coarsely.*) And as long as there are men, women will have babies, or miscarriages. (*She laughs cruelly.*)

MARÍA: You are a witch, not a midwife. You have no faith, you believe in nothing. José will come back. We will win the revolution. We will have schools and hospitals, and the people will own the land and plant and grow and . . . and . . . (*She falters.*) I will have José's children. (*She clutches at her stomach and falls over groaning.*) ¡AY! ¡AYYY! ¡Ayyyy!

PARTERA: (*Goes to work in the darkened room, placing the miscarriage in part of the sheet, wrapping it up and placing it in the basin. She forces* MARÍA *to drink from a bottle. Then she forces* MARÍA *to listen to her.*) Now, if you forget what l tell you, I am leaving a note for you under the Santo Niño. You need him now, if you live. You owe for this job. I am old, you understand, I have to live, eh?

MARÍA: (*Nods weakly.*) Water . . . Please . . . water.

PARTERA: (*She pours a glass of water.*) You are to go to the Valencia Hacienda and clean Sra. Valencia's house. I have collected for the work. We will be even. Agreed?

MARÍA: (MARÍA *shakes her head numbly.*) I will go.

PAPÁ *enters carrying a bundle, a mochila, and a rifle, across his back.*

PAPÁ: (*Whispering.*) María . . . María . . . where are you? (*He sees her prostrate on the floor and shoves the midwife aside roughly.*) María, you are sick . . . You didn't tell me?

MARÍA: It doesn't matter, José. It doesn't matter now.

PARTERA: (*Picking up her basin and sheets.*) Remember our bargain, dear. (*She moves towards the door.*)

PAPÁ: What bargain? What bargain? (*He asks* MARÍA, *then he grabs the midwife.*) What bargain, you vulture?

PARTERA: Our bargain: if she doesn't keep it, I'll put a curse on you.

PAPÁ: A curse? I'll put a bullet through your thieving heart!

MARÍA: (*Weakly.*) José, let it be. I will pay her.

PAPÁ: We have paid with blood and her service is for the revolution. We fight to rid this country of superstition and fear. (*To the midwife.*) Now go! I have paid you with your life.

PARTERA: (*Hurrying out the door, screaming.*) I curse you, José Jaramillo, I curse you. You, you, will never have a son.

PAPÁ: Out, you witch! You hag. You traitor to your *patria! Desgraciada, ladrona, puta.*

MARÍA: José, I will pay with my work—it is not much. She will curse us. *Por Dios,* she will curse us.

PAPÁ: Superstition! The revolution will cure that. Look, (*He fumbles in his sack and pulls out a package.*) *azul,* blue corn meal, (*another package*) maize, (*a bottle*) brandy to give you back your strength, (*another package*) *frijoles.* You will get your strength back.

MARÍA: I owe a debt to the midwife.

PAPÁ: You have paid with our son. No one can pay a higher price than that. Now listen, we took Torreón and our troops are moving this way. Tonight we take the supply depot and we join the main body in the morning. We are winning, *querida.* Mexico will be ours. Mexico for the people. (*He helps her lie down.*) You must meet me at the bridge. My *compadre* Luis and his wife will be here soon to help you. *Adiós, querida* . . . soon . . . soon. (*He leaves. An explosion is heard. Lights come on.* MARÍA *sits up rocking the pillow and crooning. She gets up to light the candle in front of the Santo Niño. She kneels and begins to pray. She sobs in between.*)

MARÍA: *Santa María, Madre de Dios, ruega por nosotros, pecadores, ahora y en la hora de nuestra muerte, amén.* Protect him! *Santo Niño,* protect him! (*The strains of music are heard faintly, then louder and louder. The Mariachi, singing "Las Mañanitas." The door flies open, the lights go on and* PAPÁ *walks in, a bottle in one hand, a present in the other.*)

MARÍA: José!

PAPÁ: Happy birthday, *corazón. Feliz día de tu santo.* (MARÍA *rushes to him, wiping tears and sobbing from happiness and relief. The rest of the family stumbles in rubbing their eyes. The children peek through the doors.*)

BEN: What-ta-hell is going on around here?

ESPERANZA: It's Mamá's birthday. Oh, Papá, you didn't forget, you never forget. Mamá was feeling so bad.

The old man starts pouring drinks for everyone. The Mariachi start playing a Mexican corrido. PAPÁ *grabs* MARÍA *and starts dancing.* CARLOS, ESPERANZA, *and then the two teenagers look in.* BEN *motions for them to come in, and they all start to dance. The Mariachi then sings a ballad for* PAPÁ *and* MAMÁ. *The lights go out.*

ACT I—SCENE THREE

Revolutionary music as curtains opens. PAPÁ *stands by the couch right,* MARÍA *at the couch, and* JOHN *on stage left.*

PAPÁ: Did you get your check?

JOHN: They had a mix-up at the Employment Office.

PAPÁ: I need that money. Your brother-in-law is like a coyote after a chicken. He complains daily about our living here. I want to give the jackal his due.

CARLOS: (*As he walks in.*) Hi, everybody. Say, John, I just saw Dave. He said you lost your tail at the dogs last night.

PAPÁ: What is this? You mean the racing dogs? Where the fools throw away their hard-earned money? (*To* JOHN.) Now, you add lies to your dishonor?

MARÍA: Please, José, we don't want trouble. It is not our house.

PAPÁ: A pack of jackals. Is this what I call a son? You would let me dishonor myself and live in this haggling woman's house while you throw away your money? *¡¡¡¡Desgraciado!!!!*

JOHN: (*Looking at* CARLOS.) I tried to win some money so I could give it to you, Papá. So you wouldn't have to put up with Ben's griping.

MARÍA: José, let it be. The money is gone.

PAPÁ: Look at him: he cannot hold a wife. He cannot hold a job. And he wanted money for me? I work for my money. I don't ask beggars for gifts.

JOHN: (*Whining.*) I was doing it for you and Mamá.

PAPÁ: You are corrupt. This city has made you a cheat and a liar. I taught you to work like a man, but the army took you and made a mouse out of you.

MARÍA: Please, José.

JOHN: You talk about work and revolution. Well, what has it got you? A lousy old rifle and a stolen cross.

MARÍA: Juan, respect your father.

PAPÁ: (*Advancing toward* JOHN.) I'll teach you, *sin vergüenza.*

MARÍA: Please, José, don't shame us in this house.

PAPÁ: (*Stops, dejected, he looks long at* JOHN.) Leave my sight. *¡Pícale!*

MARÍA: (*Touches* PAPÁ's *sleeve.*) He's young, give him a chance. He is your son.

PAPÁ: He is not my son! He is the son of this city. We came here with money, with pride, and look at it! How can you raise a Villa, a Zapata here? How can you start a revolution when the people are beaten down? When this city corrupts them, tears their pride, out of them, spits in their faces and they take it. He is not my son . . . He belongs to this city of hypocrites, of fools, of weasels who suck the blood from your body before you are even born. Look at him. (*Points at* CARLOS.) He reads his books to get what the gringo has. Will he remember the poor, the weak, like the father of our country, Don Benito Juárez? Will he fight for the *campesino* with his brains? No!! He will disappear in shame and in all of this corruption.

MARÍA: *Viejito,* Carlos is a good boy. Juan has had trouble with his wife. Please, *Viejito,* don't judge. We are old and maybe their life will be better.

CARLOS: Papá, I won't forget, I'll never forget. (*He closes his book and walks over to the window.*)

ESPERANZA: (*Walks in.*) Did you hear there are F.B.I. men searching the neighborhood? Those meetings they held at the old movie house—they were Communists.

CARLOS: Commies? Everybody goes to those meetings. All the old people go to have coffee and cake, and talk. (*He looks at* PAPÁ.) Papá and Mamá go every Tuesday. They don't even listen to those people. The old people talk to each other in Spanish and the organizers talk to themselves in English.

ESPERANZA: Oh, my God. The papers are full of the crackdown. This guy McCarthy is getting them all. Oh, Papá, you shouldn't go there.

PAPÁ: I'm a man. I decide for myself where I go. Let the chicken cackle, I have a mind of my own. (*A loud knock at the door,* ESPERANZA *opens it. A young man walks in.* JOHN *walks in from the other door.*) *Puro molestar y molestar no dejan a uno decansar en paz.*

F.B.I.: (*Shows his identification and badge.*) Henderson, Federal Bureau of Investigation. José Severino Jaramillo? (*He looks at* PAPÁ.)

PAPÁ: I am José Severino Jaramillo!

F.B.I.: Come with me. You are under arrest.

PAPÁ: I have stolen nothing.

F.B.I.: Do you have a card from the United Workers Union?

PAPÁ: Yes, they promised to get me a job, I have it here.

F.B.I.: Okay, you'll have to come with me.

MARÍA: No! He is an honest man.

ESPERANZA: There must be some mistake. Wait, mister. Tell us, explain.

F.B.I.: Check down at the Federal Building.

CARLOS: Why, he's no Communist. He's a lonely old man. You can't take him. He couldn't name Lenin, Marx, or Russia. He goes there for coffee, cake, and conversation. For Christ's sake, waste your time on the real enemy.

F.B.I.: He was there, all right, and he's coming with me.

PAPÁ: Unhand me, gringo. (*He jerks his arm out of the* F.B.I. *agent's grasp.*) I'll walk like a man. (*The agent takes the Old Man out the door.*)

MARÍA: Take me. Take me with him. *Madre de Dios,* take me with him. (JOAQUÍN *clings to his father's legs.* CARLOS *pulls him away. The agent and Old Man go out the door.*)

JOHN: (*Re-entering.*) They said they were going to deport him.

MARÍA: ¡*Tatita Dios!* Save him.

JOHN: Don't worry, Mamá. You were born in San Luis. You're an American citizen. They won't take you. (MARÍA *turns and looks at* JOHN *coldly.*)

MARÍA: Where he goes, I go. I have always been at his side. We have been hungry together. We have suffered and been happy together. I have borne him eight children. Three died at childbirth. Lino died for this country, and José always was there or working, working in the fields. When it rained, I held the lantern for him and Lino, so they could work all night to thin the beets before they swelled. If he is happy, I am happy. His wounds I have healed. I have watched over him sick and dying. If he dies, I will die with him.

ESPERANZA: Don't cry, Mamacita, everything will be all right. (MARÍA *rushes to the trunk and drops to her knees before the statue of the Santo Niño de Atocha standing on the trunk.* JOAQUÍN *and* ESPERANZA *kneel beside her.*)

MARÍA: Oh, blessed *Santo Niño,* do not forsake us, save us from this misery. Bring him back, bring him back. He knows no fault. *Oh, Virgencita de Guadalupe,* hear me, you who are our blessed saint, whose face is like mine, who is our very own. Bring him back. Help us through the winter. Take us back to the green fields. Take us back. I will never complain of the aching bones or the hot sun and muddy fields. He is all we have. He is all our love. Oh, Virgin, kind and good, on my knees I'll crawl for you, just say the word, I'll give my life to see him proud and strong and free again. There is nothing here but problems and misery. Oh, even my family have become strangers. This city is cursed. *Santo Niño, Virgen, Madre de Dios,* protect my love, my man. Bring him back to us. Send us to the fields. (*The family has all been silent, watching. The lights fade out.*)

ACT II—SCENE ONE

CARLOS *walks in with a young Anglo.* MARÍA *is sitting on the sofa praying her rosary.* ESPERANZA *is dusting the furniture.*

CARLOS: Mamá, this is Mr. Goldman. He was appointed to represent Papá.

MARÍA: *Muy bien.* (*She doesn't move. She sits with rosary in her hand moving the beads.*)

CARLOS: This is my sister, Esperanza Sánchez.

ESPERANZA: Glad to know you. Please sit down.

GOLDMAN: Glad to know you, Mrs. Sánchez. Glad to know you, Mrs. Jaramillo. (*He says the Jaramillo correctly.*)

MARÍA: (*She looks up, stops the rosary.*) May we offer you coffee?

GOLDMAN: Thank you, but I must rush back to the office. My secretary is preparing a motion for release of your husband.

MARÍA: (*Eyes brighten.*) He is coming home?

GOLDMAN: Yes, Mrs. Jaramillo, your husband has never taken out his citizenship papers and they cannot try him. Although they do want to deport him.

MARÍA: To where? He has been here since 1915. He knows no one there.

CARLOS: Mamá, Mr. Goldman says he can beat that, too.

MARÍA: Beat?

CARLOS: He won't have to go.

MARÍA: If he goes, I go.

GOLDMAN: Don't worry, Mrs. Jaramillo, I'm pretty sure it won't hold up in court.

CARLOS: (*Looks at* LINO's *picture.*) How can they? My oldest brother died a hero for this country. And Papá and Mamá are Catholics. Communists don't believe in God. (*He looks at* GOLDMAN.)

GOLDMAN: Your father is just a hard-working, proud old man confused by this city. He'll be all right.

ESPERANZA: Everything will be all right, Mamá. (MARÍA *prays constantly.*)

GOLDMAN: He'll be home this afternoon, Mrs. Jaramillo. (*Teenagers burst into the room, turn radio on, and start dancing*).

DEL: All right, Tina. Knock it off. It's my turn.

TINA: Just a minute, I have to hear this song.

ESPERANZA: Turn that off and get out of here. (*She turns the radio off.*)

DEL: You know Dad said we could.

TINA: Gee, Mom! (*Pouting.*)

ESPERANZA: (*With finality.*) Get out. (*To* GOLDMAN.) Excuse them. I'm sorry they don't understand.

GOLDMAN: I understand. I'm having the same trouble at home. (*To* MARÍA.) Your husband will be home. (*He shakes everyone's hand and leaves.* CARLOS *walks in.*)

ESPERANZA: He's coming home. (*She and* MAMÁ *embrace.*)

MARÍA: *Gracias a Dios.*

CARLOS: (*Re-entering.*) He's okay. Papá likes him, so he must be a pretty good guy.

ESPERANZA: They say that someone in the neighborhood was the informer.

CARLOS: Yeah, you can't trust anybody in this city. This city is rotten.

ESPERANZA: (*Looks at him.*) You sound just like Papá.

CARLOS: I wish I could be like him. But everything is so mixed up, I don't know who I am. (Starts reading.)

ACT II—SCENE TWO

Revolutionary music loud and clear as curtain opens. PAPÁ *rushes in.* ESPERANZA *and* MARÍA *are sitting at the table cleaning beans.* MARÍA *jumps up crying as she runs to him. He brushes her aside.*

PAPÁ: Where is your man? (*To* ESPERANZA.)

ESPERANZA: He's at work. He has an important job now.

PAPÁ: Yes, he is out there licking the boots of the government man. He is an informer and a jackal. (*He rushes to the trunk and takes out his rifle and inserts a shell.*)

MARÍA: José, what does this mean? You are home, let us be happy.

PAPÁ: (*To* ESPERANZA.) Your husband is a weasel, and for my honor and your freedom I am going to kill him.

MARÍA: José, no, no, you have Joaquín.

PAPÁ: Better he be the son of a dead man with honor than a son of a live coward.

ESPERANZA: Papá, tell me what is wrong. What has Ben done? Tell me.

PAPÁ: You do not know? He is a witness for the government. They want to send me to Mexico. He is an informer. They bought his soul for gringo *pesos.* They put me in jail because he said that I am an enemy of this country.

ESPERANZA: Papá, are you sure?

PAPÁ: As sure as the bullet I put through his heart.

ESPERANZA: (*Crying.*) You can't do that. He is my husband. The father of my children.

PAPÁ: A poor choice you made. You married a weasel. A blood sucker.

ESPERANZA: I never met anyone else. You never let me meet anyone. Then when I was old enough, I met Ben. He was the only one I ever knew, and if he is not the man you expected, then it's your fault that I married him. Blame yourself, don't blame me. (*She runs from the room.* PAPÁ *slowly puts down his rifle, takes the cartridge out and puts it back into the trunk.*)

PAPÁ: *¡Muchachos malcriados!* We must find a way to start again. (*Turns to* MARÍA.) Where is Joaquín?

MARÍA: He is probably late from school. He'll be home soon.

PAPÁ: This city is no place to raise a boy. (*Loud voices are heard. The door flies open . . . two policemen enter. One has* JOAQUÍN *by the collar.*)

JOAQUIN: Papá! Papá!

POLICEMAN: Is this your boy, old man?

PAPÁ: He is my son. Take your hands off of him.

MARÍA: He is a good boy.

1ST POLICEMAN: Good boys ain't out all hours of the night.

2ND POLICEMAN: We're taking him to Juvenile Hall.

PAPÁ: What has he done?

1ST POLICEMAN: We chased him last night. He was out after curfew. He got away.

2ND POLICEMAN: We just thought we'd let you know where to pick up your chili bean.

PAPÁ: Chili bean? What is curfew? You come here to insult us?

MARÍA: He is but a baby.

PAPÁ: I said unhand him, gringo.

2ND POLICEMAN: Watch your language, gramps.

PAPÁ: If he has done wrong, I will punish him. (*Pulling* JOAQUÍN *back. They struggle.* 2ND POLICEMAN *steps up and hits the old man with his club.* MARÍA *screams.* PAPÁ *manages to get* JOAQUÍN *behind him. The other swings his club.* MARÍA *and* JOAQUÍN *pull at the one holding* PAPÁ. CARLOS *and attorney* GOLDMAN *rush in.*)

GOLDMAN: What's the meaning of this? (*The policemen stop.* MARÍA *and* JOAQUÍN *sit* PAPÁ *down. He is bleeding.* JOAQUÍN *runs for water.* MARÍA *wipes the blood away.*)

1ST POLICEMAN: Who are you?

GOLDMAN: I'm an attorney, and I represent this man.

2ND POLICEMAN: Well, we're booking this Mex for assault, interference, disturbance, and resistance.

GOLDMAN: You two had better listen and get this straight and good. You are in the home of these people. (*Sharply.*) Do you have a search warrant or an arrest warrant? ANSWER ME! (*Policemen look at each other.*)

GOLDMAN: You have violated these people's constitutional rights. Do you hear me? (*Policemen look at each other.*)

1ST POLICEMAN: The boy is under arrest for violating curfew.

GOLDMAN: He's staying right here. If you two fellows want an assault suit on your behinds, go ahead and take him.

CARLOS *is eyeing the policemen bitterly with his fists clenched.* JOAQUÍN *stands to the right of his father watching stoically.*

2ND POLICEMAN: Ahh!! Let's get the hell out of here. (*The policemen walk out mumbling to each other.*)

CARLOS: Is he all right, Mamá?

MARÍA: (*Sobbing.*) We don't have a chance. We don't have a chance.

GOLDMAN: Are you all right, old man?

PAPÁ: (*Stands nodding his head.*)

MARÍA: No, José, please. No. We will bring more trouble on our heads.

PAPÁ: (*He rushes to the* petaquilla, *takes out the rifle and heads for the door.*) ¡Desgraciados! ¡Cobardes! ¡Cabrones! I will die like a man. ¡Por Dios! I will die like a man.

GOLDMAN: (*Puts his arm on the Old Man's shoulder.*) Mr. Jaramillo, please control yourself. It takes courage to be calm. (*The Old Man relaxes.*) You have your family to think of. You have many problems. Let's take care of them one at a time. I only want to help you. That's better . . . that's better. They won't bother us and they will not bother Joaquín.

PAPÁ: Thank you, Mr. Goldman. You are a good man. But there is no honor in this city. I would rather be shot against the wall than to be shamed and beaten like a dog in front of my woman and my son.

GOLDMAN: This isn't exactly the right time to tell you, but I have to be honest with you.

MARÍA: Trouble?

CARLOS: Yes, we'll work something out.

GOLDMAN: Mr. Jaramillo, they denied my motion for dismissal. We will have to go to court.

MARÍA: We don't have a chance. *¡Madre de Dios¡* We have been cursed.

PAPÁ: (*Dazed.*) What does this mean?

GOLDMAN: You will have to go to trial. The authorities want to deport you to Mexico.

PAPÁ: (*Stunned.*) *Méjico . . . Méjico.* I've always thought of the old days. I try to remember the village where I was born. I don't remember too well anymore. My children, my life is here. Lino, Lino is a hero for this country. All of this land was part of *Méjico.* This is my home, my country. This is all one great shame. Now where is my home? (*He looks at* GOLDMAN, *his voice weakening.*) Where is my home? (*He puts his head in his hands.*)

GOLDMAN: (*To* CARLOS.) Come and see me tomorrow. I need a lot of information. I have to be well prepared. I want to do my best. (*He exits.*)

PAPÁ: Joaquín, what were you up to?

JOAQUÍN: I was shining shoes, Papá. I wanted to help. (*He offers money to* PAPÁ.)

PAPÁ: (*Looking long and hard at* JOAQUÍN.) No son of mine will wander the streets.

JOAQUÍN: (*Tearfully.*) But I only want to help, Papá.

PAPÁ: That is not the work of a man. Why, even shoveling manure is more honorable. You can always wash your hands when you are through. But you cannot wash away the foul things you learn wandering the streets at night.

MARÍA: You must go to school, *hijito.*

CARLOS: (*Walks back from seeing* GOLDMAN *out.*) I'll quit school and go to work full time.

PAPÁ: No!

CARLOS: It's either that or go to the welfare.

PAPÁ: Never, never, I will never accept their help.

JOAQUÍN: Let me help, please.

PAPÁ: I will find a way. Joaquín must not work in the streets. We must get through the winter. I will find a way. (*Looking at* JOAQUÍN.) Some water, I am thirsty. (JOAQUÍN *pours a glass of water. He hands it to* PAPÁ *and stands erect, with his arms crossed while the old man drinks. Curtain closes.*)

ACT II—SCENE THREE

JOHN *and* ESPERANZA *are sitting quietly as* CARLOS *walks in. He is disturbed, noticeably perplexed, and frustrated.* ESPERANZA *looks up anxiously.*

ESPERANZA: How did it go in court today?

CARLOS: Not so good.

JOHN: Did it last this long?

CARLOS: No, I stopped at the library. I've started my education all over again.

JOHN: This is no time to study, for Christ's sake. What happened?

ESPERANZA: What about Papá and Mamá? What happened in court?

CARLOS: That's why it is time to study. I watched my father and mother in court today, and I suddenly realized that I didn't know who they were and I didn't know who I was. We haven't followed in the Old Man's footsteps because we have been brainwashed by this society. You just can't compete against all of this power. But our Old Man is doing it all alone. He is a revolutionist in a fight that grows weaker as our father grows older.

ESPERANZA: What happened, (*Tenderly.*) Carlos?

JOHN: You're speaking in riddles, man. You talk like those egghead politicians. They're the only ones who know what the hell they mean.

CARLOS: It wasn't a pretty picture, watching your father and mother treated like little children, or idiots. The attorney general was either hollering at them or talking down to them as if they were little kids.

ESPERANZA: What did Goldman do?

JOHN: I thought he was so hot.

CARLOS: He was great, but the odds were against him. He protected them like they were his own father and mother. How the hell do you fight this system, especially all alone? It was hard to take. The Old Man wouldn't speak. Mamá just prayed her rosary. She went from bead to bead. It was like watching her working beets, down a row to the end, turn around and work back down another row. It was like knowing that there isn't an end to all the labor and misery of our people.

JOHN: Our people, hell! Get off that stuff. We got our own worries; there ain't nobody helping me. It's a dog-eat-dog rat race, and that's the way it will always be.

ESPERANZA: (*To* JOHN.) You're sick. I understand you, Carlos. My proud Papá and poor Mamá. She'll never budge an inch. She'll stick with him to the end. If only I were a man, I'd do something.

JOHN: Shit.

CARLOS: I want to do something, too, but first you have to know who you are and where you're going. I'm going to find out. I have to find out. Papá knows, but he can't teach us; he just expects us to know.

JOHN: Yeah. "Work, *hijo,* work." That's a bunch of crud.

CARLOS: Maybe you have been beaten, John, but it's not too late for me. It's not too late for Joaquín. Even if it's hard, you got to try. You go to school, they tear out your guts and start brainwashing you with good old American bleach that don't change your name or your color, just makes you think you're equal to die or pay taxes. Then when you go to work, they make a robot out of you and sterilize you, and then all you can have are brainwashed kids. Papá knows there is something wrong with this system, but all he has to fight it with is that rifle, and maybe that's the only way. It's our battle now.

JOHN: You go ahead and fight the battle, kid. I'm going down to Dave's to play cards. Besides, my unemployment ran out, and I don't want to be here when the Old Man gets home.

ESPERANZA: If I were a man, I'd show you.

JOHN: Try it on Mr. F.B.I.—Fat Ben Informer. (*He salutes and exits. ESPERANZA is visually hurt by* JOHN*'s last remark. She pulls out her handkerchief.*)

CARLOS: He's just trying to get even with somebody. Forget it, Sis. (*He pats* ESPERANZA *on the back.*)

ESPERANZA: It's all my fault. I wanted everyone to be happy.

CARLOS: It had to happen.

ESPERANZA: No, I'm the one who wrote to the folks. I told them how good everything was. I offered them our home, and now everything is falling apart. Oh, Papá, it's all my fault—Ben.

CARLOS: It's not your fault. It's this screwed-up city.

ESPERANZA: You remember how Ben was? He was a good worker, a good father. Then he lost his job, things got tough and I started working. It's all my fault. Oh, Ben!

CARLOS: Take it easy, things have to get better.

ESPERANZA: Will they? (*Sniffling and dabbing at her eyes with her handkerchief. Lights begin to dim except for a spot on* ESPE-RANZA.) I don't know. It was hard out in the fields, working from early morning till late afternoon, in the hot sun. And yet, when we moved from one job to the other it was like going on a picnic, everyone happy, singing and laughing. (*The sound of chil-dren laughing, spirited guitar music. A woman's voice singing. Lights dim, spot on* ESPERANZA. CARLOS *fades into back-*

ground and sits down. BEN *appears, a shadow formed in the darkness.)*

BEN: Espi, Espi. (ESPERANZA *turns, she is a young girl again, her face aglow.)*

ESPERANZA: Ben. Oh, Ben, I didn't see you at the *campo* last night. I was worried.

BEN: (*Swaggering, assuming a dignified pose.)* I went into town. I ran into good luck, too.

ESPERANZA: (*Takes a haughty stance.)* Probably with one of those town girls. They have no pride—they throw themselves at any man.

BEN: (*Pleased but insistent.)* Esperanza, I'm going to marry you. I'm going out on my own.

ESPERANZA: And your father, does he agree? And what about Papá, are you brave enough to ask him for me?

BEN: I'm not afraid of your old man. And my old man is going to help me. I've been breaking my ass for the family and now I want to take care of you.

ESPERANZA: Oh, Ben, I wish we could. I dream of it every night. I know you can make it. Mamá would be so happy for us. But you're always kidding.

BEN: Not this time, *querida.* You know where the German farm is, where the three *braceros* are doing that thirty acres? Well, there's twenty acres left, and I'm getting the contract.

ESPERANZA: Oh, Ben, you know old man German would never let them go. He pays them less than we get.

BEN: Yeah, well he's stuck this time. Remember the Holy Family Bazaar? Well, Beto García, the one with curly hair and green eyes, he was making eyes at German's daughter. He even asked her to take a ride on the ferris wheel. Well, that's it for all those *braceros,* 'cause old man German called the immigration office and acted like he didn't know they were *mojados.*

ESPERANZA: That's a rotten thing to do.

BEN: Yeah, it sure is. But that's life. So, old man German came down to see my pa. I was there and I heard the whole deal. Papá said we couldn't work German's twenty acres because the family still has thirty left to do.

ESPERANZA: That's a lot of work, Ben.

BEN: I saw my chance and I followed him into town and walked right up to German's Ford and I told him, "I understand you need some help. I can do an acre and half a day."

ESPERANZA: Ben, you lied. An acre and a half?

BEN: Well, I can do an acre and quarter, if I work late, and I figure between us we could do two a day.

ESPERANZA: Between us?

BEN: Yeah, me and you. That's almost $220.00. We could buy that '34 Ford I showed you. Only $95.00 bucks.

ESPERANZA: Ben, we're not married. You have to ask for me.

BEN: I will, *querida,* I will. Just think, then after the topping, maybe I'll trade the Ford in or fix it up and we'll go to Denver. My cousin Cleto has a good job at the packing house. He makes good money. I'll get a steady job, we'll buy a house—it will be like a dream.

ESPERANZA: What about your Dad and what about Papá? He won't like it, Ben, I'm afraid.

BEN: Don't worry, my Papá will let us live at our house and won't even charge us for food because I've already done my share of the twenty acres.

ESPERANZA: And my Papá?

BEN: Look, *bonita,* don't worry. I'll get the contract, then you just watch your Benito. Your Papá can't refuse me. I love you, Esperanza.

ESPERANZA: I love you too, Ben. We will be happy, Ben, we will be happy. (*They embrace.*)

BEN: I'll never let you down, *bonita.* (*They kiss.*)

CARLOS: (*Stands up in the dark, the sound of children, laughter, guitar music.*) I'm going to tell. I saw you, Benito Sánchez. You leave my sister alone. She's not your wife, fatso. Leave her alone.

BEN: She's going to be my wife.

ESPERANZA: (*Ignoring* CARLOS.) Oh, Ben, we'll be happy.

CARLOS: Wait till I tell my big brother Lino—he's going to kick your ass.

BEN: Go on. Go on. (*Still embracing* ESPERANZA.)

ESPERANZA: Oh, Ben, we'll be happy.

BEN: I'll be back. Just you wait and see.

CARLOS: (*Singing.*) Lino's gonna get you. Lino's gonna get you.

BEN: (*Ignoring* CARLOS.) Good-bye, *querida,* good-bye. (*Lights come on as* ESPERANZA *comes back to the present.*)

ESPERANZA: It's as if you have the bitter to enjoy the sweet. I can't remember being really truly carefree and happy for some time now. What's happened to us?

CARLOS: They're beating us down. We can't see it or hear it, but we know it's happening. We're falling off like flies in the winter, and we have no way to defend ourselves. I wonder why people like Goldman are so different from the rest of the gringos. Do you know that he is an appointed lawyer? A federal court appointment. He doesn't even get paid for it.

PAPÁ: (*Revolutionary music.* PAPÁ *walks in.*) Did you hear them? Did you hear them? (*He mimics the attorney general.*) "Now Meester Jar-meelo—my name is Jaramillo. My name is Jaramillo! They took our land, they rob us of our dignity and now they change our language. They even want to change our names! The judge sits up there like he is God Almighty, and that *prosecutor.*

CARLOS: Prosecutor, Papá.

PAPÁ: Whatever he is, he shouts like a crazy woman, like a coyote in heat. And those people sitting in the box like vultures eyeing another corpse. What do they know of me? Why should they decide my fate? A man must choose his own destiny. Did you see Benito sit up there and lie like Judas himself? What did he say, Carlos? What did he say, Carlos? (ESPERANZA *takes on a hurt and strained expression.*)

CARLOS: He said he was an undercover man. That he was working for the F.B.I. I'm sorry, Sis, but he was a complete jerk.

ESPERANZA: Oh, God, why did this have to happen? He can never come into this house again. Oh, Ben, why did you do it?

PAPÁ: What kind of justice do they give a man? If they want to destroy me, let them do it with honor. I am not a mouse that they can play with like a cat. I looked at Benito. If he hates me so much, why couldn't he settle it like a man. I am old, but my knife is sharp—him or me. That's the way it ought to be.

CARLOS: Take it easy, Papá.

PAPÁ: No, no, he could never ride into the wall at Zacatecas with the machine guns spitting death all around, ride right into the face of death with a tequila bottle full of powder to throw into the laps of the *pelones*. What a sight! And now they are killing me and destroying me with words. *¡Qué desgracia!*

ESPERANZA: Papá, maybe we can get help from the Don Sánchez. He is in business and is in politics.

CARLOS: I already called him. He heard that we were broke and he acted like I had yellow fever.

ESPERANZA: I heard he helps some people.

CARLOS: Only if he can make money off them; he's just a city slicker *contratista* with an accent.

PAPÁ: I know that man. If Benito is a weasel, he is the father of all weasels. The revolutionist bleeds and the politicos get fat.

CARLOS: Papá, Mr. Goldman says you have to help. You don't answer the questions. You have to speak up.

PAPÁ: For what? I see only distrust and dislike in their eyes.

ESPERANZA: (*Gaining composure after the comments about* BEN.) Where's Mamá?

PAPÁ: She stopped off at the church to pray.

ESPERANZA: You should go to see Padre Rincón, he might help.

PAPÁ: How to pray for our souls? The church is a business. We are not their business. We need help; we cannot help them.

ESPERANZA: Mamá believes, and you always taught us to pray. Maybe the priest can help.

PAPÁ: They are only men, good and bad; some of them believe, some don't. Me, I believe God is here . . . (*He strikes his heart, then points at the house.*) . . . and in your home. Pancho Villa said, "The church that shelters the poor under its mantle is one thing, and the church that shelters itself under the mantle of the poor is another." I pray, I thank God for the health of my family, for the strength he has given me to provide for my family, and now in this city, I am useless.

ESPERANZA: Everything will be all right.

MARÍA: *Bendito Dios, ruega por nosotros. Hágase la voluntad de Dios.* (PAPÁ *slowly surveys the family and the room. He assumes a flamboyant pose.*)

PAPÁ: Everything is not lost. I have a friend who will help us. I will see him tomorrow; he will help us through the winter.

CARLOS: Who do you know, Papá? Don't go talk to those guys from the Civil Union Workers again.

PAPÁ: (*Winks slyly.*) Maybe he is the devil. (MARÍA *crosses herself and bows her head.*)

ESPERANZA: Don't play like that, Papá. Things are bad enough already.

PAPÁ: Someone has to help, *¿qué no?* (*Lights fade out.*)

ACT II—SCENE THREE

MARÍA *is placing a few dollars under the Santo Niño as* PAPÁ *walks in. He looks tired and haggard.*

MARÍA: How did it go, *Viejito?*

PAPÁ: (*Throws his arms up helplessly.*) Nothing. Every way I turn, there is nothing.

MARÍA: And your friend?

PAPÁ: Ha, Jesús Vargas, is as poor as we are. He had one extra room he was giving to us. His nephew and wife *y tres chamacos* arrived from Texas starving last night.

MARÍA: Esperanza said we could move to the projects.

PAPÁ: You need furniture. We only have that *petaquilla*. I cannot even catch the bus. A man is not a man without a cent in his pockets.

MARÍA: (*She fumbles and seems to be struggling within herself. She speaks apologetically but warmly.*) José.

PAPÁ: Yes, what is it?

MARÍA: (*Goes to the Sañto Nino, takes out the few dollars.*) José, I can help. (*She offers him the money.*)

PAPÁ: Where did you get that money?

MARÍA: I worked, Viejito.

PAPÁ: Where?

MARÍA: Pajarito García was sick. I took her job for one day cleaning a woman's house.

PAPÁ: Behind my back, even my own woman betrays me.

MARÍA: José, it is yours. In Mexico I worked. It was all right then, Viejito. It is for both of us.

PAPÁ: That was for the revolution. We gave our lives and our sweat and here, I walk the streets. I beg grown men for work, *como un mendigo*. I'm ready to steal, to rob, and now my woman can work without my permission.

MARÍA: José, it wasn't important. I just cleaned a house. It was for the family. Take the money.

PAPÁ: Now I am the *mantenido* while you sneak to work behind my back.

MARÍA: José, please. I know you will find work. Until then, we have to get by. Take the money, *Viejito*.

PAPÁ: No. (*He pushes her hand away.*) No. (*He walks quickly out the door. MARÍA moves slowly across the room, the lights fade.*)

MARÍA: José, what can we do? I will never have your son starving, on the move day and night. When will it end, José, when will we win? (*The jingle of spurs is heard faintly.* JOSÉ *enters, a dark form in the faded light.*)

PAPÁ: I have a letter from my brother Melquiades. He is working in the mines in Nuevo Méjico.

MARÍA: José, he invited you a month ago and yet you still talk of winning the revolution. I was born in San Luis, Colorado. I have people there.

PAPÁ: It is hard to make that choice. But it is getting confusing. Last week we took a village. The people cheered us when we drove out the Federales. The next day we were beaten by the Federales and the people cheered them. Next week we will retake the villages and we will be hated for making their *pueblo* a battleground.

MARÍA: I cannot have a son for you, José.

PAPÁ: Juan Rojas was fighting with the Federales and he lost his coat. They were going to hang him when we took the *pueblo,* now he fights with us.

MARÍA: I can have you a son if we leave. I need rest.

PAPÁ: Yes, I thought of a new life when the enemy artillery caught us in a crossfire. The horses were crying, men were moaning when the smoked cleared. I saw the soldiers walking among the bodies, shooting the men who moved. It was like lying in a river of blood.

MARÍA: José, there is nothing to win. Brother against brother.

PAPÁ: Yes, it was like a river of blood. The entrails of the horses mixed with those of our men. A *pelón* looked down at me. He was not over sixteen. We stared at each other. There were tears streaming down his face as he cocked his rifle. An attack bugle sounded. He shot into the ground and ran. Our troops were coming.

MARÍA: José, the fighting has to stop.

PAPÁ: Only those in the army get to eat. (*He looks tenderly at* MARÍA.) We will have a son.

MARÍA: Yes and we will be free.

PAPÁ: I will never leave you. You will rest and grow strong.

MARÍA: We will name him Lino, after your father.

PAPÁ: It is not far just across the river and it is part of Mexico. Malquiades says our people still speak Spanish.

MARÍA: If it is a girl, we will name her Esperanza, "Hope."

PAPÁ: I will work every day, and when things settle down here and the wars are over, we will come back. We have given three children to the revolution.

MARÍA: Our children will be strong and free.

PAPÁ: They will fight for their people. They will be sons and daughters of a revolutionist. (*They embrace, he leaves.*)

PAPÁ: (*As he leaves.*) I'll go get my pack and get something to eat. (*He gives a hearty* grito.) *¡Ajúa!*

ACT II—SCENE FIVE

PAPÁ *is sitting on a bench. A woman sits behind a desk. She is busy putting makeup on. A policeman leans casually against the wall. The Old Man gets up slowly and walks to the desk. He shuffles self-consciously. She finally notices him. He coughs.*

WOMAN: Yes?

PAPÁ: I have been waiting five hours.

WOMAN: Oh . . . I was busy, well, let's see. What's your name?

PAPÁ: José Jaramillo.

WOMAN: What?

PAPÁ: (*Fumbles with his hat, clears his throat.*) José Jaramillo.

WOMAN: (*Impatiently.*) Spell it.

PAPÁ: What?

WOMAN: Spell it.

PAPÁ: *Jota,* ah . . .

WOMAN: Now, wait a minute. Do you have identification or do you have an immigration card?

PAPÁ: (PAPÁ *hands it to her. She looks at it.*) Jarmeelo.

WOMAN: Oh, Jaramillo. (*Jar-mil-o.*) Well, what do you want?

PAPÁ: I need . . . my family needs help.

WOMAN: Can't you work?

PAPÁ: Yes, I can work, I can work.

WOMAN: Where were you last employed?

PAPÁ: What?

WOMAN: Where did you last work?

PAPÁ: In the fields.

WOMAN: No unemployment for you. Can't your wife work?

PAPÁ: I have a son.

WOMAN: If she can find work, you could watch the children. (PAPÁ *shakes his head.*)

WOMAN: Have you been to the employment office?

PAPÁ: (*Nods yes.*)

WOMAN: Where do you live? (*Lights begin to fade out as the woman's voice increases in pitch, louder and louder.*) How much rent do you pay? How many children do you have? How many in school? How old is your wife? Are you disabled? How long have you been in Denver? How long in Colorado? What grade did you get to? How much did you earn? Where were you born? Your wife? Your children? Do you own furniture? Do you have insurance? Have you looked for work? . . .

Lights go out, spotlight on PAPÁ. *His head sinks to his chest, then the spotlight goes to the other side of the stage.* JOAQUÍN *is standing looking at his father. The spotlight remains on* JOAQUÍN *as the revolutionary music grows louder and louder. The curtains slowly close. Spotlight comes up and* JOAQUÍN, *a grown man, begins reciting the play's Epilogue, the epic poem I Am Joaquín.*

A Cross for Maclovio

Cast of Characters

MACLOVIO ..... Middle-aged civil rights leader torn between dedication and security. Driven by Messianic emotions and troubled by egocentric self-analysis. The leader.

ELENA .... Maclovio's wife, emotionally torn by her intuitive premonitions. Earthly, loyal, emaciated by fear for Maclovio.

LITA .... Maclovio's daughter, age nineteen, vital electric personality, loyal to father and his philosophies. The new revolutionist.

MANNY .... Age eighteen, an individualist, a boxer, loyal to mother and doesn't believe in father's martyrdom.

PEDRO .... Maclovio's best friend, dependent on Maclovio. Weak, but loyal.

GREGORIO ...... Militant ally who sells out to the establishment for security.

HAROLD .... Anglo liberal.

TOMÁS .... Lita's suitor, egocentric, a pretender to leadership.

GRANDFATHER .. Elena's father who is never seen, dying in his room.

TAMALE
  VENDORS .... An old man and an old woman.

ACT I—SCENE ONE

The place, the home of MACLOVIO GALLEGOS *situated in the barrios of a city in the Southwest. The time, now, 1967.*
  The set is one room and to the right an elevated level onto which the action will shift from time to time. The main room is a bedroom which will be converted to a living room. The elevated level, when not used for acting, will have a backdrop as though looking over a porch from which you can see the back yards of a barrio, clothes hanging, doors open, hazy forms of the houses, and a church steeple and cross silhouetted in the background.
  The bedroom is seen faintly. A double bed, a dresser, a night stand, a picture of Our Lady of Guadalupe, a plaster flower vase in the form of the virgin, which holds yellow roses. The bed is directly to the left of a window. To the left, a door leads to the rest of the house; the right door leads to the outside. Shadows float in and out and across the room as lights from passing cars shine through the window shade. A light hits the window. The window is square with a center frame forming a cross. Car lights moving on the outside throw a shadow across the stage in the form of a elongated cross. A dog barks. ELENA *turns, mumbles and moans incoherently in her sleep. Suddenly the shrill crow of a cock is heard. She quickly raises her head. The cock crow is heard again. She sits up and grabs her head as if checking herself to see if she is awake. The cock crows a third time, and she jumps up terrified.*

ELENA: (*Screaming.*) Maclovio! Maclovio! (*She frantically grabs up an alarm clock, tries to see the time by the light through the window, then fumbles with a small bedside lamp; she turns it on and looks at the clock. Her hair is disarrayed. She is a woman in her early forties. Her hair is long and black. Her dark eyes are big and hollowed in a strong handsome face that is etched with strain. A dog barks. She runs to the window. She shivers and pulls her robe around her; she ties the belt and pulls at rather than brushes her hair down on the sides with both hands. She slumps to the bed looking at the clock. A blaring car horn is heard and fades away. She moans.*) Maclovio, Maclovio. (*She pulls at her hair.*)

LITA: (*Rushes in, tying her robe on.*) Mamá! Mamá! What's the matter? (*She rushes to her mother.*)

ELENA: (*Looking up as if bewildered, then frightened. Then trying to regain her composure.*) Your father is not home yet.

LITA: You know that he was going to stop at the picket line after the conference, Mamá.

ELENA: (*Trying to effect nonchalance.*) I forget. I'm sorry, *hija,* I forget. Very well. Go to bed. Everything is all right.

LITA: Mamá, what's wrong? It's not like you. Last night you talked all night in your sleep. You have me worried.

ELENA: Did you hear . . . I heard. (*She falters.*) Never mind. You are so much like your father. You are beautiful like him. You have his brains and his strength.

LITA: Mamá, Mamá, it's you who has the strength; without you, Papá would be just another man.

ELENA: That's what I pray for, that he would be just another man. Not me or any other woman can hold him from where he is going. (*She makes the sign of the cross.*)

LITA: You know you are proud, Mamá. Papá is a leader. He is the leader of our people.

ELENA: (*Bitterly.*) And when he is gone who will lead them? Who will sacrifice his family, his life, for a few cheers, a pat on the back, a lot of filthy gossip behind his back? But when they need help and they have problems, they come smiling. What have they to lose?

LITA: Mamá, you're tired. Papá understands human nature and he loves them and they love him.

ELENA: Love. The gossips at the *cantinas* and the *mercados* know nothing about love. Give them a full belly and you will see that for them love is a full pocketbook.

LITA: Society corrupts. You and Papá have taught me these things. I think like you. That's part of the system we have to change.

ELENA: (*Warmly.*) You're hard-headed like your father.

LITA: (*Pleased.*) They call me a revolutionary at work.

ELENA: (*Cynically.*) Nothing will change.

LITA: (*Concerned.*) You never talked like this before, Mamá.

ELENA: Like what? (*She pulls at her hair with both hands.*) *Por Dios*, now you want to change the way I talk. (*Then guiltily.*) I'm just tired, don't worry, go to bed Lita. Go to bed.

LITA: Sometimes you frighten me. Lately you seem to be under a strain. What's really wrong, Mamá?

ELENA: (*Looking up, startled as if from a daze.*) Wrong? There are many things wrong. Maclovio at the age of forty-three still fighting against injustice against this society, this rotten system. Our son Beto overseas fighting for all the things that Maclovio is against. What will happen to us?

LITA: Papá says everything always works out for the best. I'm working. Papá gets paid once in a while from the old business.

ELENA: (*Bitterly.*) The business. Better he had never been in that business. Those who owe him money avoid him like he was the plague. And he never asks them for anything anyway.

LITA: (*Hopefully.*) Well, after tonight, if he accepts that government job, you won't have to worry about money. I heard they are offering him $16,000 a year. Think of it, Papá in a big office.

ELENA: I don't care about all the government jobs in the country or picket lines or demonstrations. (*Fiercely.*) I want what I have given. I want him. I want the man I once knew. Strong, warm with laughter pouring out of him like music.

LITA: He's strong and warm now, Mamá.

ELENA: You are so busy being militant and educated that you do not see your father. Your eyes are blinded by idolatry. You see a God. Look at a man. I can watch his back and know what he feels, what he thinks. His back is bending. He is not sure anymore for what reason he fights or for whom he fights. He's caught up in a snowball thundering down a mountain, and it gets bigger and bigger and rolls faster and faster. Before it's too late, *Madre mía,* I want him back.

LITA: Mamá, that's not true; he does know what he fights for, and to me he is a real live warm human. A real person in this hypocritical society. (*A loud groan is heard from the other room.*)

GRANDFATHER: Ohhh, Oohh, *Aayy. Ay, Dios llévame. Me quiero morir. Hija, hija.*

ELENA: Take your grandfather his pills and water, hurry, hurry.

LITA: (*Embraces her mother.*) Everything will be all right, Ma. Good night. (*She hurries through the door.*)

ELENA: (*As if in deep thought.*) Lita, there was a letter for your father in this morning's mail. Have you seen it? (*She realizes she is alone and talks to herself.*) It's not like him to not mention it. Oh, well, probably a bill. (ELENA *gives a furtive look at the clock, sits heavily on the edge of the bed, her face in her hands. The light dims on her.*)

ACT I—SCENE TWO

The light comes up sharply on the level to the right. There are chairs located in a careless U facing front stage. An old battered desk sits up stage behind the middle of the U. There is a door to the left of the stage. Seated in the middle is GREGORIO—*stout, round face, high round cheek bones, fierce eyes, firm chin. He looks and talks strong, seems to dominate the meeting. Seated to* GREGORIO's *left is* PEDRO—*slender aquiline features, boyishly handsome, smiles or gives out short laughs after everyone's statements, watches each speaker with intense interest as if each word is a gem. Seated at the right of the U is* HAROLD WINTERS. *He is a slender man who sprawls comfortably in his chair; his relaxed physical makeup does not jibe with his hawklike face that scrutinizes* MACLOVIO *as the others speak. They are passing a letter around, each taking his turn reading it, until it gets back to* MACLOVIO.

GREGORIO: This letter should be turned over to the F.B.I. They have to protect you.

MACLOVIO: Our actions seem to be bothering some people. (*He waves the letter.*) Just some crank.

HAROLD: All the same, you should turn it over to the F.B.I. A death threat is no laughing matter.

MACLOVIO: (*Smiles.*) I have about a dozen of these love letters. And as for the F.B.I., they're just auditors for police departments. You never saw them stop a lynching in the south or slow a Texas Ranger down from assaulting Mexicans. Whoever wants me has to wait in line. (*He puts the letter in his coat pocket.*)

PEDRO: (*Watching* MACLOVIO *closely.*) That's a laugh, ha, ha. They really don't know who they're dealing with. Things are getting hot around here. (*He chuckles.*) Now they want to put out the fire. The racists want to kill him, and the government wants to give him a job.

GREGORIO: They're afraid; now they want to buy off our leadership. They've done it time after time. Just look across the country and you'll see what I mean. You stir up the people, get them ready for a revolution, and the establishment comes running with a suitcase full of *pesos.*

PEDRO: (*Casting a glance at* HAROLD.) Gringo dollars, not *pesos*—they think they can buy us all. (*He laughs.*) Well, not this time. (*He beams at* MACLOVIO.) We have a man. A real man that the people will listen to, will follow to hell and back.

MACLOVIO: (*Solemnly.*) Will they? *Ah, veremos.* We will see.

GREGORIO: (*He looks at* HAROLD.) My old folks think Maclovio is the answer to all those years of false hopes and phony politicians. They definitely will not move until they hear from him.

MACLOVIO: (*Humbly.*) They have been used by liars and hypocrites for so long, it's a wonder that our people can still have confidence in anyone or anything.

HAROLD: Yes, that's the question. What will they have confidence in? I have watched you fellows work and I have to admit your people are ready to move. But where, which way will they move? You must provide a doctrine, a program. (*He looks from face to face.*)

MACLOVIO: First, we must take their damaged brains and bodies and give them dignity and pride in themselves.

HAROLD: I agree, but first you must change all of society. You must, as Marx did, create a new doctrine for a new society. (*He glances at their faces.*)

GREGORIO: Look, Harold, if we can get government programs going to give our people better jobs and educational advantages . . . If we can pressure them into hiring some of our people into high administrative positions . . . (MACLOVIO *eyes him warily.*)

HAROLD: Wait a minute, they just offered Maclovio a job. Why?

GREGORIO: Pressure, pressure.

PEDRO: It's a buy-off. We have a leader they can't touch. (*He beams at* MACLOVIO.)

MACLOVIO: (*Standing up.*) We still have a picket line at the police department. I'm going to drop by. I'll see you guys. (*He leaves around the desk and out the back door.*)

HAROLD: What do you think of the letter? Maybe he shouldn't go alone. (PEDRO *and* GREGORIO *laugh.*)

GREGORIO: Just a crank. He'll be all right.

PEDRO: (*Settling down in his chair.*) You guys should have been there when he told those agency people to stick it. (*Laughs.*) Those two fat slobs in their $200 suits and dollar cigars. (*He mimics.*) Now you're an intelligent man, Mr. Ma-er Mac- M law V-0. You will do your country and your people a great service to accept this position. Just think, 16 G's a year. And our boy looked at them real cold, like he was saying, we'll see. Well, I could almost see that finger in the back of his head telling them: Jam it . . .

GREGORIO: (*Interested.*) Did he tell you he wouldn't take it?

PEDRO: Not in words, but I know my man.

GREGORIO: Don't be too sure. $16,000 bucks is big money, security, no more picket lines, no more talking yourself blue in the face to people who believe you one day and don't trust you the next. He didn't say no, did he?

PEDRO: When he looks through those people with that Indian stare, I know what he means. I've been around that man long enough to almost read his mind.

GREGORIO: Don't be too sure. He's trying to recuperate from losing all that property that went down the drain. Elena is getting tired. Don't be too sure. (*Then charitably.*) I wouldn't blame him.

HAROLD: (*Who has been studying them.*) If Maclovio did take that job, Gregorio, you have the stuff to keep this movement going. You and Pete here could do it. (*Both men, obviously pleased, shake their heads no.*)

GREGORIO: I have a job; my wife and my kids are important to me.

PEDRO: Maclovio is living off of past business investments.

GREGORIO: Maclovio won't leave us.

PEDRO: Yeah, anyway, Maclovio won't budge an inch. He's like a rock.

HAROLD: Let's go get a bite and stop at the picket line.

PEDRO: I'm game. Coming, Gregorio?

GREGORIO: I'll be by later. (HAROLD *and* PEDRO *exit. The phone rings.* GREGORIO *glances uneasily at the door and grabs the phone.*) Hello, yes, yes, this is Gregorio Sánchez. Yes sir, Mr. Henderson. No, it's not too late. I'll be done in ten minutes. Goodbye.

Lights fade out.

ACT I—SCENE THREE

Guitar music playing softly, lights come up on ELENA *making the bed.* MACLOVIO *is entering through the door at left, buttoning a white shirt.*

ELENA: (*Shouting.*) Maclovio! (*She turns, brushes her hair down the sides with both hands, and places her hands on her hips.*) Your shirt is hanging on the door. (*She makes a complete turn and sees him.*) Oh! You already found it. (*She pauses, then adds a hint of derision.*) What is this meeting all about?

MACLOVIO: Police command, community leaders. They claim they want to better relations, since they shot the Romero boy in the back.

ELENA: Will it do any good?

MACLOVIO: I don't know, but we have to try, we have to try.

ELENA: What about the furniture payment—were you able to borrow any money?

MACLOVIO: (*Piqued and obviously irritated.*) Don't worry about that, I'll take care of it.

ELENA: (*Obstinately.*) When?

MACLOVIO: (*Disturbed.*) Elena, why, why now? You have always trusted my judgment.

ELENA: (*Turning from him.*) Where are we going, Maclovio, after you get those last two checks from Kaufman? What will we do then?

MACLOVIO: I'll find a job. I'll do something. There has to be an answer. I can see the movement growing, the people coming alive. The time is ripe. They are getting their guts back. We can start a real social revolution now.

ELENA: That job they offered you, did you stare at them, say nothing, and mean . . . shove it? Like all those other times. We can't live on dreams and social revolutions.

MACLOVIO: Can't you see they want me to sell out? They're trying to buy me.

ELENA: Buy what? Your hole in the barrio?

MACLOVIO: Well, anyway, I didn't say anything. I've been weighing it over and over in my mind. Then I think of Pedro, Gregorio, and all the old people with the hope shining in their eyes, the young brainwashed students who we have to win back, the cocky kids who take the rap for each other, and the dead ones who don't have a fighting chance.

ELENA: And your family, what about us? Oh, you don't have to worry about Lita; she's just like you: she'll give her shoes away. She talks like you, and she'll starve like you.

MACLOVIO: (*Turns* ELENA *around by the shoulders.*) Let's not argue about it now. (*He smiles forcedly.*) I might surprise you.

ELENA: You're losing your son Manny, just like you lost Beto. You're fighting quicksand; you have to give those people more than just hope or, as you say, dignity and pride. You're fighting this whole damn system, and you can't win. (*She bows her head, realizing she has stung him.*)

MACLOVIO: If I give up, who will do it? We would be in the same spot if some people didn't try and change things. There are others across this country, this world, who are willing to suffer, to die. We have to find each other. (*Futilely.*) We are not alone.

ELENA: In this barrio you are not alone? So what? The hell with the world. We have our family. Come home to us. Oh, Maclovio, I'm worried . . . I'm worried. (*She catches herself.*) I'm sorry, *querido.* (*She touches his face tenderly like a blind person feeling with her hands.*)

MACLOVIO: (*Not pacified.*) Look at me and listen closely. I don't know what drives me on. I try to figure it out—you remember, we both did. Every time I started to live what everyone considers a normal life, when I would decide to wrap myself up in my business, in our business of just living, something happened. Remember, you were doing the registration work? (*She looks away ashamed.*) Yes, it was you who came home crying that in one of the homes you visited, a woman needed a wheelchair and her husband was dying of cancer. We helped them. We started checking our old neighborhood. (ELENA *nods her head.*)

ELENA: I'm sorry. Forgive me.

MACLOVIO: It's like all the other times there were problems: you noticed them first. Each of those problems still exists; we can't cure them all. So we must fight, teach, and instruct until we have an army ready for a real revolution. Meanwhile, we work with the problems. The Romero boy was shot and killed. The people expect us to do something about it.

ELENA: (*Tenderly.*) Be careful, Maclovio. There are rumors floating around, and I'm worried and afraid.

MACLOVIO: (*Angrily.*) Old ladies' talk, gossip.

ELENA: It comes from men.

MACLOVIO: (*Irritated.*) What comes from men?

ELENA: Manny told me yesterday that he heard some men talking at the gym.

MACLOVIO: What kind of talk?

ELENA: They say the police . . . the police will get you, even if they have to frame you. They say you tackled the wrong bunch.

MACLOVIO: They're just like everyone else: once they are placed in public view, they will pull their fangs out.

ELENA: Public view? The newspapers are killing you in their editorials, and the radio stations say you're a rabble rouser and that you are helping the criminal element. And the worst part of it, some of our own people believe it.

MACLOVIO: It will pass. (*Louder.*) It will pass. We are right, and we have to win. We'll get a grand jury investigation.

ELENA: What will they do?

MACLOVIO: You're right. It's what they won't do that will be exposed, that will anger the people. And when they see the impossibility of trying to gain equality through due process, they will be ready to fight and die if necessary.

ELENA: And now only you are ready to die . . . Until then, how are we going to live?

MACLOVIO: We'll make out—don't worry. (*He straightens his shirt, puts his coat on, and starts for the door.*) Oh, by the way, take the kids down to my *compadre* Pedro's house tonight. I want to talk to you, Lita, and Manny tonight.

ELENA: (*With an air of exasperation.*) Another decision to be made by the family. A discussion where you tell us what you what, convince us you're right, and everyone is supposed to walk out feeling they took part.

MACLOVIO: Now, wait a minute, that's not fair. (*He chucks her under the chin and starts for the door.*)

ELENA: Who was the letter from? (*The door slams. She hopelessly says it again.*) That letter, who was it from? (*She pulls at her scalp and hair furiously.*)

LITA: (*Walks in holding her hair up with one hand and a comb in the other.*) Ma, can I use your hair pins? (ELENA *dully waves at the dresser.*) Ma, I'm going to the demonstration with Tomás Remo tonight. Is that okay? (*She twists and contorts as she pushes her hair, grimacing in front of the dresser mirror.*) You know him—he's really cute. Some of the guys make fun of him, but I like him. He's so intelligent. He's going to be a great leader, just like Papá. Of course, I think he'll be more businesslike. But Daddy's still the greatest.

ELENA: (*Raising defensively.*) Don't compare that mouse to your father. He dresses like a banker. I've watched them all: they hang around like vultures waiting to be recognized. I warn Maclovio, because I can feel it here. (*She touches her heart.*) When they are good or bad, when the pressure is on and their life is at stake, all their intelligence and dandy manners do them no good. They run like coyotes. They are weaklings.

LITA: Gee, Mamá, he admires Daddy and he just wants to help. At least he's not like my own brother Manny and those hoodlums he hangs around with.

ELENA: Hoodlums? They are boys concerned with living like boys. Not trying the impossible of waking our people up.

LITA: I'm sorry, Mamá, I don't want to argue with you.

ELENA: (*Tousles* LITA'*s hair and pushes her playfully to the door.*) Go on, *hija.* We should be arguing about babies and talking women's talk. Go get Trini and Cuca ready while I get Liza and Mackey dressed. We have to take them to Pedro Ramo's house.

LITA: Why? Is Grandpa getting sicker?

ELENA: I'll tell you this evening . . . Let's go, let's go. (*As they exit, Grandpa is heard offstage.*)

GRANDFATHER: (*His voice offstage.*) Hija, hija, ruégale a Dios que me lleve. Mátame, Dios en el cielo, Dios bendito, mátame.

ACT I—SCENE FOUR

Lights go out and come on brighter. The chairs are now around a restaurant coffee table. MACLOVIO, PEDRO, and HAROLD are seated.

PEDRO: (*Laughing.*) You did tear them a new one, didn't he, Harold? Those cops' faces turned to stone. Man, what a lacing.

HAROLD: You did pour it on tough, Mac.

MACLOVIO: I satisfied myself. But now I worry about who will have to pay. The kids on the streets? The people coming home from dances or parties?

HAROLD: They can't afford to now. The press is on their side, but if they make a mistake, we'll be in a position to take advantage of it.

MACLOVIO: They have been making mistakes for centuries. They are still in control. All my life I've watched them beat my people, my brothers, and the fearless, honest press is with them. Blood brothers.

PEDRO: Well, they should have been there today and got an earful. Right, Harold? (*He chuckles.*) Especially when you told them, "People can only respect those representing the law when police learn to respect the people." It went something like that. Right on the line, man. (*He laughs.*)

HAROLD: It's a good start. We need more people at the demonstrations. We need more information disseminated to the neighborhoods.

MACLOVIO: One year ago, you couldn't find two of our people who would stand up and be counted. I know they wanted to, but weren't sure how to do it; neither were we. We are still learning; it's a slow process. Now we have 150 people down at the Police

Department. We had 600 at our meeting last Sunday. Pancho Villa crossed the Rio Grande with seven men from Texas to Mexico, and by the time he took Mexico City, he had fifty thousand.

HAROLD: (*Frowning.*) We are ready to start indoctrinating them. You have to provide a doctrine, a program.

PEDRO: (*Looks worried, a dark look of distrust crossing his face. He looks at* MACLOVIO *and he blurts out . . .*) Maclovio wants justice, not doctrine.

MACLOVIO: Harold, to prepare our people for evaluation of philosophy and politics will take the most powerful de-brainwashing machine in the history of man. Did you see Pedro's face darken? That's the face of our people: distrustful, puzzled, loyal, patriotic, faithful to an imperialistic society. No money to give, but they'll give every drop of blood they have. (*He shakes his head sadly.*) True, we must change people. A horse's ass is a horse's ass in whatever stable it stands. Isms don't cure ills, but reaction changes human behavior.

HAROLD: (*Standing.*) I have to go to work now. I still think the time is ripe. (*Then in a tone of superiority.*) I'll talk to you later. And say, before I forget, you should utilize the talents of more young men like Tomás Reno. (*He exits.*)

PEDRO: Who the hell does he think he is? You see this guy every time there is an issue at stake. What's in it for him?

MACLOVIO: Security. He needs to belong. His father was a bigot and a racist. He rejects his father, and this is his way to fight him.

PEDRO: Shit, we're not babysitters. But just so's he don't start giving no damn orders. Guys like him bug me. Two months ago he was up at the legislature picketing with those old broads against high prices in their middle-class neighborhoods. Why in hell don't those bitches come down to the slums and picket? He brags he marched at Selma; now he's one of us. Where will he be tomorrow?

MACLOVIO: Where will we all be tomorrow? He's all right; he believes in humanity. He's been helping us; we can't reject him for that. More Anglos should start rejecting this rotten system.

PEDRO: They say he is pink. He could hurt our Movement.

MACLOVIO: I wouldn't care if he was red down to his shorts. You don't see red, white, and blue patriots helping us. They might help us to our graves. And before this is over, we'll be called criminals, Communists, and homosexuals. And don't forget, even some of our own people will be calling us opportunists looking for a pay-off job.

PEDRO: Well, they haven't started that about you. Anyway, not people who count. (*He falters.*) What I mean, the ass-holes who complain about everything . . . (*He laughs self-consciously.*) We got a Movement going . . . nobody or nothing is going to stop us.

MACLOVIO: (*Looking at his watch.*) Where is Tomás Reno? I have to meet the mayor and the chief of police in half an hour.

PEDRO: What about that guy? What does he want? Lead us into victory after the battle is over? I don't trust him. Besides, he reminds me of a broad.

MACLOVIO: Take it easy. We have to give him a chance. We have to develop new leaders. It's true he doesn't act too stable. But I really feel he has our people's interest at heart.

PEDRO: He hasn't been around since you got him that job at the center. He just likes to see his name in the papers. First thing he'll do is set up a P.R. committee with him as head of it. (*A young man starts to walk through the door. He is slender, very neat, and fastidious, wearing an Ivy League suit, vest and all. His face is slender and sensual; he walks very straight with a proud, haughty air. He stops at the table.*)

TOMÁS: Mr. Gallegos. (*He offers his hand.*)

PEDRO: Hi, Tom, sit down.

MACLOVIO: (*Watching him closely.*) Yes, have a chair.

TOMÁS: Thank you. (*He sits, then straightens out his coat, vest, and tie, and assumes a very business-like pose.*) Mr. Gallegos.

MACLOVIO: Call me Maclovio.

TOMÁS: Very well, Mr. Gallegos . . . I mean, Mac-lovio. I want you to know that I and the other young people of the community feel you are doing a fine thing for our community.

PEDRO: How's the job?

TOMÁS: (*Ignoring* PEDRO.) I and the other young people of the community would like to offer our support. It's high time we organized to correct the inequities that exist in our society.

MACLOVIO: (*Nodding his head.*) Thank you for your support. (PEDRO *is sliding down in his chair, looking at* TOMÁS *as if through a keyhole.*)

TOMÁS: Well, the way I see it, the time to move is now, and the only way to accomplish complete and total organization is by proper administration. (PEDRO *nods his head and shrugs his shoulders toward* TOMÁS.) We must set up committees to implement every phase of the attack. We need a special committee for the pickets, a committee for transportation, one for material, such as posters, another for getting out the handbills, and a communications committee. (*His eyes brighten.*) The most important, of course, is a public relations committee, to make sure the press, radio and TV give us the right kind of coverage.

MACLOVIO: (*A stoic poker face.*) Who will serve on all the committees?

TOMÁS: The people, of course.

PEDRO: Which people?

TOMÁS: All of our people are with us. They want to help. They'll do it.

PEDRO: Of course, you'll contact them all and teach them, right?

TOMÁS: Maclovio just has to say the word, they will help. I'd be more than glad to head the P.R. Committee. By next meeting, I'll have press releases, flyers, copies . . . and friends from the S.S.C. group will help.

PEDRO: How many of our people belong to the S.S.C.?

TOMÁS: What difference does it make? Let's use them.

MACLOVIO: (*Winces.*) The word you use smacks of prostitution and treachery.

TOMÁS: (*Defensively.*) What I mean is they want to help. Let them help.

MACLOVIO: We want everyone's help. But we need to develop our own leadership. We'll take their help, but we make the decisions. Remember that.

TOMÁS: I agree. Only, we need people with administrative and organizational experience.

PEDRO: (*Sourly.*) Yeah, like they organize ten people at their biggest rally. (TOMÁS *gives him a reproachful look.*) I'm going out to put a nickel in the meter. (*He leaves with a scowl at* TOMÁS.)

TOMÁS: (*Watching* PEDRO *leave.*) We can't depend on just blind followers. We must conduct administrative procedures, so that when one person doesn't agree, he is replaced efficiently.

MACLOVIO: (*Stops him, putting up his hand.*) Tomás, haven't seen you for some time now. I try to convince myself that you are sincere in your statements about helping your people. But don't you think it's a little too soon or presumptuous to start corporation thinking among our people? Is that what you really want?

TOMÁS: The time for change is here. We can no longer have archaic charismatic leadership. We need intellectual organizers with administrative abilities.

MACLOVIO: Who will organize?

TOMÁS: The people. I don't mean to say that they will come without you. But you will be giving them their intellectual freedom of choosing for themselves. You will help them to throw off the chains of bondage, of the *patrón* system.

MACLOVIO: I should be the ox who leads the bulls to the pen to be castrated. (*His eyes and face take on a fierce look.*) To become mechanized robots in a sterile society, a society that isn't sure when to laugh, cry, or love unless they have written directions. I should lead my people to the paradise of a Mickey Mouse, tinkertoy world that has no compassion for humanity. *Por Dios,* we live more by instinct and mistake than your kind of people do by painstaking plan.

TOMÁS: They don't have to become like that. We must play their game to be able to allow our people to become creative.

MACLOVIO: Creative? (*He chuckles cynically.*) Planned parenthood, two children, and their college trust in the bank. Creative? They are even afraid to create children.

TOMÁS: (*Stung.*) We are creative . . . you and I are leaders of the community. We create awareness. We create changes.

MACLOVIO: (*Oblivious to the "we."*) Men are impostors. (*He looks over* TOMÁS's *head.*) We try to change all the flaws and mistakes we have already made. There is only one genuine creator. Her name is woman. For me, Elena. We try to become leaders, artists, poets, musicians, and writers. She lays in bed, gives her love, and produces happiness. She doesn't copy or steal. She produces music, art, and golden words of truth. She knows what she wants and she gets it. No false dreams, no discussions, no meetings, no pickets, or demonstrations, just her world . . . no organizations, administration or bullshit. Just her world, her children, her man, life . . . life . . . (*The lights have been fading out until there is only light on the face of* MACLOVIO. *Lights off.*)

ACT I—SCENE FOUR

The lights come up on ELENA. *The bedroom has been converted to a living room, worn but clean, a sofa with a serape covering it, a coffee table, an end table with a radio on it. Two chairs, a hope chest covered by a cheap tapestry, a Santo Niño with a red vigil glass holding a candle. A large picture of a Mexican revolutionist, a picture of* BETO *in his army uniform. A Mexican calendar with a picture of Hidalgo, his horse reared and carrying a standard of the Virgin of Guadalupe. A bookcase.* ELENA *crosses the room with a glass of water in one hand and medicine in the other. A loud groan is heard from off stage.*

GRANDFATHER: Oohh . . . Ohhh . . . Ayyy . . .

ELENA: *Aquí vengo papacito. No te apenes. Aquí vengo.* (*She stops; music on the radio station stops abruptly.*)

RADIO ANNOUNCER: A meeting today at the mayor's office between the mayor, police chief Howard Hill, and militant Maclovio Gallegos resulted in chaos. Gallegos insisted on a more thorough review of police recruits and the abolishment of the Internal Affairs Bureau, the police division that investigates police brutality charges. Chief Hill commended police officers in their handling of the Romero case and said, "Only the criminal element are complaining. The law-abiding citizens are satisfied with our fine police department." The mayor said, "I welcome a grand jury investigation and will study the possibility of a citizens' review board." He further added, "We have a fine police department that serves without prejudice all elements of the city. I hope to hold meetings with the more responsible leaders of the community. Our city is known throughout the nation as having one of the finest human relation climates in . . ." (ELENA *turns the radio off.*)

GRANDFATHER: (*From off stage.*) Ay, hija, ¿cuándo me voy a morir? Ay Dios, mátame, por favor.

ELENA: (*Leaves room, scolding softly and tenderly.*) Papacito, Papá, please take this. You'll get well soon. (*She says the last weakly.* LITA *walks in taking off her earrings.*)

LITA: Mamá, Mamá, where are the earrings Daddy gave you for Christmas last year? (*She drops two earrings on the dresser.*) These things have five-and-ten written all over them. Gee, they look cheap. They turn your ears green.

GRANDFATHER: Ohh . . . Ohh . . . Aayyy . . .

ELENA: (*Coming back through the door.*) Oh, God, my poor *papá* is in so much pain. He doesn't recognize anyone anymore.

LITA: Can I use your earrings? (*She is already putting them on.*)

ELENA: Yes, yes. (*Then to herself.*) The doctor said it's a miracle he is still alive. Why should he have to suffer? He worked hard all his life. Never missed a day, loved my mother like she was a queen, and he was good to us kids. We never had it made, but there was always food on the table. He was always home, always busy. Oh, god, *Oh Virgen de Guadalupe,* is it bad to pray for death for one man and life for the other? (*She slumps on the bed, strain and wear showing in her face.*)

LITA: (*Going to her mother.*) Mamá, Mamá, everything will be all right.

GRANDFATHER: Ohhh . . . Ohh . . .

ELENA: It's all mixed up, this life. Your *abuelito* trying to die and can't make it, and Maclovio trying to breathe new life into a dead cause.

LITA: It's not a dead cause. Go into the neighborhoods, listen to the people, hear how they feel. They are alive with new hope and courage.

ELENA: (*Bitterly.*) Yes, listen to them talk in the cantinas and at the coffee tables. The men are jealous, so they hate Maclovio because he exposes their weakness by doing things they will not do. There are the loyal women and the women who look for fault because they have to compare him to their own men. You have a lot to learn, *hija.*

LITA: Mamá, Mamá, someone has to do these things, someone has to say the truth. Remember, you told me when I was a little girl how Daddy went out to face down old Bill Robinson when he was drunk. Robinson had a shotgun and wouldn't let any of the neighbors get water from the only pump on the block. (*Action can be shown by silhouette on a scrim on the elevated level. ELENA visualizes the scene.*) Yes, they came pouring out of the houses as Maclovio walked that half block to the water pump. Bill Robinson was standing there drunk, his eyes bloodshot. Once a month he got his army pension check from when he fought in the Spanish-American War. Once a month he took over the water pump. "So the Mesicans," that's what he called us, "would stay in their place." (*She is growing more animated as she speaks.*) The crowd was loud and bold till they got up to ten feet of Bill Robinson. Then the noise dropped like a hush in an empty church. Maclovio stepped forward alone. I had just got there from the *mercado.* I had run and run till my heart felt like it would come out my throat. I froze. Maclovio walked slowly until he was in front of Bill Robinson. Bill Robinson weaved, then he jammed the barrel into Maclovio's chest. He pulled back the hammer. The click sounded like a drum. (*She screams.*) Maclovio!

LITA: (*Standing mute, crosses to her mother and smooths her hair.*) I'm sorry, Mother.

ELENA: (*Guiltily.*) It's just the strain of watching your *abuelito*, of watching people use your father. I have this feeling. (*She pulls at the sides of her hair.*) I have this feeling as if I need to fight to keep Maclovio. Not from another woman, but from some unseen force. I can't explain it. (LITA *is looking worriedly at her mother. Then* ELENA *catches her eye, straightens up, forces a smile and stands up.*) He'll change this whole city. *Por Dios,* he will change it so our people will be treated like human beings. Let me show you something. (*She lifts the mattress and pulls out a small leather pouch.*) I told you about it once, do you remember?

LITA: You mean the pearl Daddy found? (*She pours a small pearl into her hand.* LITA *picks it up and looks at it.*) Is this a real pearl, Ma?

ELENA: Yes, Maclovio had won some money in a crap game down at the union hall. He took me to eat at Travali's on the north side. We were talking about signs that change people's lives. He had been offered a partnership in a beer joint by Stan Kaugman, right here by these barrios. The packing houses were going to drop some of the men from the kill floor and force wages down. Maclovio had been talking strike.

LITA: They walked off, didn't they?

ELENA: That's when he bit into this oyster at Travali's. I can still remember his face when he pulled it out of his mouth. He said, "Do you know how many people find pearls in their oysters?" I said, "No." He said, "Not very many."

LITA: It was a sign, Mamá. Papá was chosen.

ELENA: He said that. This is special. This is our sign; we'll keep it forever. (ELENA *is once more caught up in the past.*)

LITA: What did he do, Mamá?

ELENA: He went back and talked the union into a strike. We starved that winter; that's when Beto was born. Maclovio junked the alleys, shoveled snow, chased scabs down the river, broke their heads and noses and his knuckles. They finally won the strike. Then three years later, the company closed the plant down.

LITA: Just think, Tomás Reno's father probably worked with Daddy. You wouldn't know it, though. Tom's so elegant and refined.

ELENA: (*Holding the pearl up to the light.*) A dream. Give us a good sign.

GRANDFATHER: (*Loud groan.*) Ay, Dios, mátame, mátame, por favor.

ELENA: (ELENA *is startled as if awakening from a deep sleep. Then she screams.*) The pearl! I dropped the pearl! (*She crawls frantically on the floor. Hysterically.*) Lita, find it! Help me! *Madre de Dios,* help me. Oh, no . . . My God . . . No. (*The lights go out.*)

ACT II—SCENE ONE

The lights come up on the elevated side, same chairs as in Act I, Scene One, in front of the battered desk. GREGORIO *and* PEDRO *are getting ready to sit.*

PEDRO: So you landed an Uncle Sam grab-bag? What does it pay?

GREGORIO: They'll start me at 12 G's. They promised a quick raise. I can go up to 16 in a year. With all these government programs popping up, the way I see it, the guys in first will be at the top in no time.

PEDRO: Have you told Maclovio yet?

GREGORIO: That's what I'm waiting for. I'm no damn fool. I know they gave me the lookover because of my association with the movement. Of course, I'm a professional in the group relations field. I have a B.A. in sociology. Nothing they could frown on. Not like a political patronage job. You know you have to be qualified.

PEDRO: You're really a lucky man. I've been selling tires for that bastard O'Hara for eight years now. You know, they had a new region open and he put this other guy in ahead of me. I have seniority, too. I wish I had your luck, or Maclovio's gut, to tell them to stick it.

GREGORIO: Not luck, pal. This Henderson told me they want young, dedicated, militant men to really develop some programs for our people. We're going to blast the doors open . . . (MACLOVIO *is seen coming through the door. He stands listening.*) . . . to employment, change the educational procedures, wipe out discrimination and prejudice. With their money, we can do it.

MACLOVIO: (*Smiling.*) Whose money? Have the Jewish businessmen and the Catholic Church joined our cause?

PEDRO: Gregorio's a big shot. He's got a big job. Right, Gregorio?

MACLOVIO: (*Placing his foot on a chair facing* GREGORIO.) Civil rights or group relations?

GREGORIO: Actually, better than that.

PEDRO: He represents the government on job contracts.

MACLOVIO: Oh, does that mean the government is taking over the sugar refineries and agricultural corporations? Officially, I mean.

GREGORIO: (*Defensively.*) I waited till you turned it down.

MACLOVIO: Thank you.

PEDRO: His position will give him a lot of prestige. Our kids will look up to him.

MACLOVIO: That's so true.

GREGORIO: My professional ambitions are at a standstill in this city. We've started something going. I can use my experience to help other communities. I can help my people. That's why I took the job.

MACLOVIO: Yes, we started a nice, hot, roaring fire, then after it's out we have to build from the charred remains. (*Then sadly, but with genuine forgiveness.*) You'll do a fine job.

GREGORIO: Maybe you can help Pedro here get that job with the city relations committee. They'll do anything to keep things quiet. Besides, Pedro's tired of hustling tires for O'Hara.

MACLOVIO: We can't afford to ask for anything. (*Then looking affectionately at* PEDRO.) Maybe you can place him on your staff.

GREGORIO: Well, don't think I won't. As soon as I get settled. I won't forget. (*He stands.*) I have to go to a briefing conference.

See you later, before I leave. Oh, Mac, do me a favor, please. Call me Gregory from now on. (GREGORIO *leaves.*)

PEDRO: He knows what he wants. I wish I did. It would be nice to have a good job and help your people at the same time.

MACLOVIO: (*Staring out over the audience.*) Yes, he knows what he wants, and so does the establishment. Some people want security . . . some want power . . . some of us, we're not so sure.

PEDRO: And some of us want pride and dignity . . . (*He looks maternally at* MACLOVIO.) . . . for their people. (MACLOVIO *averts his head. There is tremendous strain on his face. He swats at a tear rolling down his cheek. Scene ends.*)

ACT II—SCENE TWO

Lights come up on MANNY. MACLOVIO'*s eighteen-year-old son is combing his long, wavy black hair. The radio is playing rock-and-roll music loudly. He is slender, yet heavy in the shoulders and full in the chest. His movements are smooth and casual, catlike. The old man's groan is heard over blare of the radio.* LITA *walks in, over to the radio and starts to change the station.*)

LITA: I want to listen to "Comment." Tom Reno is talking to Jim Trimble today.

MANNY: Yeah, what's that queer got to say that's worth listening to?

LITA: (*Angry.*) You can't say that. You don't even know him, and you should. He offered his help to Daddy today. And he isn't his son.

MANNY: Aw, can it! I can't understand you people who knock yourselves out for somebody else. If you don't make it on your own, ain't nobody gonna help you.

LITA: If you ever get it through your thick head that this world can be changed, and start helping instead of criticizing, you might see things differently. If you would listen to Daddy instead of thinking you know it all.

MANNY: Oh, yeah, listen to him. Like Mom did, huh? Talk the neighborhood into putting pressure on the city to build low rent homes here. Well, they did, and now all the people who were renting from us went to the new houses, and we lost everything, and now we live in one of these crummy houses. And what happened? Three years later, they are as lousy as the ones he used to rent. Horseshit! What's wrong with a Cadillac, a big diamond ring, sirloin steak, and fur coats? Old pantywaist Tomás gonna get you a diamond? Hell no! He ain't gonna starve like our old man. He'll drop the cause like a hot potato when he finds out nobody feeds a leader. Not even the people you're killing yourself for.

LITA: Shut up.

MANNY: He's used to those Ivy League suits and three squares. You gonna provide them for him?

LITA: And you? Have you ever gone hungry? Have you ever had at least a tiny bit of feeling of understanding for Papá or Ma?

MANNY: For Ma, yeah, 'cause I understand her. (*He says this dejectedly.*) I don't understand him. He teaches one thing, then you go to school, and they teach you something else. Who in the hell is right? The successful ones, or the guy out there freezing his ass on the picket line, hated by the cops and city hall prostitutes, 'cause he knows who they are, and despised by people, 'cause they know themselves and don't want to rock the boat. Giving what he hasn't got and making Ma suffer while he plays Jesus Christ . . . God damn it, doesn't he know when to stop?

LITA: You know he's right. That's what makes you mad. Because you don't want to suffer. You know what they teach at school is crap, and you know the politicians are phony. You're afraid. You're a coward.

MANNY: (*Laughing.*) Yeah, I'm a coward. That's why I won the nationals. That's why I've already whipped every lightweight in this state. Coward.

LITA: Do you ever stop to evaluate things? Do you ever want to know the truth about why we're second-class citizens in the land of the free and the brave? Do you ever read, nitwit, so you can find out who you are, and you can identify success with character and love instead of money?

MANNY: Jesus Christ. We are talking about dad.

LITA: That's exactly what we are doing. He's concerned with changing things, the hypocrisy. He's trying to educate people to think, to evaluate the reasons for war, why people are being slaughtered, and who is making the money from it. And when you figure it all out, you can understand why this system corrupts and uses people. Daddy can't live in a world like that unless he changes it.

MANNY: From what I hear, if he keeps messing around, he won't see much more of it. (ELENA *has been standing at the door. Walking swiftly, she grabs* MANNY.)

ELENA: What do you mean? Answer me!

MANNY: Nuthin', Ma, nuthin'. Lita was just giving me one of her two-bit speeches, 'cause I called Tomás Reno a queer.

LITA: You thick-headed jerk. He's not a queer.

MANNY: (*Looking at* ELENA *apprehensively.*) Well, Mamá, you won't have to worry about the future 'cause this is the hand that's going to shake the world. (*He shakes his right fist in the air.*) Manny Gallegos, the lightweight champ of the world. Furs for Mamá, two-buck cigars for Papá. Vacations in Mexico. We'll give them peons a sight to behold.

LITA: Of course, you won't know any of your old hoodlum friends then. You're so loyal. And you'll probably marry a paddy, you're so proud of your own people.

MANNY: (*Ignoring* LITA.) I'll send them tickets to watch me fight in New York City. Then I'll come home and be their leader. (ELENA's *eyes narrow.* LITA *tries to stop him with her eyes.*) I'll scale the city hall walls and throw a blonde to all my buddies. I'll tell them how they come from proud chiefs, kings, revolutionists, winos, tricks, addicts, and . . .

ELENA: (*Slaps* MANNY.) Manuel, stop it, stop it! Do you hear me? Stop it! You will not shame your father in this house.

MANNY: (*Ashamed.*) I was only kidding, Ma. (*He gives* LITA *a dirty look.*) She started it.

LITA: (LITA *turns the radio up.*) It's him, it's Tom Reno.

TOMÁS: (*On the radio.*) Yes, Jim, we realize that we must assume our role in American society and that there are responsibilities on both sides that must be met.

ANNOUNCER: How long do you people expect to picket?

TOMÁS: I . . . (*Pause.*) We haven't decided yet. Of course, I feel that an objective grand jury investigation should be held.

ANNOUNCER: Tell me, how did you get started in the civil rights struggle for your people?

MANNY: His people, bull.

TOMÁS: (*Lights begin to dim.*) My people need leadership and I felt . . .

GRANDFATHER: (*Groaning.*) Ohhhh . . . Ohhhh . . . Aayy . . . (Lights out.)

ACT II—SCENE THREE

ELENA *is lying on the couch. Her hand hangs over the edge, holding a rosary. A loud knock. She jumps up, straightens her clothes, and brushes her hair down, opens the door. It is* PEDRO; *his face is flushed. He is excited.*

PEDRO: Elena, where is Maclovio? I have to see him. (*He looks behind him.*) I've been tailed.

ELENA: What have you done?

PEDRO: Nothing, nothing. I dropped Maclovio off at the police department. He told me to pick up the kids at school and take them to my house.

ELENA: (*Puzzled.*) He must still be at the police department.

PEDRO: All . . . all right. Can I take the kids to your sister Nina's house?

ELENA: Yes, take them there. I'll call her and let her know they are coming. Who was following you?

PEDRO: I don't know. (*Before she can question him further, the old man groans.* PEDRO *rushes out the door.*)

GRANDFATHER: Ohhhh . . . Ohhhh . . . *Ay, Padrecito, llévame. ¿Por qué no puedo morirme? Ay, hija, ay, hijita.* (ELENA *starts to go to him. There is a knock at the door. She opens the door to two old tamale vendors, a man and a woman. They are both dressed in black, the Old Man in a tattered suit, the Old Woman in a long black dress, her head covered by a long black shawl. The Old Man carries a wicker basket covered with a white dish towel. The Old Man smiles a toothless grin. The Old Woman cocks her head as a groan is heard. She makes the sign of the cross.*)

ELENA: (*Confused.*) *Entren, entren. Pasen, pasen.* (*They enter. The old lady sits on the sofa, holding a shoe box. She cocks her head like a parakeet, listening for the groans of the old man.* ELENA *watches her, curious, frightened.*)

OLD MAN: *¿Vive Trinidad Córdova aquí?*

ELENA: *Sí, señor. ¿Son amigos?*

OLD MAN: (*He nods to the Old Woman. She stands up, walks closer to the door.* ELENA, *fascinated, watches the Old Woman. The Old Man is wrapping a dozen tamales. He hands them to* ELENA. *She starts to pay him. He shakes his head no.*) *Quiero ver al Señor Córdova.* (ELENA *points to the room. She starts to lead him, then stops, frozen, as the Old Woman turns her head and seems to recognize something in* ELENA, *looking through or into her. She shakes her head sadly and clucks. The old man beckons the old woman with his head. They both go in to see the grandfather.* ELENA *is frozen, holding the tamales. The two old people hurry back in and then out. They both nod to* ELENA *and shake their heads as they go out.* ELENA *stands as if petrified. A car horn sounds outside. Children laughing. The distant call of olly-olly-oxen-free. A dog barks. She sits heavily. From the outside a child's voice, "Let's play* faja.*"* MACLOVIO *walks in slowly and quietly, a peaceful look on his face. She looks up startled.*)

ELENA: Maclovio, where have you been?

MACLOVIO: I've been looking at the world . . . our world. (*He takes her in his arms affectionately.*) I've come home, *querida.* I've come home. I'm going to make it up to you, to Manny, Beto, all the children. I want my life back. (*He strokes her head tenderly.*)

ELENA: Maclovio, did you see Pedro?

MACLOVIO: This evening, love. (*He is struggling for words.*) Elena, Elena, I saw it all, as I walked home. I realized what I've done to you and the children.

ELENA: We're proud of you. Did you see Pedro?

MACLOVIO: I come home to tell you it's all over, and you want to know if I've seen Pedro. I've come home, Elena. What you always wanted. You know, it all started today at city hall. I saw myself in the mirror. I looked twice. I was worn out, my eyes bloodshot. I looked like the madman the newspapers talk about. (ELENA *is helplessly shaking her head no. He continues.*) I said, "This is Maclovio Gallegos, the leader of the people. Who in the hell do you think you're kidding? You're just another foolish little man trying to be important. You are another Tomás Reno, wanting the publicity to make you important . . . another Gregorio Sánchez, praying that after all your snarling you'll finally accept a soft job and no responsibility, that you'll finally play the game and exist."

ELENA: No, Maclovio, no. Don't do this to yourself. You are Maclovio Gallegos, honest, strong, you love your people.

MACLOVIO: (*Bitterly.*) Yes, I'm Maclovio Gallegos, honest, and that's where it stops. I'm honest, and finally, I'm honest with myself. I can't play the game anymore. (*He clutches the back of a chair.*) I walked home, and I saw men laughing, walking in and out of *cantinas.* I saw grown men playing ball with their sons. I thought of Beto and Manny. (*He chokes up.*) I've never played ball with them. I've never seen Manny fight, and I heard them talking about him at the pool hall. They are all proud of him. He'll be the next champ, they say, and his father doesn't know it. Why, just one talk on the radio has made Tomás Reno a hero. We have new leaders now. I've wasted all my years moving one grain of sand from the beach, while the tide washes in a mountain.

ELENA: That is not true. You have created the atmosphere for the young people to hold their heads high, to have identity, to be someone. Maclovio, forgive me. You have but one life, and you have to live it the way you are doing it.

MACLOVIO: (*Despondently.*) Yes, I've lived it that way. Sometimes I would tell myself, "Elena's right, I'm not going anywhere. I'm not an educated man—how can I tell people how to live?" But it was always like being in a snowball, rolling down hill. Once I got started, the snowball got bigger and bigger and bigger, and went faster and faster and faster, till . . . There's only one way out. (*He looks at* ELENA, *who is staring at him aghast. The old man groans.*)

GRANDFATHER: *Mátame, por Dios, llévame.*

ELENA: Maclovio, two old people came to the door selling tamales. They said they knew Papá. Do you know them?

MACLOVIO: Them? I met them last night at the picket. He knows your father. He said they were both from the Order of Los Carmelitos. Yes, that's why I sent them. You know I don't believe old folks' tales, but they said they could help him. I was in a hurry trying to quiet a couple of the young boys down. They were arguing with the cops.

ELENA: (*Watching* MACLOVIO *closely.*) Where did they come from? (*She makes the sign of the cross.*) Do you know them? They come in the midst of trouble. They are a sign. (*Desperately.*) Who are they?

MACLOVIO: I don't know. You're so damned superstitious, everything is a sign. How in the hell do I know where they came from.

ELENA: They smell of death.

MACLOVIO: They smell old. They are old.

GRANDFATHER: Ohhhh . . . Aayy . . . (ELENA *hurries out.* MACLOVIO *sits heavily. The door opens slowly.* MANNY *tries to sneak by* MACLOVIO's *back.*)

MACLOVIO: What are you sneaking around about?

MANNY: Nuthin'. (*Assuming a casual air, his eye has an adhesive patch on it.*)

MACLOVIO: What happened? Run into one?

MANNY: (*Defensively.*) It was a butt. I beat him bad. How's the picket?

MACLOVIO: I don't know. (*Uneasily.*) Manny, I haven't been . . . Well, we haven't done much talking lately.

MANNY: That's all right. I understand, Pa. You've been helping the people.

MACLOVIO: Well, son, I'm coming home. I want to do things with the family. I want us to be like a real family again.

MANNY: Something wrong, Pa?

MACLOVIO: Something is right, kid. I want to go watch your next fight. They tell me you'll be the next champ.

MANNY: (*Obviously pleased.*) I have a lot to learn. (*They look at each other affectionately. A knock at the door. MANNY opens it. PEDRO runs in, shouting.*)

PEDRO: The Salas kid and the Quintana kid started arguing with the bulls. They got them in the can. They beat them real bad.

MACLOVIO: (*Assuming immediate command.*) Did you get them out? Did you demand they take them to the hospital? Did the line break up? (PEDRO *does not answer, as if overwhelmed.* MACLOVIO *strides to the phone, dials.*) Are you holding Alfredo Salas and Tommy Quintana there? What are the charges? (*He hangs up quickly, calls another number.*) Where is J.C.? I need a bond . . . I don't give a damn, give me the number where he's at. This is important. (*He writes and starts to dial again.*)

PEDRO: (*To MANNY.*) It was horrible. We got there too late. His head looked like a sponge soaked with blood.

MACLOVIO: Hello, let me talk to J.C., right now . . . I know he's there; put the bastard on. Hello, J.C., this is Maclovio. We have two boys in jail . . . No, I can't wait till tomorrow. They are in bad shape . . . Listen, you fat bastard, you don't do me this favor, I'll call a boycott on you. Get down there! I'll get the money. Yes, yes, I'll sign. Yes, I'll let you hold the title to my car. I expect you in ten minutes. (*He hangs up warily. He looks apologetically at MANNY and shrugs his shoulders.*)

MANNY: (*Walks up to him and puts his hand on his shoulder.*) You're the real champ, Pa. (*The phone rings.* ELENA *comes hurrying into the room.* MACLOVIO *motions to her to answer.*)

ELENA: It's Johnny Salas. He's crying.

MACLOVIO: (MACLOVIO *walks to the phone half-heartedly. Turns from the phone.*) Alfredo Salas. He's dead.

PEDRO: They're going to get us. They're going to get us all.

MACLOVIO: (*Sharply.*) Keep your head. (*To* ELENA.) Check on the children.

ELENA: They're all right. They're down at Nina's.

MACLOVIO: Nina's? I thought . . . (*He looks at* PEDRO.)

PEDRO: (*Blurts out.*) I thought I was being followed. That's why I suggested another place. Someone has been following me.

MANNY: (*All this time,* MANNY *has been watching with consternation.*) Oh, they wouldn't do that! Maybe to hoods, but not to pickets!

MACLOVIO: (*Coldly.*) Alfredo Salas is dead. (*He touches his coat by the breast.*) The police aren't the ones to fear so much as the bigots and the twisted, warped minds of this society. (*To* PEDRO.) Take my car and leave yours. Go check on the kids. People will be calling to see what our next move will be. (PEDRO *looks fearfully at the door.*) Manny, go with him. (*They leave. He turns to* ELENA.) They smelled of death, did they?

ELENA: Let's all go to Nina's. Please, Maclovio!

MACLOVIO: And the old man?

ELENA: (*As if suddenly realizing something.*) He's asleep. He's smiling. Maclovio, who left that shoe box full of dirt in his room?

MACLOVIO: (*Irritated.*) No. We stay right here. No racists are scaring me out of my own house. (*A knock on the door.* ELENA *answers.* HAROLD *and* TOMÁS *rush in,* GREGORIO *right behind them. They start speaking at the same time.* HAROLD *wins out.*)

HAROLD: This is the time you've been waiting for. The people are inflamed. You can start teaching them the right philosophy.

TOMÁS: I've already written the press release. We start a giant march on city hall. We can formulate our demands tonight. It'll be the biggest news story in the country.

MACLOVIO: (*Looks blandly at* GREGORIO, *who has been standing by himself.*) What do you suggest?

GREGORIO: We must take careful steps. We can only make matters worse if we act hastily.

MACLOVIO: Who do you represent, I mean officially—the people or the government?

GREGORIO: I leave tomorrow. (*He acts self-conscious.*)

TOMÁS: We can't let them get away with it. Listen to this. "Militant leaders of the west side community, led by Maclovio Gallegos, community leader, Tomás Reno, president of the Young Militants, and Harold Wilson, president of the S.C.C., have demanded the immediate arrest of the two officers guilty of killing young Alfred Salas in . . ."

HAROLD: Hold it, Tomás. Hold it! (*Looking at* MACLOVIO.) What do you suggest, Mac? If you go, the people will follow. You started this; now they expect you to carry it out. (MACLOVIO *looks at* ELENA *almost apologetically.*)

GREGORIO: I have to leave. I have to pack my things. (*He shakes* MACLOVIO'*s loose hand.*) Good luck. Goodbye, Elena. (*He leaves, his head down.* ELENA *has sat quietly praying her rosary. She gets up and goes to her father's room.* PEDRO *rushes in.*)

MACLOVIO: Where's Manny?

PEDRO: He's a chip off the old block. He went for his buddies; those guys are ready to fight.

MACLOVIO: (*Visibly alarmed.*) We need order and control. (*He is once more the general, sure, confident.*) Let me read those press releases. (TOMÁS, *unaware of what he is doing, jumps up as if to attention, hands the papers to* MACLOVIO *eagerly.*) Harold, you and Tomás make the rounds of all the radio and TV stations. Then call the union shops. Call the liberals. Start writing form letters to all elected officials for the people to sign. We'll hold a meeting at city hall. Make up flyers. Start writing slogans. (*Determined.*) The death of Alfredo Salas will turn this town inside out. (HAROLD *and* TOMÁS *are leaving, anxious to get started.*) And . . . oh . . . (*He reaches into his breast pocket.*) . . . take this damn letter and milk it for all it's worth. Expose the racist bastards. (ELENA *has appeared at the door as* MACLOVIO *has been talking.*) And if all this doesn't work, we'll answer violence with violence!

ELENA: (*Screams.*) Maclovio, don't go! (*He looks through her, continues directing orders. The crow of the cock is heard once-twice-thrice. She looks at* PEDRO, *who turns his head as if has heard it, too.* HAROLD *and* TOMÁS *hurry out.*)

ELENA: (*Trying to get* MACLOVIO'*s attention. He pecks her on the cheek. He and* PEDRO *rush out. She shouts to herself.*) Papá is dead! He's free! The earth in the box, they touched his feet, dead, oh, thank God! It's a sign, everything is a sign. He's free! Maclovio, you're trapped, we're all trapped . . . (*A loud explosion is heard. Flashes of light, red, blue, streak through the window.* PEDRO *comes running through the door; he is terrified.*)

ELENA: Where were you?

PEDRO: (*Tearfully.*) Maclovio is dead.

ELENA: It was your car. It was your car. (*She stared at him, her face twisted in hate, agony, and inquisitiveness.*)

PEDRO: Yes. Yes, I know. Something held me back; I was afraid. (*He mumbles, his face begging forgiveness.*) Maclovio started the car.

ELENA: (*Screaming.*) You heard it! Didn't you? You heard it! (*She shakes the numbed, fearful* PEDRO.) You knew! You knew! (*She pushes him away roughly.*) Oh, God, you knew! We both knew!

PEDRO: (*Shaking his head, disavowingly.*) He sent me. (*Pleading.*) Elena, he sent me.

ELENA: (*Fiercely.*) Go . . . Go . . . Go . . . Tell the militants . . . Tell his people . . . Tell the crumbs and the bums . . . Tell the political whores, the hypocrites! Tell the new leaders and the followers! The leeches and the parasites . . . . Tell the world Maclovio is dead.

(*Her voice rises more shrilly.*) He is dead . . . gone . . . gone . . . (*Then quietly, almost restrained.*) Go, Pedro. Tell them there will be no cross for Maclovio. He was just a man, my man. (PEDRO *stumbles, dazed, numbly sobbing, out the door. She gazes fiercely, relentlessly, at his sagging figure as he passes through the door. She turns, slowly catching a sob, her body shaking and trembling. She turns to the audience, as if suddenly realizing their presence. She walks front stage. She starts to speak, at first in a hushed voice, then stronger and stronger. This can also be played with shadows of people on the scrim as they gather to see the dead* MACLOVIO.)

ELENA: Maclovio is dead. I have nothing to live for. My life is spent. Lying awake tortuous nights for the sound of his footsteps, his healthy laughter, the touch of his coarse lips, the strength of his arms, and the heat of his body. Maclovio is dead, and so is his dream, his cause. And you, by your apathy, your smugness, your attitudes, you allow the slaughter to continue. The holocaust of burnt-out lives, mutilated bodies, and dried-up spirits. The dismembered and blood-soaked bodies of children . . . the warped minds of defectors . . . the pain of the addicts and derelicts . . . the whimpering of beggars and thieves . . . the social disease of corruption . . . the evil smell of bigotry and hate . . . the bloodstained fingers of exploitation . . . the gnarled hands of greed . . . the corpulent stench of success . . . the destruction of honor and dignity. These are your rewards. (*She looks into the audience.*) There will be no cross for Maclovio. He is gone. He was only a man. (*She points to the audience, or at figures on scrim.*) You killed him! YOU KILLED HIM! (*She turns slowly, her face in her hands. The lights dim as she walks upstage. As the lights go out, she moans.*) Maclovio . . . Maclovio . . .

The lights dim. The horn of a passing car blares and fades. A dog barks. The light passes through the window, casting the shadow of a cross across the stage. Slow curtain.

CHAPTER IV

Poetry

The following description of La Escuela and poetry selections by
Rodolfo "Corky" Gonzales are reproduced from the original Escuela
Tlatelolco brochure published in 1973 by La Escuela y Colegio
Tlatelolco Board. It is updated at the end.

La Escuela y Colegio Tlatelolco

La Escuela y Colegio Tlatelolco is an applied philosophy, a Chicano creation in the struggle to preserve and augment La Raza de
Bronce and our home, Aztlán.

Tlatelolco is an independent, family-oriented "Centro de Estudios" where Chicano ideas, culture, values, experience, feelings, and
knowledge emanate to develop and offer alternative models for Chicano education and educators.

The Founding of Tlatelolco

Following the First National Youth Liberation Conference in
1969, the Crusade for Justice, a Chicano civil and human rights organization, began a summer Freedom School. The goal was to provide
Chicano children and youth in the Denver area an opportunity to study
their history and to reinforce pride in their language, culture, and
identity as Chicanos.

One-hundred fifty students ranging in ages from four to eighteen
enrolled in Freedom School to learn Spanish, history, music, folkloric
dancing, geography, printing, sculpting, and contemporary world and
national affairs. The classes were held at the Crusade for Justice and
were taught by volunteer certified teachers and parents knowledgeable
in various fields. All instructors provided bilingual/bicultural instruction. The result was a family school in which the parents and children,
together, shared a learning experience.

In the summer of 1970, the Freedom School enrollment doubled.
Three professors were recruited from Monterrey, Nuevo Leon, Mexico, to teach advanced Spanish, Mexican history, economics, political
science, and mathematics. Certified teachers and parents were again

utilized to teach other subjects with the same methodology as had been used the previous summer.

Some of the experimentation undertaken in Freedom School involved extensive team teaching with built-in progression. Students were exposed to group teaching with the intent that they progress and compose part of the teaching team. To encourage course involvement and in-depth study, the students were exposed to peer group learning. Peer group learning discouraged individual competition by introducing self-development with the sharing of knowledge. Research was the basis of class study. Students and instructors were encouraged to research the background and history of study material. The result of this was the development of more accurate and new material.

Students who attended the summer Freedom School expressed dissatisfaction with public and parochial school systems to which they returned during the fall. They noted a deficiency in these institutions in relating curricula and teaching methods to their needs. They also experienced frustration with the instructors' ability, unpreparedness, and unwillingness to correlate their educational methods and material with the increased social, historical, and cultural awareness of the students. This awareness had not only increased students' learning motivation and provided a base for pride and identity, it also surfaced resentment that caused them to doubt the veracity of their past and possible future education. This concern was experienced not only by the students but also by their parents and individuals who had participated in the efforts of the Freedom School.

Inevitably, Escuela y Colegio Tlatelolco was founded in October 1970, as a result of the need to secure adequate educational opportunities for the Chicano—independent, alternative education.

The name Tlatelolco was adopted from Plaza Tlatelolco—La Plaza de Las Tres Culturas—in Mexico City, Mexico, where on October 2, 1968, the Mexican military massacred more than three hundred people (the majority of them students) who were actively protesting the injustices and poverty wrought by the Mexican government.

Tlatelolco is also the site where Spanish priests opened the first school for Indians and mestizos and, prior to that, where the children of Aztec royalty were taught.

Tlatelolco's Educational Philosophy

Tlatelolco's philosophical objective goes beyond effecting academic competency. We perceive education not only as the intellectual development of the individual for his benefit but as a social orientation and developmental process responsible for social change that will benefit a collective group.

We, therefore, strive to increase awareness to increase as part of a collective group, La Raza. This awareness encompasses La Raza's real state of social, economic, political, educational, vocational, and environmental conditions in this society. As educators, we dedicate ourselves to developing Chicano perceptive abilities in order that we can analyze these conditions and apply our awareness, knowledge, and energy collectively to achieve needed social transformation.

Tlatelolco is based on La Familia Concept. Since students, teachers, and parents are able to relate to one another as a familia, arising problems and obstacles can be overcome and the school is able to progress. We are all one Familia de La Raza. If a student has a problem, he can feel free to approach his teacher or brother and seek consultation he can relate to and trust. The parents work with the staff, and communication is ongoing. In this way we learn to work together. There is no separatism to block the road to education. *Carnalismo* is the common, living practice at Tlatelolco.

Education being the main purpose of this Centro de Estudios, the educational program provided is not solely for the benefit of the students at Tlatelolco, but for all La Raza as well. All knowledge is shared; what one knows is taught to others. Every student then becomes an instructor who must share what he learns and help educate our people.

Using nationalism as a base upon which to build our education, we create cultural awareness and reinforce pride in our language and way of life, building positive self-images to counter the psychological destruction of our people.

We devote our educational efforts and ourselves to bring about change for the benefit of La Raza de Aztlán.

Physical Plant

Tlatelolco was originally located where it was founded, the Crusade for Justice building, at 1567 Downing Street in Denver, Colorado, Aztlán.

This facility housed an auditorium, a gymnasium, a cafeteria, classrooms, a photography laboratory, a film laboratory, a silk-screening shop, a newspaper library, the *El Gallo* offices, an art gallery, two machine reproduction rooms, a combination curio shop and bookstore, a lounge, Tlatelolco offices, and the Crusade for Justice organization offices. Future plans included acquiring larger facilities for the sole operation of Tlatelolco.

In 1988, after the Crusade for Justice building was sold to the U.S. Postal Service, La Escuela moved to Servicios de La Raza located at 41st and Tejon Streets in Denver's northwest side. It was housed here until 1995 when the reconstituted Board of Trustees purchased a former Catholic school, at 2949 Federal Boulevard, its current home.

Tlatelolco

TLATELOLCO TLA-TE-LOL-CO TLATELOLCO
La Plaza de las tres culturas
La calle de sangre de niños guerrilleros
La escuela de liberación chicana
Ahora se comienza y nunca llega el fin.

TLATELOLCO TLA-TE-LOL-CO
La educación nunca se acaba
mientras que los ojos de los niños
están abiertos y los sueños son posibles.

TLATELOLCO TLA-TE-LOL-CO
History is the past,
and history is in the making.
The future is yours and ours.
Minds and muscles leap like
running antelopes and grasp
the food of knowledge like
hungry jaguars in ancient jungles.

TLATELOLCO TLA-TE-LOL-CO
We have made the beginning of history
and the future can only bring success.
Our souls bound together into one solid family.

TLATELOLCO TLA-TE-LOL-CO
Where laughter rings constantly
instead of hourly mechanical bells
where frustration and happiness mingle freely
as all life should.

El Gallo: La Voz de la Justicia, 4/3 (April 1971): p. 7.

TLATELOLCO TLA-TE-LOL-CO
Open up the doors to ancient secrets
open up our minds to future solutions
prepare us to settle for no less
than total liberation.

TLATELOLCO TLA-TE-LOL-CO
Liberate our minds to enter
plazas of wisdom.
Liberate our hearts to share the
fruit of all knowledge.
Liberate our bodies to work for
the good of La Raza and
all mankind.

TLATELOLCO TLA-TE-LOL-CO
Make us into a family
create of us a tribe
teach us to build a nation.

TLATELOLCO TLA-TE-LOL-CO

El Ballet Chicano de Aztlán

La Escuela Tlatelolco had a large Mexican ballet troupe, El Ballet Floklorico de Aztlán. It publicized the Crusade for Justice and was a fundraising activity for La Escuela. The following is a previously unpublished poem Gonzales wrote to honor the dancers in 1970.

Ballet Chicano de Aztlán
From the womb of stolen land
from concrete streets and steel barrios

We are La Raza Nueva
MESTIZO . . . We are the New Chicano!

From fertile eggs of emotion,
joy and beauty
Our hearts and bodies
dedicated to our people
We are the New Chicano!

La Zandunga weds
and binds us all,
La familia de La Raza
Tehuantepec gods tie us
to the revolutionary beauty.

Adelita . . . Adelita . . . Adelita
eyes flaming for justice long overdue.
Feet marching to victory
Jarabes, Espuelas, Zapateados
Niños y viejos
Dancing . . . Singing . . . Laughing
from Michoacán to La Plaza
de las Tres Culturas
From blue waters de Veracruz

to las doradas de Chihuahua.
We are the New Chicano!

Jarabes, Zarabandas, Madrugadas
Jalisco ya no llores
Tilingo Lingos stir the heart
Adelita points the way
Jesusita dedicated her soul
to rediscover our roots
Paint our proud history
teach a glorious future.

Recreate our love, our passion
our beauty and our loyalty.

We are the New Chicano!
Dance . . . Sing . . . Shout
Gritos de dolor—Gritos de amor
Bailes de fantasía
Carnalismo del alma

¡VIVA MÉJICO! ¡VIVA AZTLÁN!
¡VIVAN LOS CHICANOS!

Adiós, Miguel

MIGUEL J. RUYBAL

Born: March 13, 1960
   Alamosa, Colorado
Died: July 7, 1969
   Denver, Colorado
Buried: Mogote,
   Colorado, Aztlán
Son of Gloria and Leonel

Mike went back to the
Valley to take only a
small part of the earth
which was once ours.
His spirit will make
that valley ours once
again.

   Adiós, Miguelito,
      mis lágrimas no te pueden despertar
   I cannot trade my life for yours
   I can only live to make your memory
   beautiful and worthwhile.

Oh, Guerrillero pequeño,
      lleno de amor
         orgullo
            y pasión
   You were living proof
   That La Causa
      is love

El Gallo: La Voz de la Justicia 3/8 (Oct. 1970): p. 8.

Carnalismo
beauty
and
A boy named Miguel.

My chair will be empty
Our office (yours and mine) desolate
Our Coro will always have
a missing voice.
The Gallitos have lost a Gallo.
The Virgin will miss her Juan Diego.

I'll miss your hand
walking up and down the stairs.
It was a game,
I wasn't helping you
You were helping me
and
All your brothers and sisters
who walked and talked
in the halls and the stairways.

You taught us love,
gave us hope and inspiration.
Oh, Guerrillero, pequeño,
Lead us on to that Chicano Paradise
Abrazos
Fiesta
Amor
Carnalismo
EQUALITY!

Sing "Yo Soy Chicano"
one more time.
Put up your guard like a man,
Teach, Hermanito,

So that we can all profit
from your wisdom and your love.

The trip was short,
    the lesson priceless.
Your life was a symbol
    a falling star
        more than an omen
            A poetic reason
            A sparking light
A tiny hand
    warm
        tender
            honest.

You were born to create
LIFE in others
Your days were numbered
    but well spent.
Cuauhtémoc born to symbolize courage
    and Liberation
Che born to revolution
Zapata born to lead
Quetzalcóatl born to teach
Christ born to redeem
Miguel born to La Causa
Lágrimas y quejadas no te pueden
    despertar.

Your life was a model
    A lesson
        Un Grito
            de amor
                A pearl
        A vision

Of what all men
    should be.
Hijo de una madre morena
    y noble,
Son of your mother's tears
Blood of your father's heart
Alma y espíritu de
    tu Padre Guerrillero

Adiós, Adiós, Miguelito,
niño de La Cruzada
    Gallito valiente
        Guerrillero Pequeño
ADIÓS, MIGUELITO RUYBAL.

A Chicano's Trial

JUDGE.
    JURY.
        PIGS.
            FALSE CEILING.
FALSE MOUTHS.
        GUNS.
            LIES.
                COMPROMISE.
DEFENSE:
    white,
    kiss,
    beg,
    crawl,
    compromise.

PROSECUTOR:
    white,
    blood,
    society,
    majority,
    establishment,
    prostitutors,
    persecutor.

JURY:
    dead,
    racist,
    white,
    vultures,
    bored,
    fools.

Previously unpublished poem, written in 1972.

JUDGE:
  executor,
  white,
  political,
  prostitute.

JUSTICE:
  white,
  blind,
  racist,
  christian,
  lie, lie.

PEOPLE
  CHICANO,
  carnalismo,
  love,
  silent,
  proud,
  together.

WITNESSES:
  Ours:
      brothers,
      friends,
      reasons,
      here,
      how far?
  Theirs:
      pigs,
      liars,
      sadists,
      white,
      blue,
      racists.

COURT:
   due process,
   closed doors,
   white justice,
   corruption,
   prostitution,
   dead masks,
   white maggots.
Equals,
      no compromise,
      no tears,
      no marching,
      no songs,
      no reform,
      only
      resistance.
   Equals,
   R E V O L U T I O N !

The Revolution

The revolution stands in life's
        dark shadows,
Waiting impatiently for her, his
        troops.
The revolution cries like a baby,
        sings like a woman and
        works like a man.
The revolution watches brainwashed
        Chicanos, talk reform . . . and
        preach war.
The revolution watches pasty-faced
        boards and commissions trimmed with
        brown window dressing.
The revolution bleeds, while the
        politicos get fat.
The revolution sees Mexicans
        turn into gray gringos and
        Negroes try to turn white.
The revolution vomits . . .
The revolution watches and waits,
        while men turn into whimpering
        Dagwoods . . . and women into
        frigid establishment prostitutes.
The revolution watches our boys,
        prance like Ivy League fruits,
        and swagger like money-eyed
        Eye-talians . . .
        Sing like co-opted sequined jive asses,
        brag like washed up vendidos
        and kiss the man's ass.

Previously unpublished poem written in 1973.

The revolution watches brown
>   mannequins with dyed yellow hair,
>   talk like Boston . . . and look
>   like the Virgin of Guadalupe.
>   "Yeah-yes your number
>   pulease Miss Gaa-leg-os
>   speaking."
The revolution watches: humble
>   Mexicans kiss the cossack
>   of fat avaricious priests of
>   hidden bank accounts,
>   praise pale, ulcered teachers,
>   hold hands with hypocrite politicos,
>   bend to sweat, and mimic
>   tough hard-boiled, rednecked Hemingway
>   bosses.
The revolution waits and watches
>   brown figures crawl
>   across the gringos' earth
>   while babies starve, mothers
>   moan, old men toil
>   and young men kill and die.
The revolution watches from the
>   black barrio corners,
>   waits over the shoulders
>   of men, women, niños and
>   points to roads and plans
>   for future escalations.
The revolution wields
>   a surgical knife to cut the
>   cataracts of confusion from
>   the eyes of los ciegos.
The revolution cleanses
>   and burns the wax from
>   ears of lily-livered tapados,
>   and

vacuums, sawdust-filled brains
who say, "Look at me. I did it.
You can do it, too,"
become the gringo stooge.
The revolution laughs at fools
and calls to all Chicanos
"Freedom . . . Liberation . . . Love . . .
Carnalismo . . . Aztlán."
Take what's ours, don't beg.
The answer lies
in the powder keg
of action . . .
The revolution lights the fuse.
The revolution waits . . .

Mis hijos guerrilleros, 1973

We teach.
    We preach.
        We march.
            We sing,
the song of revolution.
(Freedom. Liberation. Justice.)
to young minds.
Blood of our blood.

RESIST . . . RESIST . . . RESIST
It bombs in your ears.
Resounds in the virgin
cavern of your minds.
And plants itself in fertile purity.

The old scars of our ancestors,
blaze livid red and
scream of past atrocities.
Beg for angry vengeance.

RESIST . . . RESIST . . . RESIST . . .
You don't have to
    spell oppression.
Your people are oppressed.
You don't have to
    understand exploitation.
Your people are exploited.
You don't have to explain economics.
Your people are economic slaves.
You don't have to
    learn about automations.
The masters push the buttons.

FREEDOM . . . FREEDOM . . . FREEDOM . . .
To be a man.
To be a woman.
Is freedom!
Talk, words, rhetoric,
without deeds.
Belongs to cowards,
(as we were).
Shielded behind sad excuses
(now is not the time).
Then let us claim
our time and history.
MIS HIJOS GUERRILLEROS,
the time has come
        for action.
Time is growing short,
Like a sputtering fuse.
The masses of our people
are the powder keg.

Together . . . together, because
one lonely hand,
one strong body,
one pure mind,
one single rifle
one solitary resistance,
cannot liberate, eradicate,
justify, conquer
a mass of infected
brainwashed drones.
Teach, mis hijos guerrilleros.
Teach, truth will win out.
Justice is indestructible.
Honor cannot be tainted.
Love is incorruptible,

but flesh alone cannot
resist lead bullets.

Teach and heal.
The eyes of babies can see.
The blood of martyrs
cannot be erased.
We must cure
the contaminated.

Life is short.
Life is beauty.
Life tastes and
feels so good
while age consoles us
by saying our time
was not the time.
You cannot be restrained, Young Lions.
Guerrilleros de mi Raza,
Your time is now,
    prowl the barrios.
Hunt through the mountains.
    Search the Pueblos.
Look to the campus,
for hermanos, carnales
    y soldados.

Mis hijos guerrilleros,
I see your youth
blossom like a wild
    spring flower,
surge forth like a stream
    of pure mountain water,
scream in animal ecstasy.
Your eyes are sparkle and light.

Flex your bronze muscles.
Live a thousand joys.
As I watch their dull faces
of gray boredom,
that will never know,
    Why?
You shout.
RESIST . . . RESIST . . . RESIST . . .
While they plod on down
countless rows of nothing,
like numbed plow horses
As you whinny
    scamper and breathe
Life and fire.
Your time is NOW!
Our time is NOW!
We form the revolution
    Together. Together.
Mis hijos guerrilleros
We live or die together.
Your courage is mine.
If you die first,
I will shed a river
    of tears,
Then spill an ocean
    of *Blood* . . .

He Laughed While He Danced, Luis Junior Martínez

Only that night in
its turbulent
            blackness
can speak of
            truth.

Only we of
            tortured silence
can remember
sorrow of
trumpet shrieks and
whining bullets
 red flashing
 eyes of eager
 patrol cars
gone mad.
Sparks of flying
leaden splinters that
ricochet off
 the walls of
            Death.

And
 the tears of a
people . . . mingle
with blood in
Screaming
 helpless youth
looking for a haven
in a jumble
 of
confusion and fear.

Previously unpublished poem written in 1973.

A lover's voice
a prophesy
of death
to come
a single name
a siren cry
to match that
terrifying night
            Junior . . . Junior

And he laughed, while
he danced.

A boy
turned man
by fate and
        consequence
a choice to know
the truth.
Something
that few mortals
do
or dare try.

In black alley way
shadowed by
city walls of brick
and ugly mortar.

No witnesses
    except
a fearful moon
and deaf mute
black
    Sullen
        Night.

He called upon
his ancestors,
  his brothers,
   his principles
and found
  a gun.

He had a choice
  of steel bars
  and concrete floors
or
a meteor into
        space
lightning burst
of sun and a
  mutilating
power exploded
        forth.

One lone resistance
  to match a
thousand hundred
        atrocities.
And he laughed, while
  he danced.

From polished
        stage
to barrio streets
a strutting
  a macho grace
a profile of
        a blade of
        steel.

In rhythm with
  life's beauty

and
    a smile to
match the sun
a gilded warrior
    in a
garbage can.
Three soggy red
roses
turn black,
where leaden darts
of hate
have pierced a
heart of love
and joy.

And he laughed, while
    he danced.
They surrounded him, like
picador y matador
    around
a fallen bull.
without knowing
    who
they killed
Guerrillero
  of deeds and
  social struggle
a symbol
to all who care.

The night shudders
as it sees a
plastic shroud
that
glitters harmlessly
who
    lies there

beneath
artificial blankets
as two blue suits
drag him
out of sight.

And he laughed, while
he danced.

The chaos of the city
thunders on, and
bloodhounds scavenge
for rewards
as the barrio wolves
howl
at a cowardly
full moon
that smiles foolishly
drown in pink
Blood.

A sleek limousine
all shine and polish
crawls
in false pomp to
the yawning doors
of a Mexican church,
to moans
and groans and
the chant of a
foreign tongue.

A priest raising chalice
of wine
but not the true blood
that only Martyrs
give.

And he laughed, while
   he danced.

In the company
      of friends
a long hollow night
laughter
      smiles
      wine to revive
recollections.
A dance with you
in the middle
 of the floor
a flurry of color
a stamping of feet.

Dawn follows noon
over the pass
the whir of rubber
      on asphalt ribbon
to the place of your
      ancestors' womb.

A trail to our
      birth
to nestle in nature's
embrace and earth
the songs and voices
sifting through
      evergreen boughs
and piñon fingers
to echo
in the valley's lap.

And he laughed, while
   he danced.

We left you in
    charge
of your homeland
to feed
    the roots
of whispering pines
and water the thirst
of dusty quelites
    and nopal
to the oration of
    frogs
the neigh of a black
    horse,
the hoot of an owl
and a
symphony of crickets
while the wind
    strums
a tune
on the strings of
a wild plum tree
the magpies gossip
    off tune
about blood on
the grinning moon.
the dove understands
and he mourns.
We leave you.

We leave you guerrillero
in the company of
mountains and hawks
and dancing in the
spirit of the wind,

And he laughed, while
    he danced.

From San Cristóbal purity
to the noise of
the city jungle,
where square elephant
            boxes
pulled by diesel
black bears
and giant beetles buses
pushing their way
through the throng
into noisy intersections
and crawling concrete
            arteries
that shutter off
last night's gory
            adventure
as blood stains
            give way.

Somewhere a machine gun waits
to avenge your death.
They'll call it terrorism as it
spews its noisy
answer to a martyr's murder.

The morning eyes look upon the
serpent's death, then the parrot
screeches obscenities and shouts
through tobacco-stained yellow
beak.
            terrorists, terrorists

And the crocodile smiles through
yellow, cherry juice teeth, straightens out
his tie and burps a cadaver
bubble as he says we shall
make them pay.

The parrot screeches "Terrorists"
We shall make them pay
a hundred million blind
mocking birds, say amen and scream
terrorists, terrorists, we shall
make them pay.

Then they flock together and
fly to perch on the
gravestones of their children
and pound their chests Amen . . . Amen . . .

While the parrots wait for another dawn
to learn a new world from the crocodile
and yesterday's printed lies are
swallowed down a toilet bowl
to be recycled and reconciled
with the substance from which
it came

The vampire bat in his wine-stained
priestly cassock eyes those who do not
say "I am not worthy"
to vent his wrath and
green venom of castigation
daring not to believe.
He dispatches hordes of hawk-
taloned blue jays to aid
his eery reformation.

They sing the praises of willing
sacrificial lambs who passively
like the ox accepts pious death
and exchange for fame and favor
from the ruling class and
leader shepherd of a willing

flock of suicidal mocking birds
Amen . . . Amen . . . Amen . . .

While those who choose because
of understanding of life's written
and unwritten scriptures of resistance
to the enslavement of humanity
are placed upon the pedestal of
infamy and disgrace
and above the din and clamor
of a city gone mad
Walking tall among the humbled
drones of mind-warped servants
His eyes were pure without
cataracts to blind.

His ears were filled with
music of the truth when
leaden darts of murder clothed
in society's good name
          send
him back to nature and
possibly obscurity.

Above the parrot's screech and
curious roar rising from the jaws of
serious pompous alligators and the mocking birds—"Amen."
its image stayed and stayed
for all to see and learn.

Because . . .
          He laughed when he danced
Not in the bull ring of death or
the squared circle of violence
but in the arena of life,
of human dignity of courage

of bright dreams
and warm wings of love
and . . . He laughed while
    he danced
and he danced
while he laughed.

A Boy, Juárez U.S.A.

His eyes were mine,
deep, fathomless, glittering
with life and curiosity.
His face was mine.
    A boy with torn pants
    worn and scuffed shoes.
A dirty boy, a real boy,
nothing less, nothing more
alive . . . ALIVE.
But, where was the dream?
The dream of the future.
       the dream of life and living.
A young face with the resignation
    of an old man.
You cannot change what is,
The earth, the bitterness,
    of man born to toil.
A house full of screaming,
    hungry children, a mother
    wrinkled before her time.
A father floating in a sea
    of despair, an escapee
    to the never, never land of
    tinsel and glitter
    and vacant rooms,
And a boy dirty
    with no dream.

A crowded, noisy barrio:
Hustle now or feel
    the pains of hunger.
Hustle or sleep in darkness.

Previously unpublished poem written in 1973.

Play the game . . . join the system.
        Hustle, Hustle
A boy, with, majestic poise;
        Cuauhtémoc, Villa.
        confident brown dignity,
In a sea of white maggots,
the squirrel cage.
        A pawn? A prince?
A boy with dirty fingernails
        with no dream.
Where is the battlefield?
        To put that confidence,
        that fierce pride,
        to lead the way
        to conquer man's
                inhumanity,
                greed,
                        hustle,
                                tinsel,
        dog eat dog . . .
A boy's eyes of gleaming
        wonder
        with no dream . . .

Eyes of ebony,
        deep of Indian soul.
Brow of Iberian steel.
        Patience of oriental time.
                enemy of man's artificial goals.
Earth bound, Father's son,
        victim of man's confusion.
U.S. Dollars,
        Go-Go girls.
                Scotch on the rocks.
                Bug-a-loo.
                        375 Horsepower.

Superman.
Lunar Lunacy.
Yellow hair.
Coca Cola.
John Wayne.

Arrogance.
Greed, greed.
Inhumanity . . .
A face like mine.
A boy like me.
A dirty boy,
with no dream.

A barren Church.
A white man's slave.
A forgotten revolution.
No morning star.
Quetzalcóatl,
a mystery of the past.
The evening star, a neon sign.
"Girls, girls, American spoken here."
Tonantzín, in the Virgin's robe.
And a boy with sandpaper hands,
cracked knuckles
and a dirty face,

with no dream . . .

A face like mine
A boy like me
A dirty boy
with no dream
A barren church
a white man's slave
A forgotten revolution

No morning star
Quetzalcóalt!
A mystery of the past
The evening star
The evening star
A neon sign
Girls, Girls, American spoken here

Tonantzín
in the Virgin's robe
        and
A boy
with sandpaper hands
cracked knuckles
a dirty face
with no dream . . .

Raíces . . . Raíces . . .

Raíces . . . Raíces,
 How deep?
 How far?
 Across a continent
 and back,
 Sweeping south
 and drifting north.
 Red of western sun, binds
 the yellow oriental eastern moon
 and most velvet blood
 intermingles,
 as Aztec gods embrace
 oriental Buddhas.
 Iberian steel pierces
 the virginity of red
 man's love.
 Moorish genius cuts through
 continents.

Raíces . . . Raíces,
 of internal intercourse
 of tribal bonds,
 tempered with family loyalty.
 Raíces,
 that imbed
 far into thighs
 of mountain valleys
 and survive on desolate
 dusty plains,
 persist in barren rocky
 crevices

El Gallo: La Voz de la Justicia, 7/7 (Oct.–Nov. 1975): p. 6.

endure nopal and
cactus strength in
sandy desert solitude.
Flourish in muddy verdolagas
and dusty quelites on
abandoned sites.

Raíces . . . Raíces,
that cannot be separated,
that cannot be torn
asunder,
a network
of human fibre,
that is one.
A crown of woven flesh..
Tarascan, Apache travel north.
Oñate, of mestizo mate.
A thousand natives pure.
Love has no boundaries
Nor discrimination.
Heat upon heat
creates the bond.

Raíces . . . Raíces . . .
Countless miles deep.
Countless miles wide.
Create the tribe.
Create la familia.
Create a nation.

Raíces . . . Raíces . . .
Aztlán, your face
is brown,
your brother güero.
Your sister morena.
Indio in the campo.
Chino in the barrio.

Raíces . . . Raíces . . .
Across a continent
and back
blood of blood.
Inseparable.
Unconquerable.
Endurable.
survival of life,
of family.

Raíces . . . Raíces . . .
Alabados of Remorse.
Mariachis of Gaiety;
sadness and love.
Flamenco; strange,
harsh, violent, arabic fire.
Corridos; sad, gay. Life,
history, dance, laughter.
Cantos—cuentos—history,
tied together by a
tribalism of love.

Raíces . . . Raíces . . .
Joined together by time
and history.
Nezahualcóyotl,
Chichimeca
Victorio, Gerónimo
Mangas Coloradas,
traveling south.
your face in Juárez;
a street walker,
a shoe shine boy.
In Yucatán,
Kiko, sits under
a shade of eucalyptus.

In Los Angeles, under
a sterile prison light.
Chu! Chu! Bleeds . . .
On a canvas sacrifice,
under neon lights.
Tíos dying in streets
o, dark and slime.

Raíces . . . Raíces . . .
Reflections of yesterday
and answers for tomorrow.
From Colorado to Califas.
Texas to Arizona.
Fields of agony
in Michigan to
heat soaked valleys
of Oregon.

Raíces . . . Raíces . . .
Blood is blood.
Tías San Luis..
Primos en San Francisco.
Tíos en Zacatecas y
Chihuahua.
Compadres en San Diego.
Abuelito, Abuelita
Jefe y Jefita.

Raíces . . . Raíces,
of strength,
of survival,
of love,
of power,
from Chile to Peru.

From Mexico to Guatemala.
From El Río Bravo to the Southwest.
From the Southwest to the East.

Raíces . . . Raíces,
that sing.
We shall multiply.
We shall grow.
We shall win.
Raíces . . . Raíces de Aztlán.

El Movimiento Chicano, 1973

Marchas, boleros, cantos
y corridos.
El corazón y el alma,
inspiración de nuestra gente.
Historia cantando y palpitando
su propio legado.
Un tono alineado con
latidos del corazón y puños cerrados.
Voces de ayer,
cargado con aspiraciones
demandando restitución
y la última liberación.
Zapata, Villa, Luis Martínez
cabalgan con mil
mártires y marchan
con guerrilleros de la libertad.
Guitarras, cantadores y canciones
apagan el fuego de opresión,
inspiran a una gente noble
a luchar por La Causa.
Desde Ayala a Aztlán,
el espíritu de liberación
resuena y recita cantos
de amor y victoria.
La sangre, la canción y la determinación
nos ayudan a elegir muestro papel.
Nuestra música recluta soldados arrojados
a unirse a las filas . . . de
¡EL MOVIMIENTO CHICANO!

El Gallo: La Voz de la Justicia, 8/4 (July 1976): p. 11.

The Chicano Movement, 1973

Marches, boleros, songs,
and ballads.
The heart and soul
of a people's inspiration.
History singing and throbbing
out its legacy,
in tune with
heart beats and clenched fists.
Voices of yesterday,
laden with aspiration of the present
demanding restitution
and liberation.
Zapata, Villa, Luis Martínez
ride with a thousand
martyrs and march
with liberty's guerrilleros.
Guitars, singers and sons
silence weapons of oppression,
inspire a noble people
to struggle for Our Cause.
From Ayala to Aztlán,
the spirit of liberation
resounds and recites songs
of love and victory.
Blood, song and determination
helps us choose our role.
Our music recruits fearless soldiers
to join the ranks . . . of
EL MOVIMIENTO CHICANO!

El Gallo: La Voz de la Justicia, 8/4 (July 1976): p. 11.

América . . . América . . . América

Los ojos del mundo vigilan.
Tus pecados están exhibidos
mientras las voces de los pobres
la angustia y el sufrimiento de
los esclavizados te acusan de
>   *TUS CRÍMENES*
Ahora el mundo conoce
TUS PALABRAS de TRAICIÓN
TU INTOLERANCIA, TU OPRESIÓN
TU ENTUMECIMIENTO a las NECESIDADES
de los pobres de la humanidad.
No mendiguen, no ruegen, no se arrodillen
Rehusen patrones e ismos, solamente LA VERDAD.
Pura, sincera, el cuchillo de la humanidad corta
>   Indiscriminadamente
Tu cuero está extendida sobre el globo.
Los piojos, las cresas, la carroña están
desenmascaradas.
El pelo se está cayendo. Ahora podemos ver
>   ¡¡¡Señor ahora podemos ver!!!

Escucha con tu oído a la tierra
tantea la dirección del viento.
¡Habla una gente nueva!
La palabra antigua, *DIGNIDAD,* es la bandera,
Y los hijos de hombres orgullosos te limpiarán
de tus parásitos.
La sangre joven hierve con fiebre
Estos no son fantasmas . . .
Ellos son los hijos de ZAPATA.

El Gallo: La Voz de la Justicia, 10/6 (Sept. 1978): p. 8. Este poema fue escrito durante La Campaña de Los Pobres y La Marcha a Washington, D.C., en 1968.

Oiga los gritos de VILLISTAS.
Recuerde el valor de CUAUHTÉMOC.
Crea las palabras de JUÁREZ.
¡Aquí estamos! Los hijos de Reyes
y Jefes y Revolucionarios Sangrientos.
Oiga el golpeteo espectral de las cadenas
que ya no detienen al Negro.
Cuatrocientos años de coraje, de venganza
arden en sus venas.
Arden en los vientres de un barril de pólvora.
Sangre—Sangre de jefes,
de príncipes, de guerreros valientes.
Arrojando la carga de los negreros.
¡Qué Arda! Pero no solamente por dentro.
Llámense con ira. Hagan saber a América.
Por King y Mártires de la causa,
canten unidos
            "SUELTEN A MI GENTE"
Blanco Pobre, EMPEÑO en el
juego del Gordo.
Escúchalo, nuestro aliado,
Contra la vergüenza del Gringo.
Él conoce la pérdida de la humanidad.
Cuando el dólar se convierte en su Dios.
Todo pobre debe unirse a La Causa.
América, tus hijos te dejan para escapar
la responsabilidad de tu delito.

Hermano Indio, sangre mía
ahora es el tiempo.
Adelante, adelante, surjan jefes nuevos
con el Calor y Valor de Jefes Antiguos
tomen esos cueros cabelludos,
el rédito está vencido.
Chucherías y armas no pueden pagar por
ocupación armada.

Palabras no pueden devolverles el Búfalo
y Valles verdes y fértiles
    ni
tratados y dignidad pisoteada.
    VEINTE MENTIRAS DEL BLANCO
Surjan, bailen, canten, tomen su tierra
pero recuerden a sus hermanos del alma.
Puertorriqueño, hermano de mi nombre,
mi sangre, unan las manos. Agreguen sus
cuerpos musculares, sus bellas voces.
Limpien el cuero de la hipocresía Americana.
    GRINGO
no queremos tu imagen
no queremos ninguna parte de tu enfermedad
ni tu neurosis.
Jamás Dioses Cristianos
en lugar de Espíritus Eminentes.
JAMÁS violaciones y castaciones sociales.
JAMÁS libros y educación racistas.
JAMÁS ratas y cucarachas.
JAMÁS haremos colas en los hospitales.
JAMÁS hogares apinados y casas federales de concentración.
JAMÁS estampillas de comida o dueños de viviendas pobres.
JAMÁS puertas cerradas.
JAMÁS armas y genocidio de las minorías.
JAMÁS guerra contra hermanos.
JAMÁS piquetes o marchas.
JAMÁS confiscación de nuestras tierras por el Gobierno.
JAMÁS contratistas y patrones cabrones.
JAMÁS nos agacharemos sobre *sus* cosechas.
JAMÁS brutalidad del Gestapo.
JAMÁS
    VENDIDOS,
        COMPRADOS,
            TÍOS TACOS O

TÍOS TOMASES.
¡¡¡JAMÁS POBRES!!!
¡¡JAMÁS!! ¡¡JAMÁS!!

Conocemos al enemigo, América,
Paga tus deudas,
Rebánale la barriga al Gordo.
Pon tu casa en orden.
El mundo vigila a América.
Paga tu deuda con Justicia Social
o la pagarás con
¡¡S A N G R E!!

America . . . America . . . America

The eyes of the world are watching.
your sins are now exposed
as the vices of the poor,
the anguish and the suffering of
the enslaved accuse you of
    YOUR CRIMES
Now the world knows of
YOUR WORDS of TREACHERY
YOUR BIGOTRY, YOUR OPPRESSION
YOUR NUMBNESS to the NEEDS
of the poor of humanity.
No begging, no asking, no bent knees
No white fathers, no isms, just the T R U T H.
Pure, sincere, the knife of humanity cuts
    Indiscriminately
Your hide is stretched out on the globe.
The lice, the maggots, the carrion are
exposed.
The hair is falling off. We can see now
    Oh Lord, we can see!!!

Put your ear to the ground,
feel the direction of the wind.
A new people are speaking!
An old word, *DIGNITY,* is the banner,
and the sons of Proud men will cleanse you
of your parasites.
The young blood boils with fever
These are not ghosts . . .

El Gallo: La Voz de la Justicia, 10/6 (Sept.–Oct. 1978): p. 8. This poem was written in 1968 during the Poor People's Campaign and the March on Washington, D.C.

They are the sons of ZAPATA.
Hear the "gritos" of VILLISTAS.
Remember the courage of CUAUHTÉMOC.
Believe the words of JUÁREZ.
We are here! The sons of Kings
and Chiefs and bloody Revolutionists.
Hear the ghostly rattling of your chains
that no longer hold the Black man down.
Four-hundred years of anger, of vengeance
smoulder in his veins.
Burning in the belly of a powder keg.
Blood—Blood—of chiefs
of Princes of bold warriors.
Casting off the slave driver's burden.
Burn, baby burn! But no longer in the inside.
Flame up in anger. Let America know.
For King and Martyrs of the cause,
sing out together
        "LET MY PEOPLE GO"
Poor white man, PAWN in the
Fat man's game
Listen to him, our ally,
against the Gringo's shame.
He knows the loss of humanity
When the Dollar becomes his God.
Every poor man must join in the cause.
America, your children leave you to escape
the responsibility of your guilt.

Indio brother, blood of mine,
now is the time.
Move, Move, arise new chiefs with the
Fire and courage of Old Chiefs.
Take those scalps,
the interest is due.
Trinkets and guns cannot pay for armed
occupation.

Words cannot give you back the Buffalo
and Valleys green and fertile,
     nor
treaties and dignity long trampled.
     TWENTY WHITE MAN LIES
Arise, dance, sing, take your land
but remember your brothers of the Soul.
Puertorriqueño, hermano of my name,
my blood, join hands. Add your muscular
bodies, your beautiful voices.
Cleanse the hide of American hypocrisy.
     GRINGO
we don't want your image,
we want no part of your sickness
or your neurosis.
No more Christian Gods
in place of Great Spirits.
NO MORE rape and social castration.
NO MORE racist books and education.
NO MORE rats and roaches.
NO MORE waiting lines in hospitals.
NO MORE tenements and project concentration
        camps.
NO MORE food stamps and slumlords.
NO MORE closed doors.
NO MORE guns and minority genocide.
NO MORE war against brothers.
NO MORE picket lines or marches.
NO MORE Government confiscation of our land.
NO MORE Contratistas or Patrones Cabrones.
NO MORE bending over *your* crops.
NO MORE Gestapo brutality
NO MORE
     VENDIDOS,
        SELL OUTS,
           TÍO TACOS or
           UNCLE TOMS.

NO   MORE   POOR!
NO MORE!! NO MORE!!

We know the enemy, America,
Pay your debts,
Slice off the Fat man's belly.
The world is watching, America.
Pay your debt with social justice
or pay the price in
      B L O O D!!!

¡¡Cuídate, Méjico!!

Dicen que los españoles
conquistaron a Méjico
y que las madres indias
ganaron la batalla contra
los padres gachupines.
Y ahora los gringos
están chingando a los dos.

¡CUÍDATE, MÉJICO!
de los Bank-Americards
Pepsi-Cola, Woolworths, Hiltons
Pittsburg Paint
y las colonias Yanquis.

Hijos del Sol,
dueños de la tierra
morena, blanda y mejicana,
no se dejen.
Y como don Benito Juárez
no les den ningún
puño de sudor ni fe
a los explotadores.
Ellos que vienen con dólares verdes
y corazones negros.
Sonriéndose con los dientes para fuera
y las bolsas llenas de plata.

¡CUÍDATE, MÉJICO!
De los que te van a matar.
Hoy no vienen con armas.
Vienen riéndose con la mano traicionera
y bolsas llenas de verde.

Mañana te despiertas
como tu hermano, Puerto Rico,
un títere sin cabeza,
un hombre sin dignidad,
menos los soldados
de la Independencia.

¡CUÍDATE, MÉJICO!
Tus hijos mejicanos
los Chicanos de U.S.A.
ya saben vivir dentro
del estómago del Tiburón,
ya conocen bien su brutalidad
su racismo,
su odio a los mejicanos,
negros y raza de color.

No te dejes, Méjico lindo,
patria de nuestros abuelos,
tierra natal de toda mi raza
de bronce.

¡CUÍDATE, MÉJICO!
De los dientes del Tiburón.
Nosotros ya estamos en su estómago.
¿Cómo nos puede mascar?

¡CUÍDATE, MÉJICO!
Cuídate del otro lado,
nosotros cuidaremos
dentro del cuerpo del monstruo

Raza Siempre . . .
Hermanos y Fraternidad . . .

¡CUÍDATE, MÉJICO LINDO!

CHAPTER V

Correspondence

Editorial

EL GALLO was born out of frustration and determination for the truth. The truth about our people is never printed in the major newspapers. The sponsors of EL GALLO found it necessary to found and financially support a newspaper that would be the VOICE of the people.

Fully realizing that to start a newspaper is one thing, but to keep it going is another, they pledged to financially support this publication for the first six months of its existence. We are banking on the people to keep it going from then on. Subscriptions and advertising will have to be our mainstay, but the realistic approach and dedication of our sponsors will give us the needed push to prove to the public and especially to the advertisers that we are here to stay. We need your support to make EL GALLO a lasting success and the real VOICE of the People.

El Gallo

1265 Cherokee St. Denver, Colorado 80204

Phone 222-0825

Editor Rodolfo "Corky" Gonzales
Production Manager Juanita M. Domínguez
Sales Manager Steve Castillo
Photography Robert Sandison
Art Bill Longley

Writers: Bill Vásquez
Kelly Lovato, Jr.

Published by The Crusade for Justice

El Gallo: La Voz de la Justicia, 1/1 (June 1967).

A Message to the Democratic Party

May 15, 1967

Mr. Dale R. Tooley
Demo. C'nty Chairman
Denver Club Building
Denver, Colo.
80202

Dear Dale,

It is with sincere and concerned feelings that I write this letter to you. As you well know, I am familiar with the machinery of the Democratic political body here in the City of Denver.

After having spoken to you last summer, I was impressed by your seemingly dedicated, liberal and progressive views. I watched for some time to see if there would be any major changes in the party under your leadership. I looked hopefully for the restoration of dignity and respect for the individual and maybe, much too idealistically, a change in the status quo which the Democratic Party has been guilty of in the past.

It is clearly apparent that the party has not progressed on any of the pre-mentioned plans so far back that the party is certainly in jeopardy of antagonizing those people who have accepted the party with open arms, induced by tradition of social progress and humanistic philosophies initiated by such men as Roosevelt, Truman, and J.F. Kennedy.

From my point of view, party politics have traveled backward instead of forward. The individual who makes his way through the political muck of today's world and more so the minority representatives suffer from such immense loss of soul and dignity that the end

El Gallo: La Voz de la Justicia, 1/1 (June 1967) and from Corky Gonzales's personal files.

results are as rewarding as a heart attack, castration or cancer! To be specific, I will enumerate a few of the mistakes that will be costly to the party in the future.

You have allowed the City Hall politicians to control and drag the party downhill with them. Regardless of the outcome of the Mayor's Race, the exposure of many of the irregularities in the City Administration by the political hacks who ruthlessly control the city and continue to sell out to the highest bidder. The arrogant intimidation of Career Service City employees to vote for the Mayor on the threat of not being promoted, placed or employed.

You, as County Chairman, have not only condoned these procedures by way of calling all Democratic employees of various departments who have placed employees of various departments, who place employees by patronage, to meetings where they are called upon to pay part of their earnings to the campaign of the Mayor.

Not since Stapleton ruled Denver by political force has there been as ruthless a City Hall political machine as exists today. A machine that you and the party have used with wanton disregard for the dignity and self respect of the party worker and city employee.

You compounded the crime of indifference to the needs of the Community, especially the minority people when you chose to appoint to the party leadership, in the districts; except for one grassroots person, Barbara Santistevan; a Blue Ribbon crew of Uncle Toms and political hacks to represent people who they do not communicate with let alone identify with.

Added to this the pressure of commitment and promise that they must support Currigan in the coming non-partisan election.

You and your cohorts have been accomplices to the destruction of moral man in this society. I can only visualize that your goal is the complete emasculation of manhood, sterilization of human dignity, and, that you not only conscientiously; but purposely are creating a world of lackeys, political boot lickers and prostitutes.

Sincerely,
R. "Corky" Gonzales, Chairman
CRUSADE FOR JUSTICE

Western Union Telegram Sent to:
Tomás y Berta Rodríguez

c/o Pancho Medrano
2346 Douglas
Dallas, Texas

From: Rodolfo "Corky" Gonzales Crusade for Justice
1567 Downing Street
Denver, Colorado 80218

Estimados hermanos Tomás y Berta Rodríguez:

Nosotros de La Cruzada para Justicia queremos aliviar el penar de las injusticias que sufren en esta nación racista.

Con el apoyo de todos los Chicanos de Colorado, Aztlán, hasta el último.

El dicho de nuestra Raza siempre será; que cuando un hermano sufre, todos sufrimos y seguiremos este pensamiento, con honor, que cuando un hermano está encarcelado todos estamos encarcelados.

Adelante con justicia, valor y verdad.

El Gallo: La Voz de la Justicia, El Año del Chicano, 3/1 (April 1971): p. 8.

Letter to Reies López Tijerina

October 20, 1972

Reies López Tijerina:

I do not plan to attend the Congreso for Land and Cultural Reform as I had earlier. Commitments here at home and my own uncompromising philosophy are the reasons for not being present with you. As you well know, in the past myself and the members of the Crusade for Justice have always taken positive action and supported those causes of the Chicano movement that were enacted for the betterment and the liberation of our people. In the past years I have disassociated myself from those people who confuse and mislead the gullible government representatives. I want no type of alignment with political prostitutes; I have no intention of creating reaction for the profitable benefit of the professional program managers. I agree on total unity. Total unity based on the ideals of liberation of the mass of our people.

Unity based on ideals and principles. One of these great issues on which all struggles are based is land. Land is the greatest issue with which to organize our people. I wish you and the Congreso a most successful conference.

The people must win and we will serve the people.

Ganaremos

Rodolfo Corky Gonzales

El Gallo: La Voz de la Justicia, (Oct. 1972): p. 3.

Discurso al Congreso de la Tierra

Por Rodolfo "Corky" Gonzales

Hablando personalmente, la dirección que escogí hace algunos años es la misma dirección que escojo hoy. El hombre que hace concesiones por ventaja política, por ganancia personal o por intereses financieros propios está tan esclavizado cuando sus bolsas están llenas como cuando está pobre. Cuando nos daban leche de polvo éramos esclavos, cuando mañana nos den crema habrá anzuelos en nuestros cuerpos y todavía seguiremos siendo esclavos. Estas gentes que ven una victoria en forma de dinero mientras que todavía tienen que hincarse y agacharse al establecimiento, quienes todavía tienen compejos de inferioridad, no están más liberados que los animales enjaulados, "aunque la jaula sea de oro".

Hay demasiados mejicanos en las ciudades hoy en día tratando de ser americanos mientras esperan que los ancianos se mueran y les dejen sus tierras, las cuales venden inmediatamente a los gringos. Esto no es diferente de la mayoría de los políticos, los profesionales y los comerciantes de nuestro grupo que venden su dignidad, su hombría y su valor de mujer al que le pague más. Ellos, como las masas de nuestra gente, todavía son esclavos.

En el pasado decíamos que luchábamos contra un gobierno injusto, una sociedad racista, un estado policial y un montón de ladrones. ¿Cambiamos pues, nuestra opinión, cuando se nos ofrece un programa, una posición o una recompensa a una persona a cambio de capturar y apresar a las masas de nuestra gente? Yo, personalmente, no puedo cambiar mi punto de vista de ayer por las promesas de mañana. No puedo, ni podré, cambiar mi filosofía por temor al desacuerdo, la incomodidad, la prisión ni aún la muerte.

El Gallo: La Voz de la Justicia, (Oct. 1972).

I. La tierra y su relación a nuestra gente y al movimiento

No hay ninguna cuestión más importante en cualquier lucha social, económica o política que la tierra. La tierra es la base en la cual nuestros valores culturales fueron creados. La tierra, entonces, es necesaria para crear una nación con una filosofía política construida en la unidad, la unidad total de un pueblo basado en nuestra historia común, nuestra cultura y nuestras raíces. Una filosofía política de compartir nuestro conocimiento, nuestra fuerza y nuestra riqueza para crear una sociedad de igualdad; para deshacernos del sistema de clases, el sistema de Dones y el sistema de patrones políticos; para crear una sociedad con dignidad y valor propio para todo hombre y toda mujer, sin importar su pobreza, su riqueza, su trabajo o su profesión; para crear una familia de un pueblo y un pensamiento, la liberación y la libertad.

¿Entonces, quiénes son los herederos sin importar títulos, patentes, o herencias? ¡Todos somos herederos! Todos somos hijos de la tierra, y la tierra pertenecerá a los que la trabajen y a los que la defiendan.

Tendremos que protegernos de los oportunistas, los capitalistas, los promovedores, los charlatanes, los demagogos, los políticos que no son del distrito que representan, y de los parásitos.

La lucha por la tierra no puede ser para la ventaja de unos cuantos o para las ganancias financieras de unos pocos. La lucha por la tierra tiene que ser una lucha de la gente.

II. La unidad basada en el concepto filosófico

¿Qué es entonces la filosofía política de la que hablo? Es la misma filosofía de nuestros antepasados: el indio, el español, el mestizo. Trabajamos juntos, compartimos los unos con los otros. Ofrecemos nuestros recursos y nuestros talentos a nuestra Raza para el benificio de nuestra gente.

El paso cultural de la identidad se ha tomado y vemos un despertar, una conciencia, a través de Aztlán. El segundo paso, el nacionalismo, siempre ha existido pero nunca ha sido reconocido o revelado, a lo mejor ha sido suprimido. Así es que usamos el nacionalismo como un instrumento para organizarnos, no como un arma para el odio, ni como un escudo para la gente que es culpable de traición. El tercer paso es comprender cómo el sistema de clases es utilizado para dividirnos. Hoy en día más que nunca rehusamos a ser clasificados por la mayoría de la sociedad como problemas sociales, como un grupo étnico de segunda clase o como cuidadanos de segunda clase. Entonces, por lo tanto, es importante que en nuestra misma familia no se permita un sistema de clases que duplique a la misma sociedad que nos ha clasificado como inferior. La lucha chicana en relación a la tierra, la cultura y el movimiento político tiene que abrazar una lucha colectiva del pueblo contra el egoísmo individual, la avaricia y el oportunismo. Nuestra gente educada en estos ideales creará una verdadera Raza Unida. Determinaremos nuestro propio destino por medio de escoger el curso de una nación, de un pueblo o una carrera competiva para el interés propio y la avaricia.

III. La responsabilidad

La responsabilidad de asegurar el éxito de los puntos que he presentado descansará sobre los hombros de nuestro liderato, que señalarán la dirección, y nuestros negociadores que representarán los intereses comunes de nuestra gente.

Necesitamos a aquellos profesionales y estudiantes que se dedicarán al esfuerzo, sin gloria, de hacer las investigaciones y el trabajo para averiguar la propiedad.

Necesitamos el brazo legal representado por aquellos abogados que tienen una filosofía en común con las masas de nuestra gente y que protegerán los intereses legales a todo costo.

De nuestros profesionales se esperará el ofrecimiento de sus recursos, sus contactos, sus conocimientos para proveer las necesidades de la supervivencia de nuestra gente.

El estudiante, quien, igual con los hijos de nuestra nación, beneficiará no solamente por medio de su participación en la experiencia práctica de hacer investigaciones, trabajo legal u organizar, pero también de ser parte de la vanguardia, mientras que sea uno de los soldados y uno de los benefactores.

Finalmente, pero de ninguna manera el último, viene la masa de nuestra gente. Sí, a pesar del hecho que en la mayoría de las conferencias, el burócrata, el estudiante, el profesional, el educador está presente como la mayoría, ésos aquí presentes hoy son una minoría pequeña. Estamos seguros que la población estudiantil chicana es menos de uno por ciento de nuestra población total, que nuestros profesionales en las profesiones de la medicina, la ingeniería, la química, la física no han empezado a indentar la superficie. Para comparar a la población estudiantil de los educadores chicanos, necesitamos un microscopio para verlos. Tenemos posiblemente, un veinte por ciento de la clase media y un gran número de aspirantes a la clase media. Después tenemos a las masas de nuestra gente que están en la necesidad y son ellos quienes sufren, y es por ellos y por nosotros que tenemos que educar, elevar y liberar.

Las revoluciones no tienen éxito cuando unos cuantos intelectuales deciden que la gente está oprimida y luego incitan e instigan a la gente a que reaccione. El liderato cambia de manos, pero la gente no ve ningún cambio. Es nuestra responsabilidad de educar a la gente para que cuando tomen una acción también reciban los beneficios. Porque es la gente que se sangrará. Sí, son los revoluncionarios que se sangran mientras los polítcios se engordan. Cuando nuestra gente comprende qué y quién está peleando, entonces estará de acuerdo con una filosofía colectiva de una familia, una nación, luchando por la liberación, el amor y la humanidad.

IV. Las metas

Nuestras metas se podrán numerar primero como la supervivencia y la preservación de nuestra gente, nuestros hijos, nuestra cultura, nuestra identidad, nuestros valores y nuestro amor propio.

Necesitamos establecer un plan de acción. Necesitamos determinar cuáles recursos tenemos y cuáles necesitamos. Necesitamos determinar dónde empezar y dónde utilizar a nuestros negociadores, nuestros organizadores, nuestra asistencia legal y nuestras tropas.

¿Quiénes serán los representantes en el Congreso y cuáles serán sus responsabilidades? ¿Quiénes son los ciudadanos; quiénes son las masas? ¿Hemos de buscar unidad cuando quizás no estamos de acuerdo con la dirección? ¿Si la gente que representamos se compone de liberales, conservadores, reaccionarios, patrones, peones, dones, políticos, racistas, podremos esperar una filosofía como la que he delineado? Porque la tierra sin la gente está desolada; un pueblo sin tierra está sin hogar; una nación sin tierra está colonizada, esclavizada y oprimida.

Me gusta recordar las palabras de un gran hombre, un hombre verdadero, Ricardo Flores Magón, quien era un periodista mejicano y un revolucionario. Dijo, "Cuando me muera yo, mis enemigos dirán, aquí está un loco; mis amigos dirán, aquí está un soñador y un tonto, pero nadie podrá decir que fui un cobarde o un traidor a mis ideales y a mis principios".

Ricardo Flores Magón también dijo, cuando se le ofreció un perdón, que si aceptaba el perdón estaría admitiendo culpa por un crimen. Fue un revolucionario quien luchó por la justicia y la liberación de un gobierno tiránico. Fue asesinado en la Penitenciaría Federal de Leavenworth.

Los principios de Magón no son fáciles para que un hombre común los cumpla. La libertad es la realidad cuando ya no está uno controlado por nadie. Una gente libre tendrá que formar una nación libre, una nación libre tendrá que tener tierra y para tener todas estas cosas tendremos que liberarnos del instrumento de nuestra opresión que es el capitalismo, la avaricia y el establecimiento que hoy está en el poder. No podemos ser acusados de subversión o de derrocar el gobierno cuando no queremos ni asociarnos con mentirosos e hipócritas. Es nuestro deber ofrecer un ejemplo de principio y de honestidad a la lucha por nosotros mismos y por nuestra gente.

Message to el Congreso on Land and Cultural Reform

Personally, the direction I chose some years back is still the same direction I choose today. The man who makes compromises based on politics, personal gain and personal financial interests is as enslaved when his pocket is full of money as when he was poor. When they gave us powdered milk, we were slaves; when tomorrow they give us cream there will be a financial or political hook in our bodies and we will still be slaves. Those people who see victory in the form of full stomachs and pockets full of money while they still squat and bow to the establishment, who still have inferiority complexes, are not any more liberated than animals in a cage, even though the cage is made of gold.

There are too many Mexicans today who are living in the city trying to be American while they wait for their ancianos to die and leave them their property, which they immediately sell to gringos. This is no different from many of the politicos, professionals and businessmen of our group who sell their dignity, their manhood and their womanhood to the highest bidder. They, like the masses of our people, are still slaves.

When in the past we said that we are struggling against an unjust government, a racist society, a police state and a pack of thieves, do we then change our opinion when we are offered a program, a position or a reward to one person to capture and imprison the masses of our people? I personally cannot change my views from yesterday for promises of tomorrow. I cannot and will not change philosophy for fear of disagreement, discomfort, prison, or death.

I. Land and Its Relationship to Our People and the Movement

There is no greater issue in any social, economic or political struggle than land. Land is the base on which our cultural values are created. Land then is necessary to create a nation with a political philosophy constructed on unity, unity of a total people based on our common history, our culture and our roots. We need a political philosophy of sharing our knowledge, our strength and our wealth to create a society of equality; to do away with competitiveness, jealousy, greed and power madness; to do away with class systems, the Don System and the political patron system; to build a society with dignity and worth for all men and women, regardless of their poverty, their wealth, their work, or their profession; to create a family of one people and one thought, liberation and freedom.

Then who are the heirs to the land regardless of patent and title or family claim? We are all heirs, we are all children of the earth, and the land will belong to those who work it and those who fight for it.

We must protect ourselves from opportunists, capitalists, promoters, charlatans, demagogues, carpetbaggers and parasites.

The struggle for land cannot be for the opportunity and financial gain of a few. The struggle for land must be a people's struggle.

II. Unity Based on Philosophical Concept

What then is the political philosophy that I speak of? It is the same political philosophy of our forefathers: El Indio, El Español, El Mestizo. We work together. We share together. We offer our resources and our expertise to our people for the benefit of our people.

The cultural step of identity has been taken and we see an awakening and awareness coming alive across Aztlán. The second step of nationalism has always been present but never been admitted or exposed; more likely, it has been suppressed. So we use nationalism as a tool to organize, not as a weapon for hatred nor a shield for people who are guilty of treason to protect themselves. The third step is understanding how the class system is used to divide us. Now more than ever we refuse to be classed by the majority society as social problems or a second-rate ethnic group or as second-class citizens. Then it is important that in our own family we cannot allow a class system, a duplicate of the same society that has stamped us as inferior. The Chicano struggle in relation to the land, culture and political movement must embrace a collective struggle of the people against individual selfishness, greed and opportunism. Our people educated around these ideals can and will create a real Raza Unida. We will determine our destiny by making a choice of a nation, of one people or a competitive race for self-interest and greed.

III. Responsibility

The responsibility for securing the success of the points I have made will rest on the shoulders of our leadership, who will point the direction, and our negotiators, who represent the common interest of our people.

We must have those professionals and students who will dedicate themselves to the unglamorous task of research and work which will provide the fact of ownership.

We must have our legal arm represented by those lawyers who have a common philosophy with the masses of the people and who will protect the legal interest at any cost.

From our professionals will be expected the offering of their resources, their contracts, their know-how to provide the necessities of survival for the people.

The student along with the children of our nation will not only profit by his involvement in practical experience in research, legal or organizing work, but from being part of the vanguard while being one of the soldiers and the benefactors.

Finally, but not last by any means, come the masses of the people. Yes, despite the fact that at most conferences the bureaucrat, the student, the professional, the educator is present as a majority, those here today are a small minority. We are sure that the Chicano student population is less than 1 percent of our total population, that our professionals in the areas of medicine, engineering, chemistry, physics have not even scratched the surface. In comparing the student population and the Chicano educator we need a microscope to see them. We have possibly twenty percent in the middle class and a large group of aspiring middle-class Chicanos. Then the masses of our people are in need and it is they that suffer and it is for them and us that we must educate, elevate, liberate.

Revolutions are not successful when a few intellectuals decide the people are oppressed, then incite and instigate the people to react. The leadership changes hands but the people see no changes. It is our responsibility to educate the people so that when they take action, they also receive the benefits. For it's the people who will bleed. Yes, the revolutionaries bleed while the politicos get fat. When our people understand what and whom they are fighting, they will then agree on a collective philosophy of one family, one nation, struggling for liberation, love and humanity.

IV. Goals

Our goals can then be listed as, first, survival and self-preservation of our people, our children, our culture, our identity, our values and our own self-worth.

We must establish a plan of action. We must determine which resources we have and what we will need. We must determine where we will begin and where we will implement our negotiators, our organizers, our legal aid and our troops.

Who will be representatives in Congress and what are their responsibilities? Who are the citizens, who are the masses? We should seek unity even though we are not in agreement on the direction. If the people we represent are composed of liberals, conservatives, reactionaries, patrons, peons, dons, *políticos, racistas,* can we look towards a philosophy as I have already outlined? Because a land without a people is barren, a people without land is homeless, a nation without ownership of land is colonized, enslaved and oppressed.

I like to remember the words of a great man, a real man, Ricardo Flores Magón, who was a Mexican journalist and a revolutionary. He said, "When I die my enemies will say, here lies a madman; my friends will say, here lies a dreamer and a fool; but no one can say that I was a coward or a traitor to my ideals and my principles."

Ricardo Flores Magón also said when he was offered a pardon, that if he accepted a pardon, he would be admitting guilt of a crime. He was a revolutionary fighting for justice and liberation against a tyrannical government. He was murdered in Leavenworth Federal Penitentiary.

The principles of Magón are not easy for common men to live up to. Freedom becomes a reality when you are no longer controlled by anyone. A free people must form a free nation; a free nation must have land, and to have all of these things, we must cut ourselves off from the instruments of our own oppression, and that is Capitalism, greed and the establishment in power today. We cannot be guilty of subversion or attempting to overthrow the government when we want no part of associating with liars and hypocrites. It is our duty to offer an example of principle and honesty to the struggle for ourselves and our people.

Letter to the Editor

Rocky Mountain News
Ashton

In regard to the questions concerning some statements, allegations and charges made by various persons (known or unknown) about myself and THE CRUSADE FOR JUSTICE to the Rocky Mountain News, I will only say that I refuse to take part in a Roman Circus that can only entertain the News readers and do considerable harm to the Chicano people and community.

I will not be part of a gossip and rumor situation for the benefit of the power structure and those misled individuals who would consider themselves spokesmen or leaders of any segment or the whole of the Chicano Movement.

We have taken a position of independence and follow a philosophy of self-determination. We do not claim to have the answers to alleviate all the problems of the Chicano people but we are steadfast in our beliefs that we can provide the solutions and the direction by providing the model through our own efforts, i.e., the establishment of a Learning Center (ESCUELA TLATELOLCO), a day care center, a ballet, a prisoner rights division, a legal defense committee, a newspaper, a source center, a social services division, a leadership development program, an athletic program, a community media committee and economic base. These then are the components that we feel are necessary for the development and education and growth of any progressive group.

We do not claim ownership or control of the Chicano people, but we have assumed the responsibility of educating and influencing the people by our example.

In conclusion, I can only ask that if we are not important in this community and if our actions have no effect, then why are we the subject and interest of so many parties in power, petty politicos and office

The Denver Rocky Mountain News, (May 29, 1974).

holders? We can only reason that our effectiveness is measured by the reaction generated.

I'm led to repeat an old adage related to me by my uncle: "The higher you rise, the better target you are for bricks."

We will withstand the bricks, the attempts to destroy us as an organization and the futile efforts to divide us as people. WE SHALL ENDURE.

"We Will Endure"

In regard to the recent bombings which have resulted in the deaths of five of our people, we want to respond as an organization and as people to the illegal tactics, the cloak-and-dagger methods of the military forces of Boulder, Denver, and Colorado; and also to the lack of human compassion in the inhumane handling of information about the deceased to their relatives and loved ones; and finally to the irresponsible journalism that has prevailed throughout these days of tragedy.

It is our belief that the military apparatus deployed by the U.S. government in the control of colonized countries across the Third World is being put into practice here at home, at the expense of those people who struggle for social justice, commonly known as "activists." By utilizing state, local and federal police agencies to stomp out and wipe out any resistance to the status quo or the "establishment," it is the exact replica of the military apparatus that represses and controls other countries, i.e., the C.I.A., the C.B.I., the F.B.I., the Secret Service, Right Wing Reactionaries, Civilian Aid & Information, Vigilantes, A.I.D. and L.E.A.A.

Contrary to the television programs depicting police heroes, such as "Barnaby Jones," "Mod Squad," "Kojac," "Mannix," who single-handedly break the crime-rings, in reality any man who is even accused of being dangerous or armed is confronted by an army of guns, grenades, automatic weapons, armored vehicles, helicopters and high-powered rifles. Because we understand the magnitude of the situation, we have reason to suspect conspiracy in the death of Reyes Martínez, Neva Romero, Una Jaakola, Florencio Granado, Heriberto Terán, and another unidentified person, as well as the critical injuries of Antonio Alcantar. The odds of coincidence of the same occurrence within forty-eight hours are inconceivable. The percentages of six people and one critically injured in two separate instances, in that span of time, in the same city, would be astronomical.

Editorial, *El Gallo: La Voz de la Justicia,* 6/3 (June 1974): p. 2.

The victims, who are speechless and defenseless forever, are the ones who are further victimized while their homes are searched by way of illegal search warrants. Are the dead the guilty parties?

To our knowledge, as of yesterday, May 30, Mr. and Mrs. Martínez, parents of Reyes Martínez, had not been notified by officials of their son's death. Mrs. Granados has never been informed officially of her husband's tragedy.

We further question why the Boulder Police Department has been so secretive in its release of information and about its investigative procedures?

The families of the deceased should have access to all the information and evidence in regard to their loved ones.

Finally the press, by insinuations and imaginary journalism, has maligned not only the dead but the living. Although it is stated over and over again that no one saw the immediate explosion in the first case, we quote from the mouths of radio hams and newspaper clippings: "It was assumed that they were assembling a bomb." Who is assuming? We say the press is the speculator, with an eye toward indicting the dead.

The *Denver Post* states, "After the explosion, early reports indicated that material from the Denver Crusade for Justice was found in the vehicle. Chicano activists in the Boulder area said they fear that they will be targets for other explosions." We demand to know what the material was and we accuse the *Denver Post* of a malicious, vile attempt to confuse the public and plant seeds of distrust in our people. It is not hard to understand that when we support the law students, the media does not mention our organization; when we support the medical students, the prisoners, the struggling union groups, youth, the poor and the dispossessed; and when we attack racism, discrimination, irrelevant education, unfair welfare issues, the newspapers fail to mention us. We are well aware of yellow journalism and its effects, and we want those people of the media who are a disgrace to honest journalism to know that we cannot and will not be broken by scurrilous and cowardly insinuation.

We will not be shamed or frightened away from claiming our brothers and sisters who we have recently lost. While they lived, they contributed to the cause of their people. They gave of themselves possibly more than any one of us will ever know. They gave proof of their solidarity with the causes and the people they believed in, and we offer the same to them.

In ending, I would like to say that this letter I received yesterday, which was mailed no doubt after the Monday bombing, is proof that other people are involved either in alliance or conspiracy with the murder of our people.

We have reason to suspect that we are dealing with highly skilled killers, who have access to the most technical and sophisticated resources and materials. Their methods have been used in Vietnam, the Dominican Republic, Cambodia, Africa, Asia, Chile, and across South America.

We intend to survive, no matter the odds against us. We will continue with our work and encourage our people to continue the struggle for liberation despite coercion, threats, or death.

CHAPTER VI

Photos

Corky Gonzales as professional boxer, 1948. He was ranked by *Ring Magazine* as the number-three contender in the World.

Corky Gonzales in cape made from his wife's wedding gown, 1950. Corky was inducted into Colorado's Sports Hall of Fame in 1988. In 1999, *The Denver Post* listed corky as the fifth greatest boxer to come out of Colorado in the last 100 years.

Rodolfo "Corky" Gonzales in 1955 when he ran for District 8 Denver City Councilman.

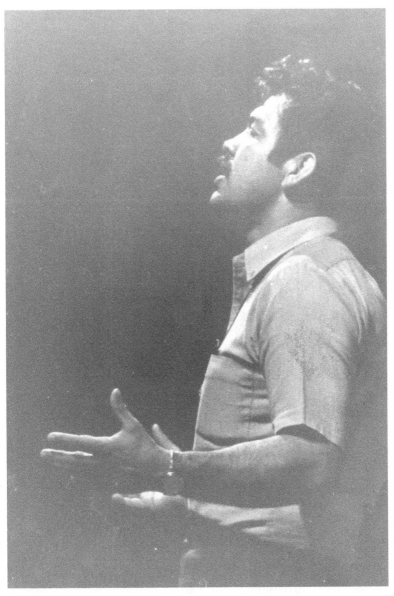

Rodolfo "Corky" Gonzales speaking at the First National Chicano Youth Leadership Conference held at the Crusade for Justice Building in Denver, Colorado, from March 29 to 31, 1969.

Rodolfo "Corky" Gonzales and members of the American G.I. Forum of which he was a founding member.

Rodolfo "Corky" Gonzales at Catholic Church Hall for a fundraiser dinner for Reies López Tijerina's La Alianza Federal de Mercedes, 1967.

Rodolfo "Corky" Gonzales being honored for his epic poem, *I Am Joaquín,* Denver, Colorado, 1967.

Rodolfo "Corky" Gonzales speaking at the 1971 Cinco de Mayo Celebration, Pueblo, Colorado.

Rodolfo "Corky" Gonzales and César Chávez of the United Farm Worker Organizing Committee at the Denver Grape Boycott Rally held in Denver, 1967.

The Crusade for Justice Building from 1968–1987 located at 16th and Downing Streets in Denver, Colorado, and site of the three National Chicano Youth Liberation Conferences held in 1969, 1970 and 1971.

Rodolfo "Corky" Gonzales at 1979 Denver rally commemorating the death of Luis Martínez, Jr. who was killed by Denver Police in 1973 and whose death inspired Corky's poem "He Laughed While He Danced."

CHAPTER VII

Selected Bibliography

Books

Acuña, Rodolfo. *Occupied America: A History of Chicanos.* New York: Longman, 2000.

Anaya, Rudolfo A. and Lomeli, Francisco A. (Eds.). *Aztlán: Essays on the Chicano Homeland.* Albuquerque: University of New Mexico Press, 1993.

Fleischer, Nat. *Nat Fleischer's The Ring Record Book, 1950 Edition.* New York: The Ring Shop Inc., Madison Square Garden, 1950, p. 393.

García, Ignacio M. *United We Win: The Rise and Fall of La Raza Unida Party.* Tucson: The University of Arizona Press, 1989.

García, Mario T., ed. *Border Correspondent: Selected Writings, 1955–1970, by Rubén Salazar.* Berkeley: University of California Press, 1995.

Gómez-Quiñones, Juan. *Chicano Politics: Reality and Promise, 1940–1990.* Albuquerque: University of New Mexico, 1990.

Gonzales, Rodolfo. *I Am Joaquín/Yo Soy Joaquín: An Epic Poem.* Toronto/New York/London: Bantam, 1972.

_____. *I Am Joaquín: An Epic Poem.* Denver: The Crusade for Justice, 1967.

_____. *I Am Joaquín: An Epic Poem.* Denver: La Escuela Tlatelolco, 1991.

Gutiérrez, José Angel. *The Making of a Chicano Militant: Lesson from Cristal.* Madison: The University of Wisconsin Press, 1998.

Marín, Christine. *A Spokesman of the Mexican American Movement: Rodolfo "Corky" Gonzales and the Fight for Chicano Liberation, 1966–1972.* R and E Research Associates, Inc.: San Francisco, 1977.

Martínez, Elizabeth S. and Vásquez, Enriqueta. *Viva La Raza! The Struggles of the Mexican American People.* New York: Doubleday, 1974.

Muñoz, Carlos, Jr. *Youth, Identity, Power: The Chicano Movement.* New York: Verso, 1989.

Nabokow, Peter. *Tijerina and the Courthouse Raid.* Albuquerque: University of Mew Mexico Press, 1969.

McKissack, Elena Aragón. *Chicano Educational Achievement: Comparing Escuela Tlatelolco, A Chicanocentric School, and a Public High School.* New York & London: Garland Publishing, Inc., 1999.

McWilliams, Carey. *North From Mexico: The Spanish-Speaking People of the United States.* New York: Praeger Publishers, 1990.

Meier, Matt S, and Ribera, Feliciano. *Mexican Americans/Americans Mexicans: From Conquistadores to Chicanos.* New York: Hill and Wang, 1994.

Steiner, Stan. *La Raza: The Mexican Americans.* New York: Harper & Row, 1969.

_____. "The poet in the Boxing Ring." *The Changing Mexican-American: A Reader.* Ed. by Rudolph Gómez. El Paso: University of Texas, El Paso, 1972.

Vigil, James Diego. *From Indians to Chicanos: the Dynamics of Mexican American Culture.* Illinois: Waveland Press, Inc., 1980.

Vigil, Ernesto B. "Rodolfo Gonzales and the Advent of the Crusade for Justice." *La Gente: Hispano History and Life in Colorado.* Denver: Colorado Historical Society, 1998.

_____. *The Crusade for Justice: Chicano Militancy and the Government's War on Dissent.* Madison: The University of Wisconsin Press, 1999.

Booklets/Pamphlets/Newsletters

Gonzales, Rodolfo "Corky." *Escuela y Colegio Tlateloloco.* Denver, Aztlán: Escuela y Colegio Tlatelolco, 1973.

Official Program of the Twenty-Fourth Annual Awards Banquet. Denver: Colorado Sports Hall of Fame, February 15, 1988.

Tribute to Rodolfo "Corky" Gonzales. Denver: Paramount Theater, April 10, 1988.

Crusade for Justice: An Independent Civil Rights, Social Action and Community Service Organization. Denver: The Crusade for Justice, 1966.

Dissertations/Theses

McKissack, Elena Aragón. *A Case Study of Two High Schools—One Public, The Other Private and Chicanocentric.* Boulder: University of Colorado Ph.D. Dissertation, 1988.

Ortego, Philip D. *Backgrounds of Mexican American Literature.* Albuquerque: University of New Mexico Ph.D. Dissertation, 1971.

Films/Videos

El Teatro Campesino. *I Am Joaquín: An Epic Poem by Rodolfo Gonzales,* 1972 Film.

____. *I Am Joaquín: An Epic Poem by Rodolfo Gonzales.* 1972 Video Cassette. Available from La Escuela Tlatelolco Centro De Estudios, 2949 N. Federal Blvd., Denver, Colorado 80211. The original film produced by El Teatro Campesino was reproduced in video cassette format by La Escuela Tlatelolco Board of Trustees in 1991.

National Latino Communications Center. *Chicano! History of the Mexican American Civil Rights Movement: Episode I: Quest for a Homeland.* Los Angeles: National Latino Communications Center, 1996 Video.

National Latino Communications Center. *Chicano! History of the Mexican American Civil Rights Movement: Episode IV: Fighting for Political Power.* Los Angeles: National Latino Communications Center, 1996 Video.

Salazar, Daniel. *After Joaquín: The Crusade for Justice.* Denver: Front Range Media Corporation, 1985 Film.

Interviews

Gonzales, Rodolfo Corky. Personal Interview. 21 July, 1994.

Gonzales, Rodolfo Corky. Personal Interview. 9 April, 1999.

Gonzales, Rodolfo Corky. Personal Interview. 10 April, 1999.

Gonzales, Rodolfo Corky. Personal Interview. 13 December, 1999.

Gonzales, Rodolfo Corky. Personal Interview. 28 December, 1999.

Articles

Bruce-Novoa, Juan D. "The Heroics of Sacrifice, I Am Joaquín." *Chicano Poetry: A Response To Chaos* (Austin: University of Texas Press, 1982): 48–68.

Bruce-Novoa, Juan D. "The Space of Chicano Literature." *De Colores,* 1/4 (October 1975): 30–33.

Cárdenas de Dwyer, Carlota. *Chicano Literature 1965–1975: The Flowering of the Southwest.* Stoney Brook: State University of New York Dissertation, 1976.

Conde, David. "Rodolfo (Corky) Gonzales." *Dictionary of Literary Biography.* Detroit: Gale Research Inc., 1992.

Del Castillo, Ramón. "Rodolfo Corky Gonzales, Revolutionary Leader of Aztlán." *Visiones, Focusing on the Hispanic World.* Denver: Juarez Publications, 1994.

Rodolfo "Corky" Gonzales, "I Am Joaquín." *Literatura Chicana: texto y contexto/Chicano Literature: text and context.* Eds. Antonia Casteñada Shular, Tomás Ybarra-Frausto and Joseph Sommers. Englewood Cliffs: Prentice-Hall, Inc., 1972.

Head, Gerald. "El Chicano ante El Gaucho Martín Fierro: Un Redescubrimiento." *Mester* 4 (November 1973): 13–23.

Lomelí, Francisco A. and Urioste Donald W. *Chicano Perspectives in Literature: A Critical Annotated Bibliography.* Albuquerque: Pajarito, 1976.

Martínez, Eliud. "I Am Joaquín as Poem and Film: Two Modes of Chicano Expression." *Journal of Popular Culture,* 13 (Spring 1980): 505–515.

Pendas, Miguel. "An Epic Poem by Corky Gonzales: 'I Am Joaquín/Yo soy Joaquín.'" *Militant,* 37 (January 1973).

Shirley, Carl. "I Am Joaquín." *Hispania,* 58 (September 1975).

Newspapers

"The Denver Post's List of Colorado's Greatest Athletics of the 1900s." *The Denver Post.* 31 December 1999, p. 11D.

Gonzales, Rodolfo "Corky," ed. *El Gallo: La Voz de la Justicia. El Gallo* was published by The Crusade For Justice from June, 1967 until May, 1980. Rodolfo "Corky" Gonzales was its editor during these thirteen years. A complete set of *El Gallo* is on microfilm in the Western History Section of the Denver Public Library.

Government Documents

Congressional Record. October 1, 1975.

Unpublished Documents/Letters

Gonzales, Rodolfo. *The Revolutionist.* Unpublished Manuscript, 1966.
Gonzales, Rodolfo. *Cross for* MACLOVIO. Unpublished Manuscript, 1967.

CPSIA information can be obtained
at www.ICGtesting.com
Printed in the USA
FSHW020707161119
64121FS